D0379400

The Lee Girls

The Lee Girls

by
Mary P. Coulling

JOHN F. BLAIR, Publisher
Winston-Salem, North Carolina

Copyright © 1987 by Mary P. Coulling
Printed in the United States of America
All Rights Reserved

Fifth Printing, 1999

Library of Congress Cataloging-in-Publication Data

Coulling, Mary P.
The Lee girls.

Bibliography: p.
Includes index.
1. Lee family. 2. Lee, Robert E. (Robert Edward),
1807—1870—Family. 3. Virginia—Bibliography. I. Title.
CT274.L44C68   1987   973.7'092'2 [B]   87–9416
ISBN 0-89587-147-5

For
Margaret, Anne, Philip, and Sidney

Contents

Illustrations

Acknowledgments

Many persons have assisted and encouraged me during the twenty years of my research and the writing of this book.

Mrs. Hunter deButts, of Upperville, Virginia, graciously permitted me to read and quote from Lee family papers at the Virginia Historical Society. She also allowed me to reproduce a number of portraits and other family pictures. Mrs. Frederick A. Zimmer, Jr., of Columbus, Ohio, permitted me to use a copy of her portrait of Mildred Lee as a little girl.

I am deeply indebted to Dr. J. Holt Merchant, who teaches history at Washington and Lee University, and to Colonel John G. Barrett, professor of history at the Virginia Military Institute, who read my manuscript carefully and provided important information about Civil War battle lines, military tactics, and weaponry.

Professionals from historical foundations and libraries have been generous with their assistance. These include staff members at the Library of Congress; the Virginia Historical Society, the Museum of the Confederacy, and the Virginia State Library, in Richmond; Arlington House–The Robert E. Lee Memorial, Arlington, Virginia; the Rockbridge Regional Library, the Stonewall Jackson House, the Rockbridge Historical Society, the George C. Marshall Foundation, the University Library of Washington and Lee University, and Preston Library of the Virginia Military Institute, all located in Lexington, Virginia; the Enoch Pratt Free Library and the Maryland Historical Society, Baltimore; the library of the University of North Carolina at Chapel Hill; the library of Duke University, Durham, North Carolina; the library of the University of South Carolina, Columbia; Alderman Library of the University of Virginia and the Lee-Jackson Foundation, Charlottesville, Virginia; the Rappahannock Regional Library, Fredericksburg, Virginia; the Winchester-Frederick County Historical Society and the Handley Library, Winchester, Virginia;

the Westchester County Historical Society, Tuckahoe, New York; the Rutherford B. Hayes Library, Fremont, Ohio; the State Historical Society of Wisconsin, at Madison; the library of the United States Military Academy, West Point, New York; and the Jones Memorial Library, Lynchburg, Virginia.

Faculty members and other college personnel who have been helpful and supportive include: Edward C. Atwood, Jr., June M. Atwood, W. Gleason Bean (deceased), Betsy Brittigan, Barbara J. Brown, Henry E. Coleman, Jr., Marjorie B. Crenshaw, Ollinger Crenshaw (deceased), Martha R. Cullipher (deceased), E. Stewart Epley, Erin E. Foley, Jefferson Davis Futch, III, Richard F. Grefe, Robert E. R. Huntley, Maurice D. Leach, Peggy W. Hays, W. Patrick Hinely, Jane G. Hughes, Betty R. Kondayan, Samuel J. Kozak, Susan Coblentz Lane, Rupert N. Latture, Earl S. Mattingly (deceased), Lisa S. McCown, Allen W. Moger, Richard W. Orem, William W. Pusey, III, I. Taylor Sanders, J. Thomas Touchton, Charles W. Turner, Romulus T. Weatherman (deceased), James W. Whitehead, Sarah K. Wiant, Anita Williams, and John D. Wilson.

Others to whom I am indebted for specific information and encouragement are: Ellen G. Anderson (deceased), Jane Roth Baugh, Marion V. Bell, Katherine F. Black, J. Stanton Blain, Rebecca E. Bordwine, George M. Brooke, Howson W. Cole, Louise H. Coleman, Robert S. Conte, Cecil D. Eby, Elaine Eatroff, Laura T. Fletcher (deceased), Charles Bracelon Flood, Mary C. Fray, Ann A. Fuqua, Hugh S. Gwin, Janice L. Haas, Tucker H. Hill, Jacquelin Lamond, Virginia B. Lawson, Linda Leazer, Annette C. Lennig, Robert S. Link, Jr., Royster Lyle, Jr., Michael A. Lynn, Betty E. Munger, John M. McCardell, Jr., Betty C. McCrowell, Ludwell Lee Montague (deceased), Agnes D. Mullins, Murray H. Nelligan, F. Garner Ranney, Eleanor Shank, Harry Shaw, Martha S. Stoops, Mary L. Tabbut, Eleanor Lee Templeman, Lucille Watson, Clarabelle L. Weatherman, and Barbara P. Willis.

Special thanks must go, also, to members of the publishing company of John F. Blair, of Winston-Salem, North Carolina, to Mr. Blair himself, whose long years in the field of publishing are matched by a wide knowledge of history, and to his capable, imaginative staff, Gail Lathey Warner, Debra L. Hampton, and Carolyn Sakowski.

Finally, this book would not have been completed without the continuous support of my immediate family: my parents, Octavia and Philip Price (deceased); my children, Margaret, Anne, and Philip; and my husband, Sidney.

Author's Note

Very few of Mary Custis Lee's letters remain, so we cannot quote General Lee's eldest daughter as extensively as the other Lee girls. No fully authenticated portrait of Annie has been found, although an oil primitive currently hanging in Arlington House was identified as Annie by the daughter of Mrs. Lee's house servant.

Spelling, grammar, and punctuation of old letters and documents have been left unaltered.

The Lee Girls

1

Bright Flowers of Arlington

1834–1848

THE WINTER OF 1834–35 was an unusually severe one for Washington City and the neighboring Virginia countryside, and it must have seemed very long for Mary Anna Randolph Custis Lee as she awaited the birth of her second child. Still, there was much for which to be grateful. She was at home, with grandparents and doting servants to care for three-year-old Custis, and she could look forward each evening to the return from the city of her handsome soldier husband.

On fair days she could stand out on the portico of her parents' home, looking over the cobblestone streets and roofs of prim Georgetown, past the scaffolding of the unfinished Treasury Building, beyond the line of poplar trees that indicated Pennsylvania Avenue, and in her imagination glimpse the War Office, where Robert Edward Lee was carrying out his routine desk assignments. When the weather was raw, she sat in the parlor, watching the wind whip icy waves on the Potomac River, which separated Alexandria and the quiet Virginia bluffs from the brick factories and unfinished clutter of the Federal city. Three times that winter the river froze from shore to shore, thick enough to "bear a man's weight," effectively halting commercial navigation as well as the shore-to-shore ferryboat.[1] The heavy ice cover promised a full icehouse for the Custis plantation, but it also meant that for days at a time her husband was unable to be with her and little "Boo." On these nights he had to put up at Mrs. Ulrich's boardinghouse, along with congressmen and transient journalists.

Slowly the frozen ground thawed and the ferryboat traveled more regularly, but the March winds still whistled over the sodden Mall and the city's unpaved streets became seas of mud, a foot deep in places, where unfenced pigs and cattle rooted about in search of garbage. Young Lieutenant Robert E. Lee of the U.S. Corps of Engineers must have felt a sense of relief to look beyond the filthy streets and stockyards of Washington to the imposing manor house on the hill opposite, where his wife and son awaited his return. From the ferry slip on the Virginia shore Lee turned west along the river road, past a wharf and the lower portions of the plantation farm with its grazing sheep, beyond the gnarled bare trees of the apple orchard, and up the curving road flanked with great oaks and chestnuts to the front portico of Arlington.

An immense mansion with white columns and striking proportions, set against a background of thick woods, Arlington House was clearly visible from the Capitol. Visitors from abroad were awed by the beauty of its location, calling it "noble-looking"[2] and likening it to "a superior English country residence."[3] For years the plantation farm had been the scene of an annual "sheepshearing" which brought gentleman farmers from several counties to admire the "Arlington Improved," a carefully bred variety of thick-wooled sheep. Picnickers by the hundreds ferried across the river in summer for parties at Arlington Spring, drawn largely by the estate's well-known associations with George Washington and his family.

George Washington Parke Custis, Mary Lee's father, had begun making plans for his mansion in 1802, shortly after the death of his grandmother, Martha Washington. Not only did the nineteen-year-old youth need a home for himself but, more importantly, he wanted a fitting repository for the furniture, portraits, and countless mementos that had been left to him by George Washington, who had legally adopted his step-grandson as his ward. Custis engaged the services of George Hadfield, an architect then overseeing the construction of the United States Capitol, to design a home on property purchased by his father years earlier. But Hadfield's proposal for a Greek revival mansion with great columns, portico, and wings was more than Custis could afford all at once. So he built the house in stages, first the two wings, separated by a gaping hole, and finally the enormous center section, completed fifteen years later. Additional work continued on the inside of the house until after his death.

Custis always referred to himself as "the child of Mount Vernon." The son of John Parke and Eleanor Calvert Custis, he was left fatherless at the age of six months and was taken to Mount Vernon with his elder sister Eleanor to be reared by General and Mrs. Washington. A short rotund man, with features resembling those of his famous grandmother, Custis was imaginative and artistic, generous and impractical, less interested in farming for profit than in agricultural experimentation. He was an amateur painter, public speaker, and dramatist, his subject matter usually related to Mount Vernon and George Washington.

Everything that interested his step-grandfather interested Custis, including the city whose site had been chosen by and named for Washington. He attended every presidential inaugural. On Washington's birthday and the Fourth of July, he was a featured speaker at rallies and festivals. He was an officer of the canal company that built the Georgetown-Alexandria Canal to serve as a water link for commerce between the Federal city and Virginia. And he wrote plays about historic subjects that were performed in Washington to overflow audiences. His chief preoccupation, however, was welcoming the public to Arlington House. An expansive host to great men like the Marquis de Lafayette, Washington Irving, and Presidents Andrew Jackson and John Tyler, Custis also entertained everyday folk from the District, for whom he built a wharf, pavilion, and wooden picnic tables and even provided a small ferryboat, the *G. W. P. Custis*. He was never happier than when he showed admirers the great iron lantern that had hung in the front hall at Mount Vernon and the Washington punch bowl and Cincinnati china in the family dining room. Often he would carry his violin down the hill to play for the crowds or tell them tales of his early days with the general. As a rare treat for special guests, he would display George Washington's war tent, used throughout the Revolutionary War.

By the time Custis had finished building the north wing of his home, he had married Mary Lee Randolph Fitzhugh, a quiet, pious girl from Chatham, a plantation on the Rappahannock River near Fredericksburg. Mary Fitzhugh was only sixteen when she married the impractical Custis, but she quickly took charge of the ten-thousand-acre estate with its sixty or more "servants," as the Custis family always called their slaves. In less than five years she had borne four children, all but one of whom died in infancy. The single survivor was a girl, Mary Anna Randolph, born in 1808.

Understandably, the parents lavished special affection on their only child. Mary was a diminutive girl, well-read and cultivated, with a vivacious manner and sparkling eyes, characteristics that tended to minimize her lack of beauty. During her many visits with relatives and

friends, she frequently met Robert Lee, a young man two years her
senior, the son of George Washington's old friend and admirer, Henry
"Light Horse Harry" Lee. Soon after Robert's graduation from the Military Academy at West Point, the couple became engaged and began
making plans for an elaborate wedding.

Mr. Custis was not overjoyed at the prospect of Lieutenant Lee as a son-
in-law. To be sure, the young man had impeccable connections. Not only
was his father a Revolutionary War hero and a close friend of Washington's, but his mother was the youngest daughter of Charles Carter, a
wealthy and influential planter whose home was at Shirley on the lower
James River. Lee was handsome, he had made a splendid record at West
Point, and he showed promise of becoming a conscientious, if not
spectacular, engineer. But the sad fact was that Robert Edward Lee was
poor. His aging father, a brilliant military man but an unsuccessful
civilian, had lost everything through speculation and died a pauper
before reaching home after a disastrous military adventure in the
Caribbean. Lee's mother, seventeen years her husband's junior and his
second wife, had been forced during most of her marriage to rear her
four children almost alone, in genteel poverty. More disturbing, Lee's
half brother, nicknamed "Blackhorse Harry" because of his various
escapades, had disgraced the family name by seducing his young sister-
in-law, a scandal well known (if little spoken of) among prominent
Virginia families. Robert Lee had been reared in Alexandria, and the
family plantation, Stratford, had been sold to outsiders in order to pay
off debts. Not long after her husband's death, Ann Carter Lee became an
invalid, with only young Robert to nurse her in her last illness. She died
in 1829, a year before Lee came courting Mary Custis, and was buried at
Ravensworth, the home of Mrs. Custis' brother, who had befriended his
distant cousin in her impoverished state.

Mr. Custis would have preferred a son-in-law with more money and
fewer skeletons in the family closet. But his twenty-five-year-old daughter so obviously wanted to marry the fine-looking engineer, and Mrs.
Custis and her relatives thought so much of the young man, that the
anxious father relented, gave his blessing, and provided a handsome
wedding. The grand house made a splendid setting for the nuptials,
held on June 30, 1831. After five days of postwedding festivities, the
couple left for Fortress Monroe, Virginia, where Lee was assigned to
improve fortifications.

Mary Lee had been reared in luxury with parents and servants at her
beck and call, and she felt that the army quarters were very small and

very plain. Unsure of herself away from home, she did not find the social life on the post congenial, and she missed the privacy of the plantation. "The only objection I have to this place," she wrote to her mother, "[is that] it is so public. . . . What would I give for one stroll on the hills at Arlington."[4] But she did her best, cheerfully refusing her mother's offers of extra furniture, making cotton curtains for the windows, planting out rootings from the Arlington flower beds, reading a great deal, and teaching her maid, Cassy, lessons from the Bible. Long visits to Arlington eased her homesickness, but she was back at Fortress Monroe again with her husband when their first child was born in September 1832.

Custis had already changed his mind about his son-in-law; the young parents made his conversion complete when they named the baby George Washington Custis Lee. Even more pleasing was the announcement, two years later, that they would be returning to the Washington area, where Lee was assigned duty at the War Office.

At first the Lees planned to live in Washington itself, but housing was very scarce, with the few residences of quality clustered around the Capitol or three miles distant in Georgetown. Maybe the untidy appearance of the city discouraged them, or perhaps it was the lingering fear of the plague that had spread in recent years among Irish immigrants living in slums between the fetid Tiber basin and the unhealthy tidal flats of the Potomac. Whatever their reasons, Robert and Mary Lee made the choice to live at Arlington.

Thus it was that Mary Custis Lee, the eldest of Lees' four daughters, was born on July 12, 1835, in the small dressing room on the second floor of Arlington House, adjacent to the Lee bedroom. No one could have foreseen, that hot July morning, the span of history that her life would cover. On the day of her birth, Andrew Jackson was president and the country's largely rural population was less than twenty million persons, scattered through twenty-four states, most of them east of the Mississippi. Before her death in 1918, Mary Custis Lee would dine at the White House with President Woodrow Wilson under a flag of forty-eight stars, symbol of one hundred million Americans engaged in a worldwide conflict. Perhaps even more difficult to envision in 1835 was the notion that Arlington, now a haven of stability and inherited tradition, would in thirty years be the focus of the bitter sectional war that catapulted her father into history.

But the Custises were not looking into the future. They were only relieved that their daughter was safe and their new granddaughter healthy. Lee was not at home for the new arrival. In May he had been

called away on a special assignment, to survey the boundary between
Ohio and the territory of Michigan. The Custises proudly recorded the
date of birth in the family Bible and sent word to Lee that mother and
daughter were mending. Slow mails and scanty information left him
totally unprepared for subsequent word that his wife had developed
serious after-birth complications, probably brought on by inadequate
sterile technique at delivery. The doctors described Mary Lee's illness as
"rheumatic diathesis," with general soreness and lesions on her lower
extremities.

Frightened by the severity of her illness, Mr. and Mrs. Custis moved
her and the two children to Ravensworth, ten miles west, where the air
was cooler and less humid. But the painful abscesses on the inside of
her thighs refused to heal, despite the ministrations of Mrs. Custis' sister-
in-law, "Aunt Maria" Fitzhugh. In desperation, Mary Lee wrote to her
husband, begging him to come home to take care of her.

This was the first major crisis in their six years of marriage, the first
time his wife had made such a request of Lee. To be sure, she had spent
more time at home than he might have wished during those first years
before "Boo" [young Custis] was born, but she was proud to be an army
wife, and he assumed she understood that if he were to succeed in his
profession, he could not get leave whenever he wished or whenever the
family asked him to. Perhaps judging Mary's recovery this time by her
relatively easy recuperation after Boo's birth, Lee replied in terms that
seem harsh and unfeeling: "Why do you urge my *immediate* return &
tempt one in the *strongest* manner, to endeavor to get excused from the
performance of a duty imposed on me by my profession?" No, he wrote,
he would not panic and ask for early leave. Instead, he urged his "Molly
. . . to cheer up and pack up; to lay aside unavailing regrets; & to meet
with a smiling face and cheerful heart the vicissitudes of life."[5]

But these stern admonitions were quickly set aside when he returned
to Virginia early in October. Now alarmed by her condition, he hastily
moved the family back to Arlington and called in the family physician.
Lee was never again to question Mary's need for him, and after that
episode she consistently underplayed, in her letters to him, her recurrent physical disabilities.

There was no talk now of setting up a separate household. Mary
remained bedridden until long after Christmas, and by early spring,
nine months after little "Mee"'s birth, she was just beginning to walk
with difficulty. Bleeding and cupping were prescribed for her illness,
and either because of them or in spite of them, she finally began to

improve, though the "sinews under the left knee" remained contracted.[6]

As though he were trying to do penance, Lee threw himself into domestic activity. Commuting to and from Washington as before, he now began to spend as much time as possible with his daughter. Like any proud father, he confided to a friend that Mee was "quite a beauty. . . . as brown as a berry." He admitted that "I diligently *oil* her hair [apparently to make it wavy] but not a *curl*."[7] The baby seemed unaffected by her mother's illness, but she had her share of infant sickness. In the winter she developed croup, and Lee sat up all night holding her in his arms to help relieve the congestion. Later, in early spring, when Mary Custis began teething, Boo got whooping cough, and Mrs. Lee came down with mumps, he acknowledged that so much illness and his daughter's "little ways" did not "altogether suit a man of my nervous temperament."[8] Fortunately, warmer weather brought improved health for them all, and the young father's spirits soared. "The country looks very sweet now," he wrote to his friend Andrew Talcott, especially "the hill at A. [Arlington] covered with verdure, and perfumed by the blossoms of the trees, the flowers of the garden, honeysuckles, [and] yellow jasmine. . . . But the brightest flower there blooming is my *daughter*. Oh, she is a rare one, and if only sweet sixteen, I would wish myself a *cannibal,* that I might eat her up."[9]

As soon as she was healthier, Mary Lee began to take more pleasure in the baby, who was fat and healthy, "a clear brunette," according to the young mother's description, "with brown hair very fine large black eyes a *perfect* little mouth & respectable nose."[10] When Mrs. Lee was able to walk outside again, she enjoyed watching the two children playing in the Park at the front of the house under the careful supervision of "Old Nurse," who had cared for their grandfather Custis at Mount Vernon.

With his wife in better health, Lee could once again begin thinking about his future. He had been promoted to first lieutenant in 1836, a slow advance for a man who had been in the army for seven years. As soon as Mary was well enough, he requested a new post, believing that if he were ever to hope for advancement, he would need new experiences and varied assignments. His orders came through in April of 1837, but he did not leave for St. Louis till midsummer. He was still at home when the third Lee child was born, a second boy, named William Henry Fitzhugh after Mrs. Custis' brother. The long name seemed too ponderous for such a tiny fellow, so the baby was quickly nicknamed "Rooney." "I am the father of three children," Lee declared, "so entwined around my heart that I feel them at every pulsation."[11] He might have added that, at the same time, he carried increasing responsibility for his rapidly growing family.

This time Mary Lee had none of the complications that had plagued her after Mee's birth, so he departed with few apprehensions and genuine enthusiasm for the new job, to supervise the dredging and improving of the inner harbor at St. Louis in an attempt to save that community's shipping industry on the Mississippi. He found, however, that the farther he got from home, the more he missed them all. "I am very anxious my dear Mary," he wrote from Des Moines, "to get back to see you all and learn of your proceedings, as then alone I can expect pleasure." He even dreamed about the children "nearly every night, and our last romp together was a race on the hill, in which the little woman flew like a gazelle, and far outran the *Boo*. . . . How is the little darling and her bright eyes."[12]

When Rooney was two months old, Mary Lee took the children west to the Blue Ridge Mountains to visit relatives and to get away from the heat and humidity of the Washington summer. Far away, Lee worried over his wife's problems with discipline, especially while she was visiting. He knew that she tended to get impatient with noise and confusion—"my brats are squalling around," she once declared in exasperation[13]—yet she was too lenient, he felt, and did little to curb Boo's *"reputation* of being hard to manage, a distinction not at all desirable, as it indicates self will and obstinacy." Once she returned home, he was sure she would "put them under a proper restraint . . . which you were probably obliged to relax while visiting among strangers." At the same time, he was aware that she was having to play the dual role of mother and father. "We must endeavor to combine the mildness and forbearance of the mother with the sternness and perhaps *unreasonableness* of the father. . . . I pray God to watch over and direct our efforts in guarding our dear son, that we may bring him up 'in the way he should go.'. . . Dear little woman [daughter Mary Custis]. I am so glad she is hearty again and I long to see the great improvement in the little one."[14]

As winter approached, ice floes on the Mississippi effectively blocked work on the project, so Lee came home for Christmas, traveling by riverboat, stagecoach, and the newly opened horse-drawn railroad. Christmas at Arlington was always a festive occasion and having "Papa" home made it more so. Wide-eyed, the children listened to stories of "Indians paddling their canoes along the river, dressed in all their finery & blankets, and some not dressed at all."[15]

When it was time for him to return to St. Louis in the spring, Lee decided to take his wife and the two boys back with him. Mee had been sick, so she would remain at Arlington with her grandparents. With two wildly excited youngsters, Kitty the servant, and assorted trunks and hampers, the Lees left for Baltimore to stay for a few days with Lee's brother-in-law and sister, Mr. and Mrs. Louis Marshall. Only fifty miles and a few days away from Arlington, Boo began missing his sister. "He was affected to tears," Mrs. Lee wrote to her mother, "at repeating the little poem you sent him about 'I have a little sister.' . . . Tell her her Mamma sends her a thousand kisses & has been looking all about town for a pair of garters for her."[16] After a long, tedious journey to Pittsburgh and down the Ohio River, they finally reached St. Louis, where Mrs. Lee was discouraged by their small quarters and the merciless insects. "Mee must keep up her spirits & think of me out here almost devoured alive with moschetaes [sic], for they are as thick as a swarm of bees every evening."[17]

Back at Arlington, life must have seemed depressingly quiet and lonely for five-year-old Mary Custis. She had never known life without Custis, and now he and Rooney were "steamboating" without her. Her father had written that "they convert themselves even into steamboats, ring their bells. . . . fire up so frequently, and keep on so heavy a pressure of steam that I am constantly fearing they will burst their boilers."[18] Descriptions of their adventures may have made the child decide, at that early age, that someday she would do her share of traveling, an ambition she fulfilled to the utmost in later years. It is interesting to note that one of her first long journeys, in 1870, was a trip on the Mississippi River, with a prolonged stop in St. Louis.

But if she felt neglected by parents and brothers, little Mary Custis certainly was the center of attention at Arlington. It was probably during this period alone with her grandparents that the child began to absorb so much of the history and meaning of her Mount Vernon connection. One can visualize Mr. Custis, stooped and balding, as he walked through the high-ceilinged rooms with the dark-haired little girl, identifying paintings of Washingtons and Custises and the wistful portrait of the beautiful paternal grandmother she had never known, Ann Carter of Shirley. Many years later, Mary Custis Lee remarked that she knew more about the family portraits and the Mount Vernon mementos than any other member of the family, for she had "received my knowledge of them first hand from my grandfather himself."[19]

There is a hint in the correspondence between St. Louis and Arlington that the child was rebellious and obstinate as well as lonely. In a letter to Mrs. Custis, Lee expressed concern over Mary Custis' willfulness, which he hoped might be "laid to the door of her *vivacity*" and not a "harsher name."[20] Not a few of Mary Custis Lee's traits as an adult may be traced back to this period alone with grandparents and servants to wait on her every whim—alienation from family, loyalty to Arlington and its traditions, and a determination to put her own desires ahead of the concerns of others. "You know, she is not sympathetic with weakness, nervousness," her youngest sister, Mildred, wrote years later, "& is always absorbed in self, first and foremost."[21]

By the spring of 1839, Mrs. Lee was anxious to get back home, for she was expecting another baby. She was not only apprehensive about giving birth on the frontier, but she also realized that the two boys would be easier to manage if she had the assistance of her parents and "Old Nurse." Rooney in particular was a youngster always into mischief. "Rooney is playing around me pulling my pens, paper & ink," she wrote her mother from St. Louis, "& is now trying to throw his Papa's hat out of the window. . . . I find it rather tiresome to nurse all day such an unsettled brat, tho' his Father has come to the conclusion that there is not such another child in all Missouri & that he would not exchange him for the whole state."[22]

Lingering river ice and a delay in Lee's emergency furlough, however, kept the family from traveling until May. The journey took eleven long, wearing days, by steamboat up the Mississippi and Ohio rivers, then by bumpy stagecoach across Virginia from Wheeling. Lee recorded that on the trip "the children [were] all in a row" and that Mrs. Lee, now eight months' pregnant, was "much fatigued" by the end of the journey.[23] With genuine relief, he settled the family at Arlington and hastened back to St. Louis. The return trip without his noisy companions was lonely. "You do not know how much I have missed you and the children, my dear Mary," he wrote. "To be alone in a crowd is very solitary."[24]

On June 15, 1839, only five weeks after she reached Arlington, Mrs. Lee gave birth to her second daughter, Anne Carter Lee, named for Lee's beautiful mother. Just as there had been concerns after Mee's birth, so there were special apprehensions about this second little girl. Word reached Lee from Mrs. Custis that the baby had been born with a reddish birthmark, and the anxious father wrote for more information. "None of the descriptions [of "Little Raspberry," as he called the new arrival] . . . have satisfied my paternal longings. Does the mark you mentioned fade at all, or retain its original hue? It has been some *whim wham* of that *Mama* that has caused it," he claimed, referring to the widely held theory that a scared mother would produce an abnormal child. Looking to the future, he determined to help the baby overcome the disfigurement, should the birthmark remain. "We must endeavor to assist her to veil if not eradicate it by the purity and brightness of her mind." He then added poignantly, "We have a nice little parcel of [children] now . . . God grant that they may all be preserved to us, and grow to be our joy and comfort."[25] Of the seven Lee children, Annie was the only one to die before her father.

By late summer Mrs. Lee felt well enough to travel again. Taking the four children, her mother, a number of servants, and numerous trunks, she ventured as far as Kinloch in Fauquier County, forty-five miles west of Alexandria. Lee worried that such a ménage would be overwhelming, and his views were echoed by her host and cousin, Edward Carter Turner, in a wry entry in his diary for July 26, 1839: "At night Mrs. Custis & Mrs. Lee (her daughter) with a squad of children, Negroes, horses, and dogs arrived."[26]

Home again after their holiday, Custis and Mary Custis began school under their mother's direction in the small classroom beside the Custises' first-floor bedroom in the north wing of the house. Here they learned to read and write and also studied geography using an old terrestrial globe, on which were "traced all the principal voyages and discoveries, from Columbus in 1492 to Vancouver in 1795."[27] Most children of well-to-do plantation families started their rudimentary education at home, either with their mothers as teachers or with a governess. Like her mother before her, Mrs. Lee was well qualified to instruct her growing family. As a young bride at Fortress Monroe, she had occupied herself by reading Latin and French, and in St. Louis she had written home for both Latin and Greek dictionaries. She read Goldsmith, Southey, and Coleridge and kept up with Godey's *Lady's Book* and *Harper's Magazine*, as well as the four daily newspapers to which her father subscribed. These papers enabled her to keep up-to-date with current affairs and politics, an interest most unusual among women of her acquaintance. She inherited her father's talent for painting, and later critics would characterize her work as superior to the enormous historic canvases that Mr. Custis labored over.

The routine of plantation life scarcely changed from day to day, or even from generation to generation. Every morning Custis, Mary Custis, and Rooney breakfasted with their mother and grandparents, after which came family prayers led by Grandmother Custis. The two older children moved on to their studies, while Rooney played in the upstairs bedroom or out of doors with his "Mammy," and the baby rocked in her cradle. In good weather the youngsters roamed the plantation from the deep woods behind the mansion to the sloping Park in front or ran along the garden paths, watching their mother and grandmother digging in the rose beds where the yellow Safronia and sweet-smelling Bon Silene roses bloomed. Custis and Rooney quickly forgot details of their years in the West, and they found it hard to remember a friend from St. Louis who sent Christmas gifts by their father when he returned home for the holidays in December of 1839.

Now Lee was eager for the whole family to join him in St. Louis. The Custises were not enthusiastic about the idea; rather they suggested that he resign and take up permanent residence at Arlington. He replied that he had "thought much on the subject of our coming out here . . . and have yet seen no 'impropriety' in the step but on the contrary it has appeared to me highly *proper* to be as much as possible with my wife and children." He acknowledged that their lives would be simpler if "we would locate ourselves at Arlington," but such a change would be possible, he said, only if "I would have *$20,000 a year* to put everything in apple-pie order and make us all comfortable."[28] He must have been unpleasantly aware that Mr. Custis' lavish ways and impractical management of the estate signaled financial trouble in the future.

Perhaps the Custises prevailed upon their daughter to remain at home. More likely, Mrs. Lee felt that she would have an even harder time with four children in St. Louis than she had had with two. Whatever the reasons, Lee left alone in late spring to complete his tour of duty, worried over his wife's heavy responsibilities. "Do . . . let the mending, shopping, etc. alone till the Fall," he wrote to Mary Lee during the summer months. "You must take care of yourself too, Mama."[29] Mrs. Lee did need to conserve her strength, for she was already expecting another baby.

The money for the harbor project ran out in the fall of 1840, and Captain Lee returned home once again for Christmas. Two months later, on February 27, 1841, his third daughter and fifth child was born, Eleanor Agnes Lee. Agnes was only twenty months younger than Annie, and the parents found the closeness overwhelming. Lee wrote to a friend about "the arrival of another little Lee, whose approach, however long foreseen, I could have dispensed with for a year or two more.

However as she was in such haste to greet her Pa-pa, I am now very glad to see her."[30]

For a few months the baby slept in the dressing room behind the Lees' bedroom, where adults could guard her from her inquisitive siblings. To the front of their parents' bedroom, Custis and Rooney shared a large, sunny room that looked out over the Potomac River. Across the hall from the boys' room was the "Lafayette Room," so called because the Marquis had stayed in it when he visited Mr. Custis in 1824. This room, with a spectacular view of the river and Washington, was young Mary Custis', furnished with an enormous four-poster bed. Behind the Lafayette Room and across the hall from her parents' room, Annie slept alone in a fourth bedroom in another high four-poster, which had belonged to George Washington, with steps beside it so the little girl could crawl in and out by herself. Within a short time, Agnes was moved in with Annie, and "the Girls," as their parents dubbed them, became almost like twins, sharing everything.

Warmer weather lessened what Lee called "the confusion in the Wigwam," for the children were able to spend most of their time outdoors. They quickly discovered that their father was a more adaptable playmate than the baby, and Lee found himself transformed into "a horse, dog, ladder, and target for cannon."[31]

In May of 1841, Captain Lee left for a new duty, repairing forts at the entrance to New York Harbor. The house assigned for the family's use at Fort Hamilton was in need of extensive repairs, and there was an epidemic of measles on the post, so Mrs. Lee and the children delayed leaving Arlington until summer. For seven-year-old Mary Custis, the move marked the first time she had been away from Arlington for longer than short visits. The ocean scenery of the "Narrows" (the straits between Brooklyn and the opposite shore) and the crowded quarters at Fort Hamilton must have seemed strange after the expansive vistas of Virginia. There were occasional trips home for holidays, several prolonged winter stays while Lee did off-season duty at the office of the chief engineer in Washington, and a special journey to Arlington in the fall of 1843 to await the arrival of Robert E. Lee, Jr. But except for these visits, the Lees were at Fort Hamilton for nearly five years, learning to enjoy saltwater bathing and becoming used to the sights and sounds of trans-Atlantic shipping. "Last night we were returning from Mrs. Stanton's by the brilliant light of the moon," Mrs. Lee wrote her mother, "when we heard afar off in the stillness of the night the rolling of immense paddles in the water. . . . [P]resently a gun & then a rocket announced the arrival of the *Great Western*," one of the first oceanic paddleships, tying up to the wharf in New York City.[32]

Though his engineering duties seemed dull compared with the innovative work he had been doing at St. Louis, Lee was grateful to have his wife and six children with him. "The little Lees are growing finely," he wrote to a friend.[33] His wife had her hands full, teaching the three older children, supervising the play of the younger ones, and keeping her daughters clothed in the latest fashions. "Daughter" (Mary Custis) and Custis were reasonably amenable to studying, but Rooney preferred to spend his time swimming and playing "with an iron hoop & beater."[34] As often as possible, Mrs. Lee took the three younger children swimming, though sea bathing was still a daring innovation among well-bred ladies. She was willing to take time to clothe herself and the two little girls in elaborate, cumbersome bathing costumes—black stockings, long skirts, and even corsets—in order to stimulate their appetites. The exercise and fresh air, she hoped, would especially help the health of tiny Agnes, who "scarcely eats enough to keep a new bird alive."[35]

Being so near New York City, Mrs. Lee was acutely conscious of current fashions for her growing daughters, though she was never especially interested in looking stylish herself. "Plain tight bodies with very long waists are much worn for little girls," she wrote her mother.[36] "I have a cardinal [a short hooded cloak] for Annie, cut out like 'Daughter's,' which will answer for this winter; next year I will present them both with something prettier."[37] She requested that the Arlington seamstresses make a few pairs of sleeves for Agnes, "as her arms get much burned in the sun & she has not many long sleeved aprons."[38] Even baby girls were not supposed to lose the pale complexions considered so lovely among highborn Victorians.

At Arlington the family had always had dozens of cats; at Fort Hamilton they acquired their first dog. Soon after his arrival Lee had rescued a spaniel swimming the Narrows. Presumably the pup had been someone's pet and had fallen overboard during an excursion cruise. Lee named the dog Dart and wrote home about the castaway. When Dart produced puppies shortly thereafter, the children were permitted to keep one, a floppy-eared creature called Spec. The dog followed the youngsters everywhere, even to church. One Sunday, in retaliation for a previously disrupted church service, Spec was left behind, shut up in an upstairs bedroom. Nothing daunted, he jumped out an open window, landed on his feet two floors below, shook himself, and trotted away to meet the delighted children as they entered the church door. After that, Spec attended church as often as he liked.

Swimming, watching ships come and go over the horizon, and enjoying Spec were the activities the older Lee children remembered best about their years at Fort Hamilton. Their parents looked back primarily to two serious accidents that occurred during their stay. After they had been on the post about a year, Annie one day picked up a pair of shears that someone had carelessly left within her reach. Too young to understand the danger, she ran the point of the scissors into one of her eyes. Here was a far more conspicuous scarring than the infant birthmark, which by now had apparently disappeared. Lee never got over this injury to his "gentle Annie," and he was always especially tender toward the child, who grew increasingly self-conscious about her appearance. When he wrote his will in 1846, just before going into battle, he included a particular provision for Annie, who "from an accident she has received in one of her eyes may be more in want of aid than the rest."[39]

The other mishap involved Rooney, a boy whose life was constant motion, noise, and confusion. His mother wrote home wearily from Fort Hamilton a comment that echoed her earlier feeling in St. Louis: "As soon as Rooney comes in the house there is commotion."[40] Late in November of 1845, when she was out of the house saying Christmas farewells to neighbors, the irrepressible young man slipped away to the barn, where he began playing with a razor-sharp straw cutter. Within moments he had taken off the ends of two fingers. The post surgeon tried to sew the fingers together again, and for many nights Lee sat by the boy's bedside to keep the injured hand immobile while Rooney slept. But three weeks of therapy were unsuccessful and Rooney's hand was permanently disfigured. The invalid composed a letter to Custis, which he dictated to his father, admitting his folly and sounding only reasonably contrite. Lee added a postscript in which he moralized about the two accidents, one caused by carelessness, the other by "disobedience." But underlying the didactic comment was the father's pain. "If children could know the misery, the desolating sorrow with which their acts sometimes overwhelm their parents, they could not have the heart thus cruelly to afflict them."[41]

Rooney's accident prevented the family from being reunited at Arlington for the holidays. Custis and Mary Custis had left Fort Hamilton that fall, Boo to attend school at Fairfax Academy, Daughter to live with her grandparents and study French with a tutor. Distressed that she could not get presents to them in time for Christmas, Mrs. Lee wrote to tell Mary Custis that "her papa has got for her a very pretty book" and to notify "old Boo" that his father had purchased for him, at Grandmother Custis' request, a set of tools costing sixteen dollars.[42] "You are however to consider the present as from your Grandmother."[43] The tools would later be used by Custis and his sister to build a tree house in the Park at Arlington.

In spite of the separation and Rooney's infirmities, Christmas Day was a happy one. Though the ground was covered with snow, the air was mild enough for Mrs. Lee to take the girls to church, and Rooney was able to accompany the family out for a holiday dinner. But by evening Mrs. Lee admitted to feeling "pretty tired," for the little ones had wakened at four in the morning to see what Papa had put in their stockings.[44]

As soon as Rooney was well enough to travel, Mrs. Lee took the four younger children back to Arlington so that the seventh and last baby might be born at home. Mildred Childe Lee, named for Lee's youngest sister who lived in Paris, was born on February 10, 1846. Lee was relieved to know that "poor Mama" was over her ordeal, and he longed to kiss the baby's "fragrant mouth & feel that little heart fluttering against mine."[45]

Now the family was complete. Robert Lee was thirty-nine, his wife thirty-eight. The three boys were fourteen, nine, and two and a half. Mary Custis was eleven, with the same dark luminous eyes her father had so admired in her babyhood. Annie, with shining black hair, and Agnes, with light brown curls surrounding her sweet face, were six and almost five.

Alone at Fort Hamilton, Lee found the house terribly quiet. "I am very solitary," he wrote, "& my only company is my dog & cats. But Speck [*sic*] has become so jealous now that he will hardly let me look at the cats." The little dog could not understand where everyone had gone. "He seems to be afraid that I am going off [from] him & never lets me stir without him."[46]

It was August before Robert Lee and Spec returned to Arlington. There the proud father had time to see "Milly" for only a few days before leaving by boat for New Orleans on his way to Texas and the war with Mexico. This was his first combat assignment, and the family was understandably concerned. Much of his time in the early months was spent out on maneuvers, and he longed to have his four girls with him "to wrap up in my blankets each night. What a comfort they would be to me. . . . But I am afraid Millet would kick too much." He was grateful for every letter from home, and when he heard that Mrs. Lee had bought a piano so that Daughter could take lessons, he urged the Girls to begin studying, too, so they could "play some handsome tunes" by the time he came home.[47]

Christmas was particularly difficult after so many holidays with the children. "I hope good Santa Claus will fill my Rob's stockings tonight," he wrote to Custis and Rooney, "& that Mildreds, Agnes, & Annas [*sic*] may break down with the good things. I do not know what he will have for you & Mary, but if he only leaves for you only half of what I wish you, you will want for nothing."[48]

For their part, the children were delighted to be back at Arlington, with its woods and gardens, its riding trails and lawns. They suited their play to the seasons, making necklaces of jasmine in March, playing hide - and-seek behind the lilacs in May, watching the hummingbirds hover round the honeysuckle in June and July, and swinging on the stripped grapevines in the early fall. On rainy days they played indoors in the "Big Room," the huge unfinished drawing room in the south wing of the house, just off the central hall. Here the family stored old furniture from Mount Vernon, broken chairs and tables, bookcases stuffed with dusty books, and an old harpsichord. Agnes wrote in her diary that the room made a splendid place for make-believe, as the young people played house behind the dilapidated furniture and rode "stick horses making stables of the niches in the Arches."[49] In the evenings they gathered about the fireplace in the nursery, where Mrs. Lee or one of the servants told them stories. In hot weather they sat in the huge hall of the house, which stretched from the front door to the rear. Here there was always a breeze, blowing up from the river below or drifting down from the cool woods at the back.

In the fall of 1847, Annie and Agnes began their studies with their mother. To improve their penmanship, they took turns writing to Papa. Sometimes he replied to them together, but on February 12, in response to a special request, Lee wrote a letter from Mexico City just to Agnes.

> My dear little Agnes,
>
> I was delighted to receive your letter & to find that you could write so well. But how could you say that I had not written to you. Did I not write to you & Annie? I suppose you want a letter all to yourself. So here is one. I

am very anxious to see you again & to know how you
progress in your studies. You must be quite learned,
studying so many branches & I suppose are becoming
quite a philosopher.

The remainder of the letter concerned a little girl named Charlottita,
who lived near Lee and impressed him with her neatness. He
concluded:

I hope my little girls keeps [*sic*] their [clothes] just as
nice for you know I cannot bear dirty children. You
must therefore study hard & be a very nice girl & do not
forget your Papa, who thinks constantly of you & longs
to see you more than he can express.[50]

Two weeks later Annie had her own private missive.

City of Mexico 29 Feb 1848

My darling Annie

I was much pleased with your nice letter of December & anticipate great pleasure in the correspondence
of my little daughters. The next pleasure to seeing them,
is to hear from them & as I cannot have the first, I am
sure you will give me the second. Winter here has past.
The trees are in leaf again, & the flowers are in bloom.
Indeed the latter might be said never to have ceased to
bloom, unless the more delicate kind. The roses, violets, running geraniums, large white lillies & the various
varieties of the geraniums have been in bloom under
my window all winter. The peach trees are in blossom &
the vines & creepers are covering the arbours with their
foliage. The little humming birds are returning to their
haunts, but as the vine on my balcony is not yet in

bloom, I have not yet had a visit from *Annie & Agnes*. [The previous year Lee had named two pet birds for his middle daughters.] I think I have seen them at a distance peeping into my window however, which is what I might have expected from such saucy little hussies, & I have no doubt they will soon return to their old play ground. I shall be very glad to see them back again & only wish I could have their namesakes at Arlington in their stead. I should have nice times then & could *feel* as well as look at their little *bills*. I am glad to hear that your Grandpa's cats are so sleek & fat. But I should like to know, Annie, how they keep so fat, if they do not catch mice? Do you children feed them, or do they live on air? Answer me that Annie. There is a fine large yellow cat that belongs to a tailor down the street, & every day when I pass there, I see him sitting on a stool, half asleep, with his fore paws doubled under him, close by his master, who is sitting on another, at his work. He does not understand a word of English, but is just the colour of your Grandfather's cat & is as tame. I think too he is rather larger. There is an English gentleman here, with whom I dine very often, who has a cat very much like my Tom at Fort Hamilton. He is very fat & tame & plagues his master at table, until he gives him his dinner. So as soon as he has finished his soup, he cuts him up a chop, or cutlet, or some nice thing, in a clean plate & sets it by his chair. When he has eaten that up, unless he has had enough, he is sure to ask for more. The gentleman tells me, that his house is so filled with rats that they eat the corks out of his bottles to get at the cordial. They are quite a dissipated set. If I had Speck [*sic*] here, he would soon clear them out. He would also put a stop to the mice frolicking about my room. They live in my dressing room & every morning light they come rushing out, with as much glee as you children jump out of bed, & take their way down into the kitchens & garden. Seeing that I am a quiet man, & all by myself without even a cat or dog, they eat up my candles, bananas & impose on me in every way. I think I must bring little

Saucer [a favorite cat] up here to see if he can't stop them.

But I will now bid you good bye with many prayers for your health & safety.

Your affectionate father,

R. E. Lee

I want to hear those little tunes you play so well very much.[51]

In spite of his cheerful letters to the children, the family knew that Captain Lee had been in the thick of battle, had almost been captured, and had narrowly escaped being shot. So it was with considerable relief that they received word in April of 1848 that he was on his way to Virginia. Mrs. Lee sent a carriage to meet him in Alexandria, but in his haste to get home he missed it, rented a horse instead, and came riding up the circular drive toward the house. The children, assembled in their best clothes, kept dashing outdoors to watch for "Pa." Suddenly Spec set up a wild barking and flew down the path. The youngsters returned to report the dog's strange behavior, only to discover to their chagrin that he alone had recognized his master.

Spec seemed to be the only member of the household who had not changed. "I am once again," Lee wrote to his brother Smith a few days later, "perfectly surrounded by Mary and her precious children, who seem to devote themselves to staring at the furrows in my face and the white hairs in my head. It is not surprising that I am hardly recognisable [sic] to some of the young eyes around me and perfectly unknown to the youngest. But some of the older ones gaze with astonishment and wonder at me, and seem at a loss to reconcile what they see and what was pictured in their imaginations. I find them, too, much grown, and all well."[52] Part of the problem may have been that Lee had shaved off his moustache, "which was exceedingly becoming to him," Mrs. Lee had felt.[53] Young Rob had grown up so much that Lee mistook a young cousin for his namesake, a mistake that temporarily hurt the little boy's feelings.

It was a summer the family looked back upon with pleasure, one of the last times the seven children were all together with their parents.

Unlike many Victorian fathers, Lee thoroughly enjoyed his children's company, and he not only spent as much time as he could that summer with his sons, but he also supervised the play and study activities of his girls.

There was a high jump in the yard and Lee tried out his skill with the older boys, Custis and Rooney. He went boating and swimming with them and helped Daughter with her horseback riding. "He was always bright and gay with us," Rob wrote years later, "romping, playing and joking." The little ones were allowed to get into bed with him at any hour in the early morning, snuggling close while he told them stories about Mexico and Texas. In the evenings, while Mary Custis or Lee read aloud from Sir Walter Scott, Rob and Milly had a special duty—to tickle their father's hands and the soles of his feet, which he placed, shoeless, in their laps. If they got too drowsy after a long day of play and fell asleep, he would rouse them with his foot, "laughing heartily at and with us."[54]

Details of their father's military adventures reinforced in both Custis and Rooney their determination to pursue army careers. Perhaps some-day they, too, might be cited for bravery under fire, as Papa had been. One can picture the two boys playing out their ambitions all summer long, charging imaginary slopes of Cerro Gordo, riding stickhorses along a make-believe road toward Mexico City, or crawling through high grass to spy on foreign hordes massed for attack under the dreaded Santa Anna.

Lee had always had pet names for each of his daughters. Now that she was a young lady of thirteen, he no longer called Mary Custis "Mee"; she was always "Daughter" now, to differentiate her from her mother. Annie was still "gentle Annie," and Agnes was "Wig," "Wiggie," or "my little Agnes." Mildred, who had been in her cradle when he left for Texas, had turned into such an effervescent, vivacious little toddler that he now nicknamed her "Life" or "Precious Life," a term of endearment that he used the rest of his life.

The nicknames, the fun, and the teasing were all a part of the intimate family pattern. On public occasions the Lees were far more decorous. Years later a relative recalled watching the group on their way to church, Rob and Daughter riding first, Mary Custis sidesaddle with "Robbie" beside her—"two handsome and gallant figures they seemed to look-ers-on."[55] Some distance behind came the lumbering carriage with old Daniel at the reins, carrying the rest of the family. The Lees sat together in the gallery of old Christ Church, and little Marietta Turner remem-bered looking up at her cousins, wondering if Annie, Agnes, and

Mildred minded "the hardness of the pew and the tedium of the sermon," which lasted sixty minutes.[56]

For Robert E. Lee the homecoming had been warm and satisfying, despite the early confusion of carriage and misidentification of children. Mary and the children had adjusted without complaint to his supervision over the family again, a loving, stern oversight reinforced more by the strength of his personality than by any physical restraint or punishment. At fifteen, Custis worked hard to be just the kind of son Lee envisioned. Agnes and Annie were content simply to be together, while Rob and Mildred had eased quickly into comfortable companionship with their father. Mary Custis and Rooney perhaps showed flashes of the independence and need for self-determination that they were to exhibit in later years, but on the surface they, too, probably seemed as docile as any Victorian father might wish.

Mary and Robert Lee had come a long way in the seventeen years since their marriage, surviving the perils of war, illnesses, and accidents, and enduring long separations and the cramped quarters of unattractive army posts with children pressed too close together. Lee was a "brevet colonel" now, having been promoted for valor on the battlefield, and his hair and long sideburns were tinged with gray. Beside him, Mary Lee had matured immeasurably from the spoiled young bride whose horizons had hardly been wider than the Arlington treetops. She had traveled, she had learned to put up with tiny rooms and exhausting trips, and she had been forced to be both mother and father during the lonely months when her husband was far away. Most important, they were surrounded by all their children, Custis and Mary Custis already surprisingly mature, Rooney stretching up almost overnight, the young ones just beginning to unfold into truly distinctive personalities. As Robert Lee put it, there was "much cause for thankfulness, and gratitude to the good God who has once more united us."[57]

2

Marble Steps
and Iron Railings

1848–1855

THE EARLY EXPERIENCES of the Lee girls had been strikingly like their mother's. All four had been born in the great house and learned to walk under the benign gaze of ancestors staring down from the walls. The older ones had studied in the downstairs schoolroom, as Mrs. Lee had done, and learned their hymns and Bible verses during morning prayers at the dining room table. They had scampered and tumbled about on the Arlington acres, picking apricots, cracking nuts on mossy stones in the Grove, and playing tag along the paths in the rose garden and herb borders. Unlike their mother, however, they were seldom alone.

Yet Mary Custis Lee was often very lonely. As a little thing, both before and after the boys' trip to St. Louis, she had played almost exclusively with Custis. If he were not at home, Mrs. Lee commented, "what would Daughter do . . . for a companion?"[1] But he and Rooney began enjoying boys' games together as they grew older, while Daughter was encouraged to be ladylike, to stop building tree houses—much less to climb them—and to keep her curly hair under fashionable control. Even their schoolwork was changing, as Custis prepared for college and Rooney looked forward to a military career, while their sister was supposed to concentrate on needlework, French, and piano.

So she was perhaps the only member of the family genuinely excited about her father's next assignment, to oversee construction of a fort in the harbor of Baltimore. The new job meant that the Lees would move to a real city, with schools, shops, social life, and plenty of young people to play with.

The War of 1812 had shown the nation just how vulnerable the northern end of the Chesapeake Bay was to naval attack. Baltimore officials had petitioned Congress for years to build defenses more adequate and up-to-date than old Fort McHenry until finally in 1845, the Federal government purchased suitable property and preliminary plans were made for the new construction. But appropriations lagged far behind authorization, and Robert Lee, as supervising engineer, found himself during the autumn of 1848 with little to do at the site, though he was kept busy on several short-term projects in other places. Not long before Christmas, he moved his belongings to a downtown Baltimore hotel and began a daily schedule of commuting eight miles or more by omnibus and rowboat out to Sollers' Point flats, a sub-merged shoal located at the mouth of the Patapsco River where it widens into the bay. Here, using underwater supports, Lee was to oversee the building of a man-made island of several acres, on which a brick fortress with walls forty feet high was to be constructed.

At midcentury Baltimore was the second largest city in the United States and one of its more prosperous trading centers. Sailing clippers and side-wheel paddleboats from all over the world anchored in its commodious harbor, bringing silks, spices, and porcelains from the Orient, dry goods from Europe, and coffee from Peru. Baltimore had been one of the first cities to see commercial value in railroading, and by 1848 the B & O line was carrying thousands of tons of international merchandise to the Northeast and the Ohio Valley. From the busy docks and warehouses the city fanned out along cobblestone and brick streets to fashionable residential sections with their tall row houses and elegant Georgian brownstone mansions.

Because the area was so prosperous, housing was expensive and very scarce. After searching in vain for several months to find suitable quarters for the family, Lee finally made arrangements through his uncle, Williams Wickham, to rent a three-story brick row house that Wickham was having built. That construction seemed to move as slowly as the groundwork for Fort Carroll, with no early prospect of the family's joining him.

Shortly after he moved into the Baltimore hotel, Lee and young Rob had journeyed to the city harbor to pick up Santa Anna, the small white mustang which had been purchased in Mexico for the children's use.

The bedraggled pony was unkempt and thin from the long sea voyage, but a winter of grazing and kind treatment turned him into a handsome mount with "a most delightful gait."[2] Curried and trained by old Jim Connally, Lee's Irish valet who used to boast that he and Santa Anna were the "first men [*sic*] on the walls of Chepultepec,"[3] the pony was patient and amiable with the Lee children. His behavior toward strangers was less predictable. One small cousin, clambering upon Santa Anna's back, jerked the bridle and the animal bolted toward the stable. When the pony suddenly stopped, young Thomas Wickham "ignominiously went right over his head, to the consternation of the grown-ups and the wild hilarity of the youngsters."[4]

Though she was not overjoyed at the thought of leaving Arlington, Mrs. Lee found her life increasingly tedious and wearing as the months went by. "You know what a monotonous life I lead," she wrote a friend, "& how very stupid the fitting up of 7 children with winter clothes must make one."[5] Cold weather forced them all indoors and she became especially conscious of the children's "little feet," which were "as noisy as usual."[6]

She was even more discouraged when spring came, the woodbine and roses bloomed, and the girls began planting their own small gardens, for still the new house in a fashionable section of Baltimore was incomplete. Lee wrote home that before long the weather would be too hot for the family to move, so now they had better wait till fall. "Nobody can eat" in Baltimore's torrid summers, he wrote, "but flies." Out all day in the merciless sun and sickening humidity at Sollers' Point, he worried about his daughters getting sunburned. "Tell the girls they *must not* go in the sun without their bonnets," he admonished his wife. "Annie is getting horribly freckled and I can't allow it."[7] His daughters were only following their mother's example, for she spent most of her gardening hours with her white sunbonnet hanging uselessly down her back.

It was probably October or November of 1849, almost a year after Lee's departure from Arlington, when Mrs. Lee moved into the new house with the four girls and two younger boys. Custis remained in Virginia to attend Fairfax Academy. The new home was a long, thin, three-storied row house with white marble steps. Located at 903 Madison Avenue, the dwelling is no longer standing, but it must have been similar to others nearby which feature a vestibule opening into a dark hall running the length of the house. Opening from the hall were four rooms, one behind the other—two parlors, a dining room, and a kitchen. The upper stories contained several deep, narrow bedrooms, possibly a library, and servants' quarters. Most of the rooms were totally without sunlight, since windows were only at the front and rear. By city standards, the house was large, but Lee complained that it was "hardly big enough to swing a cat in."[8] Fortunately, the yard had enough space to stable the horses, Santa Anna and Grace Darling, and the interior of the home seems to have suited Spec and the assortment of cats who made the trip over from Arlington. (Late in their sojourn in Baltimore, Spec disappeared and was never seen again.)

Life in the big city provided the children with excitement and new adventures. Omnibuses crisscrossed the town, and at night the new-fangled municipal gas lights cast a soft glow over the streets and around Mount Vernon Place, the parklike square a few blocks away, with its tall cylindrical monument to George Washington. Art galleries and theaters offered a variety of cultural opportunities, a German band gave regular concerts, and Jenny Lind gave a spectacular sell-out performance at the Front Street Theater in December of 1850. The city even had its own dinosaur, a collection of mastodon bones carefully reassembled at the Peale Museum.

Lee's brother-in-law and sister, Mr. and Mrs. Louis Marshall, who lived nearby, quickly introduced the Lees to a wide circle of friends and relatives. From colonial times the Chesapeake Bay had served as a water link between Baltimore and plantations on the lower Potomac and James rivers. It is not surprising, therefore, that the social patterns of the city were largely Southern, though an interesting international flavor had been introduced early in the century when a Baltimore belle, Betsy Patterson, had married Jerome Bonaparte, Napoleon's brother. Jerome, Jr. and his wife were among the Lees' close friends in Baltimore.

The children's first cousin, Louis Marshall, was a first classman at West Point, but there were many other more distant relatives in the neighborhood to visit and attend school with. Only a few doors from their home was Mount Calvary Episcopal Church, where the Marshalls worshiped. Soon the Lees began attending Sunday services in the small brick edifice with its pointed stained-glass windows and square tower.

Formalized education for young women was just developing in America, and Baltimore boasted of at least four girls' "academies" or "seminaries." Mary Custis attended one of these, along with a number of cousins, but Annie probably stayed at home under her mother's instruction until Agnes should be old enough for the two of them to go to school together.

Class rolls for the Baltimore female academies have long since disappeared, but brochures and catalogs are extant, so a composite reconstruction of a typical school and its curriculum can be made. Classes were usually held in a large private home, with the principal being a refined gentlewoman or clergyman. The school year ran from early September till July, divided into two terms, with tuition averaging between six and twelve dollars per term. Studies included "orthography, reading, and writing" in the lower grades. Grammar, arithmetic, French, German, music, and drawing were added in the middle years, with history, philosophy, and astronomy saved for the oldest pupils.[9] In all the schools, scholastic achievement went hand in hand with an emphasis on "moral as well as physical and mental powers."[10]

For the first time in her life, Mary Custis found herself in the midst of a group of girls her own age. Much to her father's amusement, she spent most of her time with them. "Daughter is much taken up with her young companions," Lee wrote to Custis, "and there are regular walks in the afternoons and sundry visits on Saturdays." Like most young girls, they were beginning to be aware of the boys in the neighborhood, and Lee was delighted by this budding social sense. "I perceive," he wrote, "that their walks never extend country-wise, but always town-wise, from which I infer that they are more attracted by sightseeing than by a desire for exercise and the beauties of nature. The confabs at the corners, too, are frequent and long and their tongues try to cover their glances over their shoulders at interesting passengers. I fear they are wicked things."[11] Among Mary Custis' special friends were Esther and Mary Whitingham, daughters of the Bishop of Maryland, who also lived on Madison Avenue and attended Mount Calvary Church. The friendship continued for several years, Mary visiting the Whitinghams on the Eastern Shore of Maryland as late as 1855.[12]

While Daughter and Rooney went to school, the younger children kept busy playing hopscotch on the sidewalks and rolling their hoops on the green lawns of Mount Vernon Place. In the evenings, when Lee came home, he and the children played an elaborate game called "strategy," in which he had "us all shut up in rooms so that we couldn't get out until he let us."[13]

Robert and Mary Lee were a popular couple, entertaining at home or dining out frequently. On special occasions Mildred and Rob were allowed to stay up past their bedtime to kiss their parents goodnight. Resplendent in his dress uniform, Lee was always ready first. When his wife appeared, he would "chide her gently in a playful way and with a bright smile . . . then bid us good-bye," Rob recalled. "I would go to sleep with this beautiful picture in my mind, the golden epaulets and all—chiefly the epaulets."[14] Sometimes Mary Custis, as the eldest child at home, was permitted to attend special functions with her parents. Once she went to a wedding with them, dressed in a "new sprigged muslin which was made for the occasion with pink sash & short sleeves." Her accessories included "a white lily in her hair [and] new white kid gloves."[15]

Living in a large city and going out so much made Mrs. Lee more conscious of high fashion and available fabrics, both for herself and for the girls. "I wanted half a pound of Zephyr," she wrote to a friend in New York, "containing an oz. of any colour . . . & Mother wanted half a pound of what they call *double* Zephyr *white*, it is a *little coarser* than the common Zephyr but *very little, not* that very *thick* floss kind." She also needed, she said, "any little *cheap* trimming that would answer to trim Annie & Agnes' joseys [a fitted outer waist]. Send about 7 yds. of it." Concerned about new designs, she asked "if there is anything new in the style of sleeves. . . . Do they pink the long shawls as well as the dresses?"[16] When she could not find materials locally, she sent to New York to "Mr. Macy's."[17]

In spite of her husband's comments about Baltimore summers, Mrs. Lee decided to remain in town throughout the hot months of 1850, "as I have been so much separated from my husband."[18] She soon found out why so many of their friends had left for seashore or mountains. Agnes, Annie, and Rooney quickly departed for Arlington, and Mary Custis escaped the hot pavements and entrapped air of the row house by visiting friends in the country. With only Lee and the two younger children at home, Mrs. Lee invited her mother to come over for a visit. Together the two women read religious biographies, Mrs. Lee painted, and they enjoyed watching Rob and Milly at play. Precious Life, now five years old, had "become quite a little woman. . . . [She] sings a great many songs . . . [and] is a most finished coquette."[19] In the evenings they strolled through Mount Vernon Place, admiring the Washington Monument. Mrs. Custis wrote a friend that "really it is beautiful especially at moonlight."[20]

September brought cooler weather, the return of neighbors, and fall housecleaning. Lee reported to his friend Jerome Bonaparte, Jr., that "windows are open, brushes are flourishing, & dust flying."[21] The Lee household was smaller this year, as Custis had entered West Point as a plebe, and Annie and Agnes remained at Arlington to be taught by their grandmother. Mrs. Custis was well qualified to teach, but the little girls preferred playing paper dolls to studying. "There is only one subject in which they are diligent," Mrs. Custis wrote to the Lees, "cutting up paper into babies & dresses & articles of furniture, strewing them—leaving a trail."[22] She finally persuaded them to begin reading out loud to her on a regular basis. Each taking a turn, they read "the story of a lovely child . . . successively under the influence of strong natural passions and ultimately of divine Grace."[23] The book was the enormously popular *The Wide, Wide World,* published in 1851 under the pseudonym of Elizabeth Wetherell, a painfully saccharine tale by today's standards but a story guaranteed to make feminine readers of the period weep.*

By January it was decided that the girls needed a governess to live at Arlington and provide more professional teaching and discipline. The new instructor was "a charming character" named Susan Poor, who proved to be an imaginative guide and real friend.[24] Robert Lee had very specific and decided views about women's education which he outlined carefully to the new governess. "I particularly desire that she [Miss Poor] will teach them to write a good hand, & to be *regular, orderly, & energetic* in the performance of all their duties. I also wish her to teach them to sing . . . to sew and knit." He also hoped the new teacher would "insist on their taking regular exercise."[25]

With the Girls gone, the Madison Avenue house seemed roomier this year until Mrs. Lee began extending invitations to Virginia relatives. When he returned home from a trip to West Point earlier than expected, Lee discovered to his chagrin just how many beds were occupied. He arrived by train at daybreak, he later wrote to Custis, and walked from the station to the house, letting himself in with a borrowed key. Going upstairs to Mrs. Lee's bedroom, he knocked on the door. "But instead of admitting me, on opening the door, she prevented my entrance, saying that Emma Randolph was in there. So . . . I determined to go up & see the children. I found both Marys (who has moved to the front room, 3rd story) & Rooneys doors locked." After much knocking, someone opened the door to Daughter's room. "I walked in & found M. [Mary Custis] sound asleep & some person by her side, buried in the bed with head completely covered. I saw it was too *long* for any of the children, & having succeeded in waking M., she informed me it was Cousin Corn-

---

*Elizabeth Wetherell [Susan Warner], *The Wide, Wide World* (New York: G. P. Putnam, 1851).

elia Randolph. I had then to beat a retreat from there." As a last resort, he tried Rooney's door, which was finally unlocked by little Rob. "There laid R. [Rooney] sound asleep in the middle of the bed, Mildred on one side of him & Rob crawling in on the other. Upon investigation, I discovered that Rooney, on coming up to bed, had caught up the two little children from their room & put them into his bed. . . . I did not venture to examine farther into the house."[26]

Not wishing to experiment with another sultry Baltimore summer, Mrs. Lee and the children went to Arlington at the end of the school year in 1851, and Robert Lee was left by himself. "Times are pretty dull now in B[altimore], for Spec, the Parrot [presumably another household pet], and myself," Lee wrote to Custis. "No Mim [Mrs. Lee], no children. . . . Still at Sollers we hammer on lustily."[27] The young people passed their time visiting relatives and watching repairs in progress on the portico at Arlington. In the evenings they all sat in the cool hallway, looking out across the river at the Federal city's partially completed Washington Monument.

When September approached, Mrs. Lee took only Rob, Mildred, and Mary Custis back with her to Baltimore, Rooney remaining in Virginia to attend Mr. McNally's school. Rob and Milly had serious cases of whooping cough that fall, with Precious Life recovering first. "Milly says I must tell you that Rob is sick and she and Angelina [a favorite doll] are quite well, the latter having recently been restored by having the upper half of her cranium cemented on," Mrs. Lee wrote Custis.[28]

Fortunately, both children were well enough to make the annual Christmas trip to Arlington. Only Custis, in barracks at West Point, was missing from the family reunion, and Lee took time to write the lonely young man a detailed letter about their holiday activities. After delays caused by cold weather, they had been met at the Washington train station by Mr. Custis and old Daniel, the coachman, and one other servant, "young Daniel," riding the new colt, Mildred. Lee and Rooney decided to walk through the heavy snow across the Potomac bridge and up the steep Arlington hill, arriving only a few minutes after the heavily laden carriage. On Christmas morning, as usual, Rob and Milly aroused the household before daybreak to view their stockings. All day Mildred played with her new doll, a marvelous surprise, which was to serve as a substitute for Angelina, whose "infirmities were so great that she was left in Baltimore."[29] Lee ended the letter describing the traditional family dinner—turkey, ham, plum pudding, and mince pies.

No Virginia plantation holiday was complete without company, and there were innumerable cousins and friends at the big house. One of the guests must have been coming down with measles, for within a few weeks of the Lees' return to Baltimore all three children, as well as Rob's hapless young "mammy," Eliza, came down with the disease. Mary Custis was sick for a long time, Rob and Eliza recuperated slowly, but Mildred was soon up and about, busy with pretend tea parties for the handsome new Christmas doll, Jenny Lind.

For three years now, Lee had been supervising the tedious and expensive construction of Fort Carroll. January of 1852 found the parade ground finished and smoothed down, ready for spring grassing. The wall that ringed it to keep out seawater was ten feet high and clearly visible from the city, the barracks were nearing completion, and mountings were in place for three hundred cannon. But the original sum authorized by Congress was depleted, and legislators seemed to be losing interest. Lee was optimistic that with a year's additional work and one more appropriation the project could be successfully finished. But the Corps of Engineers had other plans. In May Brevet Colonel Lee received the surprising news that he had been appointed superintendent of the United States Military Academy at West Point, New York. The office was one of the few choice positions in the Engineering Corps, carrying with it the assurance of several years of pleasant living, a fine house, and considerable prestige. But Lee felt that he was not well qualified and asked to be given another post. The order stood, however, and early in June the family prepared to make yet another move.

The first stop, of course, was Arlington, where mother and children would wait till their new quarters were ready. The gardens were in full bloom, and for the first time Mildred was mature enough to appreciate the beauty of her surroundings, as well as old enough to be a real pleasure and playmate to Annie and Agnes. One evening, much to her delight, the Girls made her a crown of red roses, using a variety that "grew under the apricot tree—I wore it with great pride on my sunny brown curls."[30]

The Arlington rose garden was famous all over the area. Mrs. Custis had planted most of the bushes, and she and Mrs. Lee took special delight in tending them, with help from "Old George, little George, Uncle Ephriam [sic], Billy, and swarms of small Ethiopians."[31] Guests were always invited to wander through the garden, leaving with armloads of every species—pinks, reds, damasks, hundred-leaf roses (which Nurse and "Old Mammy" used for making rose water, kept in stone bottles in the storeroom), and a rich yellow variety tinged with crimson, which was Annie's favorite because it complemented her glossy black hair.

Free from the restrictions of the city, the younger children romped all over the estate. It must have been after one of these morning play sessions with Rob that Mildred came in for lunch with a dirty dress. Her grandfather reproached her, saying that his "grandmamma, Mrs. Washington, wore always one white gown a week, and that when she took it off it was as spotless as the day she put it on."[32]

Lee left for West Point in August. Within a few weeks, after the repairs to the superintendent's house had been completed, Mrs. Lee joined him with Mary Custis, Mildred, Rooney, and Rob. Annie and Agnes remained at Arlington under Miss Poor's tutelage.

The United States Military Academy was fifty years old when the Lees took up residence on the post, with fifteen faculty members and several hundred cadets. New Barracks, a commodious hotel for visiting dignitaries, a chapel, and numerous classroom buildings bounded three sides of a forty-acre parade ground, or "Plain," as it was called. Halfway along a row of faculty houses, between the cadet barracks and the quarters for noncommissioned officers, stood the superintendent's house, surrounded by an iron railing with a gate. The house was "large and convenient," according to Agnes' later description, with stables for the two horses, a garden, a pond, and a greenhouse with a "splendid lemon tree," where Mrs. Lee was able to propagate cuttings from the Arlington gardens.[33]

To help fill up the spacious rooms, the Lees had bought in Baltimore a new set of red velvet parlor furniture, which included two settees, a lady chair, and matching side chairs. These, along with their older furniture from Arlington and the Lee and Custis silver and china, enabled the family to entertain in a manner becoming the superintendent.

Within a few weeks Milly and Rob began school, attending the post academy with a handful of other officers' children. Rooney, still boisterous and growing enormously, went away that fall to a preparatory school in New York City. At first Mary Custis tried studying at the Point, but before long she transferred to Pelham Priory, an unconventional girls' seminary in Westchester County, New York. This relatively new but already popular school for young women was a special favorite among Southern families, and Markie Williams, Mrs. Lee's first cousin (once removed), was a close friend of one of the teachers. Its proprietor, the

Reverend Robert Bolton, was an Episcopal clergyman from Savannah, Georgia, who had studied for the ministry in England. To supplement his meager income, Mr. Bolton began teaching young people in the neighborhood along with his own thirteen children, and his reputation soon spread.

The school took its name from the large house that Mr. Bolton had built with architectural suggestions from Washington Irving. It must have been an extraordinary-looking structure, in "medieval English style," with a stone tower at one end and a brick tower—"to give the effect of a Jacobean addition"—at the other end. In another direction a "half-completed chamber was erected, affording the effect of an abandoned or partly ruined chapel."[34] Terraced gardens, boxwood hedges, and a small lake purported to give the appearance of an English estate. Indoors, classrooms were gloomy, with stained-glass windows, walls hung with armor and ancient weaponry, heavy oaken tables, and carved high-backed chairs.

Mr. Bolton was an admirer of Thomas Arnold, the famous English headmaster, and he adapted Arnold's curriculum for boys to his American young ladies. European history, Latin, Greek, and biblical studies were added to the more traditional women's curriculum of art, piano, and the harp. But there was also time for recreation in season— morning walks two by two in pleasant weather, ice-skating and sledding in winter months. Most of the teachers were women, including several Bolton daughters and a young New York educator, Blanche Berard, Markie Williams' friend. These were augmented by several male professors who commuted daily from New York City.

More unusual than the architecture and the curriculum was the intense religious atmosphere of the school. This strong moral influence had been well publicized by a small book about one of the Bolton daughters, published in 1850. *The Lighted Valley* is a lugubrious biography of Abby Bolton who, between bouts of increasingly debilitating tuberculosis, taught at the Priory, studied in England, traveled, and tried to persuade those about her to find peace in religion. Mrs. Lee had read Abby's story during the hot, quiet summer of 1850.*

The half-dozen letters written by Mary Custis Lee from Pelham Priory do not mention academic subjects. But her descriptions of boarding

---

*R. Bolton, *The Lighted Valley* (New York: Robert Carter & Brothers, 1850).

school life, her occasional use of French phrases, and her new signature—"Marielle"—suggest that she was an attractive, lively, eighteen-year-old girl, admired by schoolmates and teachers alike, whose poise and maturity enabled her to remain close to her family while at the same time savoring new friends and her proximity to sophisticated New York City. Only her unruly curls gave a hint of the little tomboy of years past. In a letter written in the spring of 1853, Mary Custis begged Nurse "if she has time to make me a bottle of pomatum [a sweet-smelling ointment for the hair]. . . . Mine is completely exhausted and habit and my scurvy hair have rendered it almost indispensable."[35] The name "Marielle" was one she used frequently in letters from 1853 till the turn of the century. Perhaps the heavy Gothic influence of Pelham Priory made plain "Mary" seem too ordinary.

The family was divided that Christmas, Mary Custis and Rooney traveling to West Point, Annie and Agnes remaining at Arlington. But despite her disappointment over the separation, Agnes was excited about Christmas. If only the rest of the family were with them, she confessed to her new diary, "my cup of happiness would be full."[36] As it was, she awoke before five on Christmas morning, wished the servants "Christmas gift," opened her stocking, and ran downstairs before Annie or her grandparents were up.

The diary was a gift from Miss Poor, who suggested that the child keep a journal to improve her penmanship and writing skills. Through the winter and early spring, Agnes struggled to make frequent and significant entries. She found it hard, however, to "put down every little thing, the weather, warm or cold, wet or dry, the sickness or health of the family . . . all of which items are even more tiresome to write than to read."[37] She acknowledged that "the everyday life of a little school girl of twelve years is not startling," but she continued keeping her journal until January 1858.[38] To the contemporary reader her account reveals a sensitive, observant, winsome teenager whose sense of proportion and humor were not marred by her associations with the great and the near-great.

Early diary entries mention skating on the canal with Cousin "Washy" Washington Stuart, a visit from Washington Irving to Arlington, sighting the first crocus of the season in her own small garden, crossing the river with Grandfather Custis to celebrate Washington's birthday, and her decision not to go with him to President Pierce's inaugural. Mr. Custis had never missed the ceremonies for swearing in a president so, in spite of sleet and bitter cold and his own increasing age, he took Miss Poor across the choppy Potomac to witness the festivities.

Also in the crowd that chilly day was an itinerant artist-journalist, Benson Lossing, whom Mr. Custis met and invited to Arlington for a brief visit. Accompanied by his wife and two small daughters, Lossing stayed nearly a week at the great house, listening to tales about Mount Vernon, sketching the Washington mementos, and making notes in preparation for an effusive article which he published in *Harper's Magazine* in September of 1853. Agnes and Annie were left to entertain the two Lossing girls, who were much younger and rather dull, according to Agnes' diary. She was far more interested in her new gray and white rabbits and her pet chickens—Brunetta, Aunt Stella, and Eudora.

A guest of a different sort that winter was Cousin Martha Custis Williams, aged twenty-seven, whom the family always referred to as "Markie." The orphaned daughter of Mrs. Lee's first cousin, Markie Williams began spending more and more of her time now at Arlington, becoming a special favorite and protégée of Grandfather and Grandmother Custis. "She is a lively, warm girl," Mrs. Custis wrote to a friend in 1851, "a Christian in name and deed."[39] Markie's mother had been one of three extraordinarily named sisters—Britannia, Columbia, and America Peter—who had grown up at Tudor Place in Georgetown, near enough to the Potomac to be clearly visible from Arlington. As children they and little Mary Anna Custis used to exchange messages across the river by means of elaborate signals with colored cloths in upstairs windows. "Aunt Brit" (Mrs. Beverly Kennon) was a frequent visitor at Arlington, but Markie's mother, America, had married an aide to General Lafayette, William George Williams, and the family had lived "up North." Captain Williams' death at Monterrey during the Mexican War was followed not long afterwards by his wife's. Markie and her two younger brothers, Lawrence and Orton, were taken in by the Custises and considered Arlington their second home, spending portions of their vacation time there and at Tudor Place. Lawrence had graduated from West Point in 1852 and Orton was in boarding school. During the winter of 1852, Markie moved her furniture and most of her own paintings into Mary Custis' large front bedroom at Arlington, which from then on was always referred to as "Mary and Markie's room."

When Cousin Markie went abroad, Agnes and Annie could not help feeling forlorn. News from West Point was especially welcome, and their father sent letters as often as he could, with admonitions and obvious affection.

My precious Annie [he wrote on February 25, 1853] my
limited time does not diminish my affection for you . . .
nor prevent my thinking of you & wishing for you. . . . At
dawn when I rise, & all day, my thoughts revert to you in
expressions that you cannot hear or I repeat. . . . I am
told you are growing very tall, & I hope very straight. I
do not know what the Cadets will say if the Supt's
children do not practice what he demands of them. . . .
Give much love to your dear Grdmother, Grdfather,
Agnes . . . & all friends, including the Servants."[40]

A new responsibility that winter and spring for Annie and Agnes was
to teach the slave children. Such instruction was expressly forbidden by
Virginia law, but Mrs. Custis had always done it and so had Mrs. Lee.[41]
The Girls sometimes found that outdoor fun was more attractive to their
pupils than writing compositions. Agnes noted in her diary that on one
occasion, "I had my little *dark* scholars though they were loth to tare
[*sic*] themselves from their sleigh riding."[42]

Busy with their studies, teaching, and play, the children were only
vaguely aware of their grandmother's declining health and recurrent
headaches. Even Mr. Custis, far from well himself, seemed unprepared
for his wife's sudden illness on a Thursday in the middle of April. Two
days later the doctors began looking very grave and sent for Mrs. Lee.
With no one to keep them out of their grandmother's bedroom, Annie
and Agnes hovered near the door, and Annie burst into tears. Hearing
her sobs, Mrs. Custis called the Girls to her, with arms outstretched.
They clambered onto the bed, one on either side of the dying woman,
while she held them close and tried to calm them. "How can you cry so,
Annie?" she whispered.[43] Wide-eyed, Agnes watched the heaving
breaths come more and more slowly. With the Girls still beside her, Mrs.
Custis murmured the Lord's Prayer and died.

It was one of the Girls' first encounters with death, though they had
known of slave deaths on the plantation and may have been with their
mother six years before when their cousin Lorenzo Lewis died suddenly from pneumonia.[44] Instinctively, they realized that their quiet
grandmother had been not only their mentor and friend, but also the
mainstay of the whole plantation. Mr. Custis, heartbroken and suddenly
old, was unable to make decisions, deferring all plans until his daughter

could arrive. With the sound of weeping servants all around her, Agnes crept off to her own trundle bed and "wished for Mamma."[45]

Mrs. Lee arrived a day or two later, surprisingly calm, to conduct morning prayers (which had been neglected since Mrs. Custis' illness), select a grave site, and make arrangements for the simple funeral service, which was held in Arlington's main hall with only the immediate family and a few close friends attending. Then four of the stronger servants—Austin, Lawrence, Daniel the coachman, and Ephraim the gardener—carried the small, plain coffin up the hill to a knoll overlooking the river, where the family threw "bouquets of flowers."[46]

Letters of condolence arrived from friends and family members, Markie wrote heartbrokenly from England, and there was even a eulogistic letter in a local newspaper praising the gentle woman who had been Arlington's mistress for forty-nine years. With so much to attend to, Mrs. Lee remained in Virginia with her father, but Lee could not leave West Point till after examinations, and both parents felt that the five children in school should remain in their classes to the end of the term.

Life without Grandmother seemed unalterably sad, and Agnes and Annie looked forward with eagerness to the return of their brothers and sisters. They were also unhappy over the departure of Miss Poor, who in the two years she had taught the Girls had become their close friend. "O I felt *so* sad when we parted!" Agnes wrote in the diary. But her leaving had one advantage—"it may be of benefit to my journal; it is so impossible to write unrestrainedly when you feel some one is going to look over what you have just written."[47]

Within a few weeks everyone was at Arlington, including Rooney, who by now felt so large and grown-up he asked the family to begin calling him Fitzhugh. The name seemed too formal for Agnes to use, for though he was " perfectly enormous," he seemed "just the same."[48] Most of the vacation was spent at Arlington except for a three-day excursion to Ravensworth. While the rest visited with Aunt Maria Fitzhugh, Agnes and Rob wandered outdoors and "regaled ourselves with a few peaches . . . to the horror of some little colored children on the hill who stared at us as if we were wild beasts."[49]

One Sunday evening before summer's close, Mary Custis and Annie were confirmed at Christ Church, Alexandria, and their father decided to be confirmed with them. Lee had long been a faithful churchgoer and had even served on the vestry at Fort Hamilton, but he had never formally taken the vows of full church membership. It must have been impressive for Daughter and Annie to have their father kneeling at the altar rail with them, but Agnes felt terribly left out. "I wish A[nnie] & I could have been confirmed together," she wrote.[50]

With Miss Poor gone and Grandmother Custis no longer at Arlington to supervise, Lee and his wife decided that Annie and Agnes should return with the rest to West Point. The last few days were taken up with good-byes, visits with cousins, placing a special bouquet of flowers on Mrs. Custis' grave, and making a final trip to see the pet rabbits, now securely housed in a new pen that Rooney had built at the edge of the vegetable garden. "I hugged & kissed" the bunnies, Agnes recorded, "but little did they appreciate my affection or my sadness."[51]

In spite of their reluctance to leave Arlington, the Girls found the trip exciting. They took the train from Baltimore to New York, transferring at five in the morning to a riverboat that took the n up the Hudson. Agnes liked the new house and the scenery, but both she and Annie were very homesick. "I long for Arlington," Agnes wrote, "my precious Arlington my own dear *home*."[52]

Part of their unhappiness stemmed from their acute discomfort at being surrounded by so many young men. Custis sometimes brought classmates to visit at the superintendent's house, and the Lees frequently entertained large groups of cadets. On these occasions Annie and Agnes would dutifully help set the tables, but then they would slip away, spending the evening "sitting on the steps & having a good cry," ill at ease in their new environment and longing for the old familiar scenes.[53]

The opening of classes made life easier. The Girls studied French under a professor at West Point and took piano lessons from Mr. Apelles, the leader of the post band, who gave them "long hard exercises," and made them "*thump*," presumably to keep steady time.[54] Mary Custis remained at West Point that winter, far more relaxed when entertaining cadets than her younger sisters were. Since it was a large household, with only Rooney away in New York and Custis visiting infrequently, Mrs. Lee felt fortunate to have several of the Arlington servants to help out, including a cook, a waiter, and Eliza, Rob's childhood "mammy," now a full-fledged housemaid.

By winter, Agnes wrote, "we know almost all of Custis' class," so she must not have been too unhappy when the Lees entertained the entire senior class during the Christmas holidays.[55] Though her letters and journal mention only a few of these young men by name, many were soon to become famous as leaders in the Civil War. Stephen Lee, John

Pegram, Archie Grace, Jeb Stuart, and William Dorsey Pender would all be generals in the Confederate army, while Oliver O. Howard, who ranked second in the class, was to fight as a major general against the Southerners at the Battle of Chancellorsville and other important encounters.

The most frequent cadet visitor during that year of 1853–54 was James Ewell Brown Stuart, called "Jeb" or "Beauty" by his classmates. Sturdy, restless, and an excellent horseman, the young Virginian had been in a variety of scrapes early in his college life, but by the last half of his senior year Jeb Stuart had settled down and become quite an admirer of Mary Custis Lee, whom he described as most attractive "both as regards beauty and sprightliness." He hastened to assure the family at home, however, that even "with all the array of love-seekers and heart-breakers I have escaped unscathed."[56]

Another cadet who felt comfortable at the superintendent's house was Fitz Lee, a year behind Custis and his first cousin. "Chudie," as the Lee girls called him, was far less military in his manner than Custis and found the restrictions of the Academy oppressive. Because of his various breaches of conduct, Fitz spent much of his free time walking penalty tours or confined to barracks.

There was one other cadet at the Point that winter who was to achieve worldwide fame, the future painter James Abbott McNeill Whistler. An unlikely candidate for military life, "Curly" Whistler probably wanted to stay as far away from the superintendent and his family as possible, for he managed to incur an overwhelming number of demerits for tardiness, unshined shoes, and long hair. He lasted two years at the Academy, with his final dismissal coming at the end of an oral examination in chemistry, when he was asked to discuss silicon. With the bravado born of desperation, Whistler pronounced silicon to be a gas, whereupon his teacher recommended withdrawal from West Point. If the girls saw him at all, it was probably at cadet art exhibits, for he stood first in his class in drawing.

Though Agnes made conversation with cadets with greater ease now, she still found it hard to behave in as ladylike a manner as her parents wished. "Young as I am," she fussed, "I must sit up & talk & walk as a young lady and be constantly greeted with ladies do this & that—& think so—all as if I was twenty."[57] Not only were the children supposed to behave as befitted the daughters of the superintendent, but they had to adhere to a rigorous schedule as well. In the dark winter months they got up at five in the morning, when the rising gun sounded in barracks, for breakfast was at six-thirty so Lee could be in the office by seven.

Meanwhile, back at Arlington Mr. Custis was trying to adjust to a daily routine without his wife. Fortunately, Markie Williams had returned from England and taken up residence again. Her stay with Mr. Custis meant that Mrs. Lee could remain at West Point till late spring, a necessity, she and her husband felt, since "the present welfare of the children & their future usefulness require [the] unremitted care & attention" of both parents.[58]

Markie wrote cheerfully about news from Washington and the coming of spring in the Virginia countryside. But she was also much concerned about future schooling for her younger brother Orton, a handsome, bright, but headstrong young man. Orton had his heart set on attending West Point, but Lee discouraged such hopes, believing it unlikely that two from one family could receive appointments. He told Markie that Rooney and Rob were also talking about becoming professional soldiers. "I can advise no young man to enter the Army," he counseled Markie. "The same application, the same self-denial, the same endurance, in any other profession, will advance him faster & farther."[59]

Winter lingered on in New York State, much to the disgust of Mary Custis, who had somehow hurt her foot and was forced to remain indoors, unable to skate, sled, or even ride horseback. To add to the family's discomfort, Mildred came down with whooping cough for the second time, and Agnes grew homesick all over again when Cousin Markie sent some pressed crocuses from Arlington. Agnes confided to her diary the things she missed most—"the dear old servants, & my pets, my bunnys [sic], one poor little thing is dead, my chickens, my cats, pigeons, garden in fact everything in & near home."[60] Finally, late in May, Mrs. Lee could wait no longer to check on her father, so she took Mildred out of school, and together with Mary Custis, they set out for Arlington. Annie and Agnes remained at West Point till classes were over to keep house for their father and witness Custis' graduation from the Military Academy.

June brought new cadets to the post, and both girls were incensed by the indignities heaped upon the hapless "plebes." "Poor fellows, they are teazed [sic], tormented & tricked almost out of their lives," Agnes wrote.[61] A few weeks later came final examinations, oral recitations to which the public was invited. Annie and Agnes attended the First Class exam on ethics, and Agnes went to one on national law. "Every one told

me I wouldn't understand one word . . . but to my great satisfaction I did
. . . & liked it very much."[62] She did not mention attending Curly
Whistler's disastrous chemistry recitation.

Just before commencement there was an eclipse of the sun, clearly
visible in the northeast United States. All the cadets—and presumably
the Lees—watched from the post observatory or "scattered over the
plain with pieces of smoked glass, each his own astronomer, begrim-
ming [*sic*] his face & hands," Lee wrote to Markie.[63]

On the first of July, 1854, George Washington Custis Lee was graduated
first in his class, a distinction that his sisters noted with satisfaction, since
he was younger than many of his classmates and "educated in Virginia
where 'tis thought people are so lazy."[64] Unfortunately, Custis got sick
just before the final exercises and had to miss the last hop, the commencement parade, and the fireworks. Agnes felt he was lucky to have
escaped the graduation speech—"the longest most uninteresting thing
about 'unlimited extension.'"[65]

The summer at Arlington passed too quickly for them all, in spite of
the intense heat and Mary Custis' continuing foot problems. Annie and
Agnes did their best to carry her around by making a chair with their
hands, "but she is pretty heavy."[66] The return trip to West Point was a
difficult one, partly because of Daughter's infirmities, partly because the
family had in tow a friend's small puppy whom they had kept over the
summer. "Papa & Rooney carried Sister," Agnes wrote in the diary,
"Annie her crutches, Rob, little Tip [the visiting dog], who sat up grandly
in his arms, I the cloaks of the party numbering three or four large &
heavy." At each change of cars, the group caused a sensation, as "the
Conductor would scream to 'Jack' or 'Bill' &c to come & help a lady who
couldn't walk [and] instantly two or three great men would rush up & lift
us, cloaks, crutches, dogs, & people up or down whether we would or
no."[67] Understandably, Mrs. Lee and Milly came on later at a more
leisurely pace, bringing Mr. Custis back for a visit.

During this school term, there were five Lee children living in the
superintendent's house—Agnes and Annie, who continued their French
and piano lessons; Rob and Mildred at the post school; and Mary Custis,
whose foot continued to give her much trouble. Since he was unable to
obtain an appointment to the Military Academy, Rooney enrolled at
Harvard College, where his size and leadership ability quickly made
him an important figure on the campus. Custis, awaiting his permanent
orders, was away most of the autumn on short-term engineering
assignments.

Annie and Agnes were much happier this fall, though they admitted to being "only a little glad to get back."[68] Well past their fear of cadets, they now found themselves prepared to comment on the vagaries of their male acquaintances and even to poke a little gentle fun. The students they most often talked about in letters were classmates of their cousin Fitz—Junius B. Wheeler, "about the greatest lady's man" at the Valentine's Day party;[69] F. S. Armistead, "a perfect bore"; and "Mr. Carroll, . . . as impudent as ever," who grew a "moustache . . . of the most delicate red, rather rose colour."[70] Agnes could even find amusement at the discomfort of a plebe who, searching for a topic of conversation, picked up a book by an author named Phillip and observed that "there by adding an *s* you make my name." Agnes confessed that this method was one way of discovering "to whom I was talking."*[71]

Much of the Girls' self-assurance came from their having one especially close friend, Helen Bratt, almost exactly Annie's age, who was the daughter of the purveyor of subsistence for cadets at West Point. Helen, who lived only a few doors from the superintendent's quarters, attended boarding school in New York City, but she was home frequently on weekends. The girls corresponded regularly about matters that they felt to be of vital importance—walks home from church with cadets, student concerts and art exhibits, and the new book everyone was reading, *The Heir of Redclyffe*, by Charlotte Yonge.*

Restless away from Arlington, Mr. Custis was willing to stay at West Point for only a few weeks. Custis, still without assignment, took his grandfather home and on his return brought the Girls letters from the servant children whom they had been teaching. Annie ruefully wrote Helen that the slaves' spelling and syntax did not "do us, their masters[,] teachers I mean, much credit." One began, "'I take my pen in

---

*Junius B. Wheeler, graduated 5th in his class at West Point in 1855; served as a colonel in the Union army in Arkansas, Texas, and Louisiana; later taught engineering at West Point.

Frank S. Armistead, a cadet from Virginia, graduated 34th in his class in 1856; served in the Union army on the Utah Expedition; joined the Confederate army in 1861, serving on his father's staff under Gen. Pickett; was killed at Gettysburg.

Samuel S. Carrol, graduated 44th in his class at West Point in 1856; rose to brigadier general in the Union army; fought in the battles of Chancellorsville, Gettysburg, and the Wilderness; was wounded in Spotsylvania. (George Washington Cullum, *Biographical Register of the Officers and Graduates of the United States Military Academy*, 3d ed. [New York: Houghton Mifflin & Co., 1891], 2:610–11, 664, 670–71).

Phillips cannot be identified.

†Charlotte Yonge, *The Heir of Redclyffe* (London: Macmillan, 1879).

hand to inform you of the state of my health, I is well at present, & hopes you is the same.'" Another sent an essay about the "beauties of a 'popular tree that sits on the hill-side, & this place is truly admirable, from your absent scholar Marselina.'"[72]

Helen came home for Christmas and the three friends attended a variety of parties, including one where they ate "turkey, oysters, sangaree, marmelade ice cream, cake, mottoes & all things nice." On New Year's Day "from morning till night the house was filled by officers & cadets. . . . [We] 'gabbled' or listened to it all day. . . . & went to bed perfectly 'overkim as it were.'"[73] Rooney, too, came for the holidays, sporting "a tremendous black beaver, which he says are all the fashion at Cambridge," Agnes noted.[74]

On Valentine's Day, Mrs. Lee planned an elaborate party with sixteen cadets and twelve young ladies, including Annie and Agnes. Homemade valentines had been circulating all week. "Rob & Mil. each received & sent at least a dozen," Agnes wrote in the diary. "Most of them original without much regard to rhyme or metre. Sister [Mary Custis] had a good many too. Annie & I considered ourselves much neglected I only had one," in which "I was compared to sugar—clarified at that, molasses, honey, & all things sweet."[75] The identity of the author caused considerable speculation, for Annie was sure that it had been sent by Mr. Agnel, their French teacher, while Agnes insisted that it had been sent by a cadet.[76]

Annie sent a long rhymed Valentine poem to Helen Bratt, in which she threatened all sorts of dire self-inflicted tragedies if Helen would not consent to be her Valentine. If it is original, the poem shows vigorous writing and a clever sense of humor.

To Helen

The wing of my spirit is broken,
  My day-star of hope has declined;
For a month not a word have I spoken
  That's either polite or refined.
My mind's like the sky in bad weather,
  When mist-clouds around us are curled:
And, viewing myself altogether,
  I'm the veriest wretch in the world!

I wander about like a vagrant
    I spend half my time in the street;
My conduct's improper and flagrant,
    For I quarrel with all that I meet.
My dress, too, is wholly neglected,
    My hat I pull over my brow,
And I look like a fellow suspected
    Of wishing to kick up a row.

One says, "He's a victim to Cupid;"
    Another, "His conduct's too bad;"
A third, "He is awfully stupid;"
    A fourth, "He is perfectly mad!"
And then I am watched like a bandit,
    Mankind with me all are at strife:
By heaven, no longer I'll stand it,
    But quick put an end to my life!

I've thought of the means—yet I shudder
    At dagger or rat's bone or rope;
At drawing with lancet my blood, or
    At razor without any soap!
Suppose I should fall in a duel,
    And thus leave the stage with *éclat*?
But to die with a bullet is cruel—
    Besides, 'twould be breaking the law.

Yet one way remains: to the river.
    I'll fly from the goadings of care!—
But drown?—oh! the thought makes me shiver—
    A terrible death, I declare!
No!—my Helen *will* forgive me;
    I'll stand her for a time,
For I'm sure at last she'll take me
    For her own true Valentine.

   Beneath the poem is a small sketch of a cadet standing at the edge of a precipice called Lover's Leap.[77]
   Pleased with the success of her Valentine party, Mrs. Lee decided to give more frequent dinners and soirées. Though the Girls had become much more comfortable conversing with young men, they still found so

many parties excessive. "We have had so many, averaging more than one a week," Agnes wrote, "that the whole family are heartily sick of them."[78]

One afternoon in March, Agnes was walking home across the Plain from a French lesson when a cadet called to her with the news that her father had just been promoted and assigned command of one of the cavalry regiments in Texas. The promotion to lieutenant colonel was most welcome, but the new duty meant leaving West Point and shifting to a new branch of military service. "We are no longer in the Engineers but the Cavalry," Agnes explained.[79] Annie wrote to Helen that she would like to go with her father "to see the beautiful west with its immense prairies, proud mountains, & broad rolling streams," but her notion of traveling with her father was as fanciful as her geography of Texas, for she knew that along with the rest of the family she would be journeying back to Arlington.[80]

As the girls ran from cellar to attic, sorting and packing, and watched the house get emptier till there were only four beds left for sleeping, they found it harder to leave than they had imagined. Friends dropped by to say farewell, and as a final gesture of gallantry, the whole cadet corps serenaded the superintendent's quarters with "Home Sweet Home" and "Carry Me Back to Old Virginny."

The morning of departure dawned wet and dismal. Crowds of acquaintances and cadets gathered at the wharf in the pouring rain. Even "Chudie" Lee was there, with a special permit to leave barracks to say good-bye. The family crossed the Hudson in an open boat, thoroughly soaked but straining to look back through the mist at the dock, the bluffs, and the gray towers of West Point. Agnes cried "'till my eyes were blinded."[81]

A stopover in New York City to view the Crystal Palace and a boat ride down the Chesapeake Bay soon revived them all. They stayed for a few days in Baltimore, where Mildred accompanied her parents to dinner with the Jerome Bonapartes, and Mary Custis decided to remain awhile with the Marshalls to nurse Aunt Anne, who by now was almost an invalid. Annie and Agnes were wild to get home and chafed at the delay. Finally, on the Saturday after Easter, they took "the cars" to Washington and were met by "the *two* Daniel's [sic] & the familiar carriage & horses."[82] "It seemed an age," Agnes wrote, "before we dashed around the garden fence. I sprang out on the steps kissed Grandpa, & Cousin Markie, ran out to tell the servants how d'ye do & then wandered all over the house." Everything seemed the same—house, woods, flowers, pets,

and their own bedroom, with its four-poster bedstead and a trundle bed
for Mildred, the miniature chest that had belonged to their grandmother Lee, and the old mantle with cologne bottles and a statue of the
Three Graces. Even the servants seemed not to have aged, except for
"old Mammy," now "seventy six at least" and " very weak & thin."[83]

The old house had not changed, but the four Lee girls had. In the six
years since they had moved to Baltimore, Mary Custis had matured from
a lonely child to a self-assured young woman of twenty, at home in the
city and in society, with a wide circle of friends whom she enjoyed
visiting often. As her foot gradually improved, she was able to ride
horseback for hours at a time, no longer content to sit and keep
company with the family at home.

Taller than their mother and with their hair "put up," Annie and Agnes
felt themselves to be almost as grown-up as Sister. After all, Agnes
mused, "though young in years" (she was fifteen), she had acquired at
West Point "the experience of an ancient," so that she could now "look
down upon young people generally from a great height!"[84] Annie, not
quite seventeen, was always self-depreciatory about her looks; she
characterized herself that summer as "quite a *spinster* [and] sour as
vinegar."[85] But in spite of themselves, the Girls were often still
childlike.

Annie was the more irrepressible, and she loved to tease her Cousin
Markie. One day, after she had spread manure on her small garden plot,
Annie came indoors to practice the piano. There sat Markie Williams,
"sentimental & romantic" and very proper, reading a book. "I asked her
to guess what I had been doing, so she guessed once or twice & then
gave it up, & I told 'I had been *manuring* my garden.' Oh! *Annie! how
could you*? . . . Then she asked me to tell her wether [*sic*] I had been in
the *cart* with *it*."[86]

Even the overseer found the ways of the Girls hard to get used to. One
afternoon Agnes and a companion were asked to take a message from
Arlington House to the farm at the bottom of the hill. As she trotted
down the hill on her horse, she felt her comb slip out and fall to the
ground. Agnes jumped off to pick up the comb and let go of the bridle,
whereupon the horse dashed off without her. She ran after the runaway,
her hair loose and flying behind her. "When I reached the old ox house
little Austin [one of the servants] stood holding my quiet charger," she
wrote in her journal. She remounted and glancing over the fence, spied
a group of thirty field hands and the overseer, who stared open-

mouthed at the "comical" sight—"my hair streaming down my back, my riding skirt wet & my face brilliant with my race."[87]

Mildred had been only three years old when she moved to Baltimore, so she had changed even more than her sisters. No longer a small shadow trailing after the others, Precious Life now knew how to entertain herself, playing with a favorite cat, Thomas Aquinas, or making necklaces of jasmine blossoms to sweeten the linen closet. When she was tired, she would slip away to a "wooden bench, almost hidden by a drooping branch of seringa, my favorite hiding place." Another favorite place was the Grove, that "place of mystery" where squirrels played and bluebells and grapevines grew.[88] Here, on a mossy stone, she cracked hickory nuts and first read *Dairyman's Daughter* and *Coelebs in Search of a Wife.**

As if in response to the girls' delight at being home, the woods and gardens burst into exuberant growth. Lilies of the valley, bluebells, and mock orange carpeted the paths, while lilacs, honeysuckle, and locust blooms scented the air. Agnes spoke for them all when she declared, "West Point is probably more striking & picturesque, but Arlington with its commanding view, fine old trees, and the soft wild luxuriance of its woods can favorably compare with any home I've seen!"[89]

---

*Legh Richmond, *Dairyman's Daughter* (Philadelphia: American Sunday School Union, 1810) and Hannah More, *Coelebs in Search of a Wife* (New York: T. & Swords, 1809).

Legh Richmond, an evangelical minister in the Church of England, published *Dairyman's Daughter* in 1810. The religious tale (purportedly a true story) is filled with details of humble agrarian family life and tells of a young girl, fond of pretty clothes, who is converted to a single-minded devotion to God and to the need to bring others to her newfound faith. Just before her death from consumption, she repeats her belief in eternal salvation and her gratitude for God's goodness. To modern readers, the book seems a curiously lugubrious and mature one for a little girl to be reading.

Hannah More's popular book follows the protagonist's search for a helpmate in the image of Milton's Eve. Widely read for more than half a century, these two books, really little more than religious tracts, appear hopelessly dull and saccharine to readers today.

3

Schools, Spas, and Secession

1855–1860

SOON AFTER THE FAMILY'S return from West Point, Colonel and Mrs. Lee began discussing boarding schools for Annie and Agnes, since the Girls had never had formal education in a regular academic setting. For several months their father's letters were filled with messages about appropriate schools and the need for adequate preparation. Writing from Missouri, he urged them to "labour at their french, & music . . . try to progress in mathematics & English," and write to him "in either prose or verse" as practice for future composition classes.[1]

For their part, Agnes and Annie hated to think of leaving Arlington so soon after returning home. Annie wrote to Helen Bratt that she was having "a delightful time here, except for the prospect of going to school in the fall, awful!"[2] But in spite of their apprehensions, they managed to have a busy, happy summer, filled with routine activities and a long visit to King George County, Virginia.

All four daughters loved to ride horseback. During the hottest weather, Agnes and Annie preferred riding early in the mornings, accompanied by old Daniel. They found the quiet and beauty of the scenery as pleasant as the exercise itself. "You have no idea how beautifully everything looked in the morning dew," Annie explained. "Our ride for some distance lay along a row of high hills which commanded a beautiful view of Washington with fields & meadows on one side & dark forests on the other."[3]

Summertime always brought extra visitors to the great house, and this year was no exception. A number of former cadets came to call and the girls entertained them graciously, carefully hiding their amusement at seeing their friends for the first time in civilian garb. A guest from farther away was their uncle Smith Lee, a naval officer just returned to America after serving with Commodore Matthew Perry in Japan. Along with stories of the mysterious East, he brought back gifts—kimonos and lacquerware for the girls and a Japanese kite for Rob.

July Fourth traditionally meant Independence Day festivities, but this year the weather was rainy, so only Mr. Custis chose to travel across the river for speeches and acclaim. The rest waited at Arlington till dark, when they went outside on the porch to view the annual fireworks. "After tea," Agnes noted in her diary, "there was a grand display on the Arlington Portico—of cushions shawls etc. to make us comfortable while gazing at the magnificent fireworks which were to astonish the millions. Well we waited and waited, one or two faint efforts were made," but evidently the rain had dampened the powder, and so it "was 'no go' & we went in—much scandalized by the idea of a '4th' without fireworks."[4]

Before he had left for Missouri and Texas, Colonel Lee had drawn up plans for a new furnace and major renovations for the large area in the south wing of the house. Originally planned as a formal parlor, this room had never been completed by the Custises but had been used by the Lee children as a dusty playroom. Now, ostensibly to pay tribute to Mrs. Custis but more importantly to prevent further deterioration, the Lees undertook substantial repairs. The girls spent many hours watching the transformation as walls were cleaned and painted white, woodwork, doors, and bookcases stained a dark walnut, and red velvet curtains to match the West Point parlor furniture hung at the windows. With the addition of marble mantels, a crystal chandelier, and a French clock, the room was changed from a shabby storage area into a formal sitting room. Agnes envisioned a "brilliant room" filled with "the sound of gay music & dancing, with merry laughter."[5]

For Annie and Agnes the most important event of the summer was a ten-day trip to Cedar Grove, sixty miles south of Arlington. Situated on Chotank Creek, not far from the Potomac, the estate was the home of Dr. and Mrs. Richard Stuart, cousins of Mrs. Lee. Neither girl had ever been south of Alexandria, and so they were very excited boarding the Potomac riverboat *Columbia*, accompanied by their mother and Rob, for the five-hour trip downriver. Stopping at wharves along the way to pick up relatives, the vessel finally reached the Stuarts' landing dock about one in the afternoon. Here the travelers climbed into bumpy wagons for a short drive up to the house. "The portico was filled with a mass of . . . females," Agnes wrote, "& I assure you it was with no little dread I anticipated my introduction to my unknown cousins."[6]

But the Girls found everyone friendly, and they admired the sprawling house with its splendid view of the river and "eleven or twelve bedrooms"—"plenty of room" to accommodate the Stuart family as well as "Cousin Julia Morris, the Halls, Bowies, Ella & Mildred C.[arter] & ourselves." The young people went swimming by moonlight, feasted on "crabs, fried chickens, green peas, cake strawberries & ice cream," and visited neighboring plantations. "I heard the affairs of the Lees, Carters, Childes, *Grymes & others* discussed at length," Agnes wrote.[7] If she and Annie had not already heard stories about their father's half brother, "Black Horse Harry" Lee, they perhaps learned them during this visit, for Dr. Stuart was a half brother of the unfortunate young woman whom Harry Lee had seduced.

Their trip to Cedar Grove provided Annie and Agnes with glimpses of a plantation life quite different from their own—enormous families, sprawling manor houses on isolated farms, and slave labor far more demeaning than that practiced at Arlington. Annie wrote to Helen Bratt of her astonishment that slaves at Cedar Grove were used to carry master and guests from the riverboat to shore. When she saw "the boatmen jump into the water," she wondered "who was drowning" and understood only "when the girls commenced to choose which of the [slave] men should carry them." Even her heavyset host, Dr. Stuart, "over six feet and quite stout," came ashore "on the back of a rather small negro."[8]

The Girls must have realized, too, that their mother was not like some of the plantation mistresses they met at Cedar Grove. Though she supervised cultivation of flower and vegetable gardens, ordered supplies, directed the making of servants' clothes, and dispensed medicines to the slave quarters, Mrs. Lee really cared for few domestic occupations except gardening. Unusually well educated and influenced by her proximity to Washington, she preferred reading, painting, and political discussions to housework. She had dutifully taught her daughters to sew and to oversee the kitchen, but Annie and Agnes must have recognized during their stay at Cedar Grove that, in spite of her coaching, they were more dependent upon well-trained servants than many of their contemporaries.

Aware that some homemakers were more successful and happier than others, the Lee girls gave no hint in letters of this period of any stirring of feminist rebellion. And why should they? Except for a few seamstresses and dedicated teachers, all the ladies they knew lived at home, protected and supervised by husbands, sons, fathers, or brothers. In his letters Papa frequently exhorted them to acquire domestic skills, as well as to take loving care of their mother. Their favorite authors, Sir Walter Scott, Hannah More, and Charlotte Yonge, romanticized family life and endorsed female passivity. If, while they lived at West Point, they had learned anything about the Seneca Falls Convention of 1848 or its Declaration of the Rights of Women, they omitted any mention of them. At this period in their lives, independence and feminine assertiveness were simply not relevant issues for the Lee girls.

Not long after they returned from their trip, the decision was made for Annie and Agnes to attend the Virginia Female Institute in Staunton, Virginia, along with two of their cousins from the house party, Ada and Mary Stuart, and another cousin, Annette Carter. The school was a relatively new girls' academy, under the auspices of the Episcopal Diocese of Virginia, with high standards, a varied curriculum, and a religious atmosphere.

The remaining days of the summer were filled with activity. Dressmakers came over the river from Washington to assist the Arlington seamstresses in providing appropriate school wardrobes. There were friends to say good-bye to and name tags to sew in all their clothes. Finally, at their father's insistence, Annie and Agnes paid a long overdue visit to the dentist. "Mr. Williams will not be able to do much for the preservation of the girls teeth," Lee predicted. "They do so little themselves, that by the time they finish at school, they will all have gone."9

On September 12, 1855, the two girls climbed into a carriage, with Sister as chaperone, to travel down to Alexandria, where they were joined by Annette Carter and her father and the Stuart girls with their parents, two brothers, and four sisters. Together the party traveled west across the mountains to Strasburg, then down the Shenandoah Valley to Staunton, arriving in time for a late dinner at the local hotel. The meal passed all too quickly for the nervous young people, and it seemed only minutes until the five newcomers, "attended by their afflicted relatives wended their way up to the Institute," a white-columned brick building surrounded by gardens and a fence. Here they were met by Mr. and Mrs. Daniel Sheffey, proprietors of the academy. The new surroundings, solemn teachers, and scores of unfamiliar schoolgirls were intimidat-

ing, and all the cousins "cried a little & refused to go down to tea."
Fortunately, Mrs. Sheffey was a sensible woman, accustomed to such
displays of homesickness, and so she sent refreshments to their room,
with the tea sweetened with brown sugar, a palliative "which restored
our drooping spirits."[10] Within a few days, Agnes and Annie felt comfortable enough to take stock of their environment, their fellow pupils, and
the faculty.

The Virginia Female Institute was one of six private preparatory
schools in Staunton, a railroad center near the southern end of the
fertile Shenandoah Valley between the Blue Ridge and Allegheny mountains. The town itself was built on a series of steep hills, with narrow
streets and high Victorian houses providing few opportunities to view
the green expanses and rolling countryside the girls had heard about.
All five cousins shared a room on the second floor of the substantial
building, which had been designed for use as both dormitory and
school.

Daily routine was strict, they discovered, with early morning private
devotions, two chapel services, and six hours of classroom work a day,
leaving almost no freedom to walk, to exercise, or even to be alone. The
only outings came on Sundays, when the pupils were marched down
two blocks to Trinity Episcopal Church, "carefully guarded from the
young gentlemen [of other institutions] as if we were gold." The
Sheffeys tried to get their charges into the front pews of the church
"long before . . . the formidable boys make their appearance, but they by
some strange chance always happen to arrive equally early and are
waiting for us." At the end of the service, the institute girls had to stay in
their seats till the congregation left, "but those obstinate boys have a
great deal of patience," Annie wrote, "and quietly wait for us at the
door."[11] Annie and Agnes were amused by such maneuvers, but they felt
themselves far too mature to make friends with such very young men.
After all, they had known much older West Point cadets.

Most of the 120 students at the institute were from Virginia, with a few
girls coming from the Carolinas, Georgia, Alabama, and Missouri. There
was one brave soul who had traveled from the far-off Indian territory of
Arkansas. "There are a good many common girls," Annie told Helen,
"but some of them are very nice."[12] Classwork was a challenge, for it
included algebra, chemistry, botany, natural theology, political econ-
omy, geography, philosophy, logic, New Testament, and Latin, as well as
the two subjects for which the Girls were well prepared, French and
piano.

Though the Sheffeys were the proprietors of the school and served as its houseparents or "heads of the family," as the 1857 catalog rather quaintly phrased it,[13] the academic work was under the direction of a principal, the Reverend R. H. Phillips, described by Agnes as "handsome and attractive." Mr. J. C. Wheat, also a clergyman, "smart & intelligent . . . but *no* beauty," was vice-principal, teaching in the collegiate department. French was under the tutelage of Professor Gme. de Rinzie, considered "very leinient [*sic*]," and Miss Kate Berkeley, "our cousin pretty & sweet, but quite strict & rather cold," served as assistant teacher. Piano, voice, and guitar lessons were taught by Professor J. C. Engelbrecht, "very good . . . we all like him." Professor Talbot Coleman, "the only *young* man" on the faculty, taught drawing and painting.[14] Because Professor Engelbrecht also taught botany, he had two assistants in the music department, Miss Mary Kinney and Professor Martin Saur. According to the 1856 catalog, two additional instructors were still to be procured, one to teach moral philosophy and evidences of Christianity, the second to serve as assistant teacher of modern languages.[15]

Recitations, classwork, music, and drawing lessons occupied most of each school day, with a two-hour study period designated in the evening. Pupils studied in their rooms, a practice which, according to the 1856 catalog, "promotes intellectual improvement [and] engenders a home feeling enhanced by the friendly offices of room-mates."[16] Five girls together in one room probably engendered something, but it may not always have been study! Lights were turned out promptly at ten o'clock, after which a proctor checked each room. Friday evenings were reserved for musical soirées or public recitations, activities which neither of the Lee girls found comfortable. Meals in the basement dining room appear to have been as unpopular as institutional fare in contemporary schools and colleges, and packages from home were eagerly welcomed and shared.

Both girls were enrolled in the collegiate department, for which tuition was $40 per year, in addition to basic fees of $200 for board, room, fuel, lights, and washing. Other extras included piano lessons at $60 per session, drawing and languages for an additional $20 a year each, and pew rental of $2.50 yearly. Pupils were not allowed to read "novels or promiscuous newspapers," nor were they to receive "calls of gentlemen . . . unless by letters of introduction."[17]

In spite of such restrictions, the students managed to make their own fun. One evening Annie, Agnes, and two of their cousins burnt a piece of bristol board obtained from drawing class and with the ashes painted "ferocious moustaches & eyebrows" on each other, under the admiring gaze of less adventuresome classmates. Agnes and Annette Carter were brave enough to wear their masculine makeup down to supper, but when they heard that Mrs. Sheffey might "censure" them, their courage faded, and they hastily wiped away the evidence with pocket hand-kerchiefs.[18] In a more lugubrious vein, several of the boarders decided one night to cover themselves with sheets, pretending to be the ghost of a fellow student who had recently died. Fortunately, the plan to "come in the girls' rooms in the middle of the night to frighten them" never materialized. Agnes thought it "dreadful that some few of the girls will be so wicked" but "rather expect[ed] they merely said so in fun."[19]

More conventional costuming occurred during several student "balls." One friend, Annie reported, came as Martha Washington, complete with wig, hoop skirts, and an accomplice in blackface to carry her train. Others attired themselves as American Indians and Chinese. Several dressed like boys "& if there had only been some *real* boys," Annie commented, "I think the girls would have been perfectly happy."[20] On one special occasion Agnes assisted Ada and Annette to dress up as Revolutionary heroines, with whitened hair "powdered . . . and combed . . . over tremendous cushions." The effect, she reported, "was becoming but curious."[21]

While her sisters were studying in Staunton, Mary Custis, still restricted by her slowly healing foot, amused herself by making leather frames for Grandfather Custis' historic paintings. Her father had requested that she undertake to teach Mildred and Rob at home, though he recognized that she would not find the task easy, in part because of her tendency to be too dictatorial. "She must exert her self control & ingenuity," he wrote, "by making it agreable [*sic*] as well as instructive. . . . [A]s much can be accomplished by the *suaviter in modo* as the *fortiter* in re."* "Any one can *insist*," Lee continued, "but the wise alone know how to desist."[22] Mary Custis may have taken his advice too literally, for several years later, noting that Mildred misspelled *Saturday* by inserting "two *ts* (Satturday)," her father suggested that Sister had not "pile[d] on enough of 'those extra lines.'"[23]

---

*"Gentle in manner but resolute in action," motto of the Earl of Newborough (translated in *Dictionary of Latin Quotations*, ed. H. T. Riley [London: Bell & Daldy, 1866], 445).

When Annie and Agnes left for Staunton, they were uncertain about getting home for Christmas, but permission was granted and they returned for two happy weeks. Rooney was home, too, and to make the family circle almost complete, Colonel Lee arrived for a short furlough. The mood of the household was cheery, almost exuberant, with "Mill & Bobbie . . . about as bad as ever," Annie felt.[24] The only sad note was the loss of one of their favorite servants, "old Mammy," who had been found dead in her quarters two days before Christmas. The girls had loved to listen to her talk about Mount Vernon and "Ole Mistis," as she always referred to Mrs. Washington. The general, in Mammy's eyes, was "only a man," but Mrs. Washington had been perfect, a good manager, and a great beauty.[25]

The vacation went swiftly, passing "like a dream," as the young people skated, coasted, and enjoyed heavy December snows. On the morning of departure, the roads were dangerously slippery and Lee worried about the long trip back to school. "We left about four," Annie reported, "long before light & it was looked upon as a very remarkable enterprise, if you knew the laziness of Arlington; all is quiet till between *eight* or *nine*. It was pouring rain, the hills & road covered with sleet. . . . Pa had some fears about a very steep hill, so one of the men accompanied us on foot, also with a lantern to see us safely & *notch* the wheels if necessary." The farther west they traveled, the heavier the ice became. "The mountains were beautiful, all iced & frozen over, each little blade & twig was stiff & shining with its coat of crystal."[26]

Staunton remained snowbound for nearly four months, with the Staunton newspaper reporting one last "furious snow storm" on April 20, a date when one might have expected trees to be in full leaf.[27] Winter doldrums were accentuated by the dismal weather and a new infirmity for Agnes—swollen, painful fingers and feet.* Though she read all the books her friends could collect for her, she was bored and homesick and longed for her father. "He is now in Texas O so far away he seems. I love him so much . . . Now we do nothing but study & look forward to

---

*Agnes' recurring symptoms sound like the beginning of rheumatoid arthritis, the debilitating disease that afflicted her mother and later her brother Custis. There is a possibility, also, that they were manifestations of rheumatic fever, since chills and fever were sometimes mentioned in conjunction with complaints about painful joints. Her early death at the age of thirty-two makes one wonder if she might not have had serious heart disease, which could have developed from rheumatic fever.

next summer."[28] Several days later she expressed her loneliness again: "I only know I want to go home. "[29]

Two breaks in the routine helped to pass the long second term. The Girls were invited to eat Sunday dinner at a private home in Staunton, where the mother of a classmate provided "turkey, fish, peas, ice cream, marmelade, pound cake, jelly, pineapples, & ginger etc. for hungry school girls." The understanding woman not only fed them sumptuously, she also included a number of young gentlemen among the guests. Agnes found the visitors even more interesting than the exotic menu. "The idea of Mr. S.——'s lambs being in such close contact with the wolves was terrific," she confided to her diary.[30]

The second treat was the opportunity to attend a concert given in Staunton by Madame Teresa Parodi, an Italian dramatic soprano then on tour in the United States. Mr. Engelbrecht was so eager for his pupils to have the chance to hear the great singer that he offered to buy a ticket for any student who could not afford one and promised to rent a hack if it rained. Persuaded by his generosity, the Sheffeys relented, and the young people took their seats in the right-hand section of the town hall, filled with enthusiasm. The *Staunton Spectator* called the performance "a great concert . . . from the lips of the unrivalled cantatrice," but the girls were less effusive.[31] They appreciated Madame Parodi's voice as long as they could close their eyes and did not have to look at her—she wore "pink gauze decidedly 'bas' a vast amount of jewelry & . . . [was] remarkably *un*pretty.[32]

Fortunately, both girls were good students and they enjoyed most of their curriculum, which this term included geometry and rhetoric. "What do you think of our studying Geometrie [*sic*]?" Annie asked Helen Bratt. "Are we not blue stockings & I assure you we think ourselves quite skilled in the art. We are going to effect *wonders* & to raise our sex above the weak trammels of novels & fashions."[33] Agnes was not quite so confident about an upcoming examination in rhetoric. "I don't believe I know two questions *properly* in the book."[34]

At Arlington Mildred and Rob lost their teacher when Mary Custis left to visit friends in Baltimore. It is possible that Markie or Mrs. Lee took over the tutoring. But whatever her scholastic arrangements, Mildred stayed busy tending the family's cats and her brood of chickens, about which she and her father kept up a lively correspondence. Lee wrote her from Texas that he had seven hens which he kept in an open coop on stilts because "there are so many reptiles in this country that you cannot keep fowles [*sic*] on the ground. . . . Soldier hens however must learn not to mind rain." For a time, he told her, he had kept a rattlesnake as his only pet, but the snake "grew sick & would not eat his frogs, etc. & died one night." [35] He suggested that to compensate she send him a kitten in her next letter.

The quiet routine at Arlington was broken in April by a visit from a young teacher at Pelham Priory who had come to spend a week with Markie Williams. Blanche Berard and Markie had been friends for years, and Markie used to visit the Berards at West Point when Blanche's father taught French there. At the end of her week's stay, Blanche wrote a long letter to an acquaintance about her impressions of Arlington, the sparsity of its furnishings,* the beauty of the woods and fields, and her appreciation of "the *first spring wild-flowers*—beautiful beds of trailing arbutus." The young schoolteacher also enjoyed a Sunday afternoon walk with Mildred to attend the servants' church service in a "little school house." But she was appalled by the slovenly housekeeping and "shiftlessness" of the slaves. "Just fancy," she wrote, "waiting for tea . . . until 8 o'clock *because* they couldn't *find anything to milk the cow in.*"[36]

In Staunton spring rains and May sunshine finally melted the snow, bringing flowers, sudden heat, and more homesickness. "It is so hot we can't study," Agnes wrote to her father, "so I can not help thinking and talking *only* of home."[37] She acknowledged to Helen Bratt that she "ought not to complain but still in the Spring when flowers came & every thing was bright, idle & *free* I sighed & longed to be the same."[38]

The Girls did not return home until July, however, after examinations and a public exhibition of music, both vocal and instrumental. The final performance, held in the school parlor, was an elaborate affair, with numerous guests invited. All the pupils wore "white muslin—the senior class in white sashes, middles blue, juniors pink."[39] Agnes was the seventh girl to perform, and she became exceedingly nervous awaiting her turn before sitting down on the piano bench with a weak smile to play Paganini's "Witches' Dance." Annie performed variations on "La Violette." A valedictory address and presentation of awards concluded the long evening.

---

*The Lee family bedrooms upstairs were furnished with beds and dressers but with little of the additional bric-a-brac that many Victorians felt to be essential. Perhaps this accounts for Miss Berard's comment that the upper rooms of Arlington House "are all large, but we should think them terribly unfurnished" (Blanche Berard, "Arlington and Mount Vernon, 1856," *Virginia Magazine of History and Biography* 57 [1949]: 152–53).

Both girls received a number of awards as well as report cards filled with 6s, the highest grade, which pleased their father. "I am very glad to hear that Annie recd so many prizes," he wrote to Mrs. Lee. "I am also very glad to hear of Agnes success. She is less constant than Annie in her application, but I am in hopes will improve with years. . . . Both of them wrote me very pretty letters . . . but said nothing of their medals."[40]

Although they professed not to like "Staunton Jail," as they sometimes referred to the institute, Annie and Agnes had obviously matured and made many friends during their first year away at school. Annie was still self-conscious about her looks, describing herself as "long and gaunt, sharp as a razor . . . 'nose communing with the skies,' sharp voice and long fingers, with the sourest expression imaginable," but her sense of humor had not deserted her.[41] She laughed at Custis and called him an "old crone" for giving her so much unrequested big-brotherly advice.[42] She also insisted on calling Helen Bratt "granddaughter" to compensate for being nine days younger than her friend (Helen Bratt was born on June 10, 1839, Annie on June 19 of the same year).[43]

Agnes sometimes felt that she was not as popular as Annie. "I can't expect you to care for me as much as you do for Annie," she wrote a friend, "but can't you love me *some* in return?"[44] But like her sister, she had learned to live in close quarters with strangers, adjust to regular classroom work, and adapt herself to a variety of academic disciplines. Most important, both girls had gained the poise to meet new situations without the supportive influence of home and family.

Returning to Arlington in high spirits, they found an unhappy surprise awaiting them. During the spring their mother had become virtually bedridden with arthritis, a fact she had avoided mentioning in her letters. "Oh! how strange it seemed," Annie wrote, "not to see Ma waiting for us, but she [has] been an invalid upstairs for nearly a month with rheumatism."[45] They were delighted, however, to have Rooney home from Harvard for the summer, and they now found Mildred old enough to share their fun. "Miss Milly is *quite* a young lady in her *own* estimation," Agnes confided to Helen, adding that the little ten-year-old spent "her time when not more agreeably [sic] engaged in reading *love* tales."[46] Perhaps it was just as well that Colonel Lee was too far away to supervise Mildred's choice of books, for he disapproved of novels and romances. Such books, he felt, depicted "beauty more charming than nature," and thus influenced children "to sigh after that which has no reality, to despise the little good that is granted us in this world & to expect more than is given."[47]

Mrs. Lee's arthritic pains were so acute that the doctors advised her to try one or more of Virginia's hot springs, spas "much celebrated for rheumatic cures," Agnes explained. So in July Mrs. Lee left for Warm Springs, two hundred miles southwest by railroad, taking Rooney, Mary Custis, and Rob with her. Mildred was permitted to visit the Stuart cousins at Cedar Grove, and Annie and Agnes were left at Arlington, "mistresses of the mansion," with special responsibility for "Grandpa . . . and two yellow cats, by names '*Old Tom*' and '*Young Tom*.'"[48] Mr. Custis was probably easier to care for than the felines whom he spoiled outrageously, permitting them to curl up in the center of his favorite armchair, while he was left to perch precariously "on the edge . . . to allow Pussy undisputed possession."[49]

Stimulated by the warm mineral baths and cool air, Mrs. Lee returned in August able to move about the house with less difficulty. Suddenly it was time to get Rooney off to Harvard for his senior year and to help Annie and Agnes with final preparations for their return to school. "We put off everything for the last two weeks," Annie acknowledged, "& then what with visitting [*sic*], dining out, & being visitted [*sic*], we were in a perfect hurrey scurrey."[50] Both girls approached school with enthusiasm, eager to see the new classroom building and meet the new teachers, and they did not seem to object to the addition of another Carter cousin in their already crowded dormitory room. Agnes in particular felt "so much more confident in myself so much more independent!"[51] She had not been in school long, however, before she became ill, suffering the "most curious pains in my chest & back. . . . The next morning I found my face considerably covered with pistules." She had come down with a severe case of chicken pox, with "painful itching & burning . . . in my eyes & everywhere else."[52]

Fortunately, she was well by Thanksgiving, when Mr. Phillips declared a day's vacation, provided the young people finished their homework, even though Virginia had not yet officially made the day a holiday. With twenty-four hours to themselves, the students put together a series of tableaux, or living pictures, imitating illustrations from their Victorian novels. Annette Carter portrayed a sleeping maiden, "her hair loose about her face & white drapury [*sic*] thrown around her," while the newest roommate, Mary Carter, dressed up as *Ivanhoe's* Rebecca, wearing a "velvet mantle bound around with beautiful white fur, her head adorned with lace veils & jewels."[53]

Christmas of 1856 found the family scattered, Colonel Lee in Texas, Custis a second lieutenant on duty in Savannah, Annie and Agnes in

Staunton, and the rest of the family at Arlington. Because he could not send gifts all the way to Virginia, Lee gave presents to the children of friends on the post at Fort Brown. "Tell Mildred I got a beautiful Dutch doll for little Emma Jones," he wrote, "one of those crying babies, that can open & shut their eyes."[54] He had not forgotten how much Angelina and Jenny Lind had meant years before to Precious Life.

His own Christmas present was a package of more than thirty letters, the first from home in four months. Unfortunately, not all the news was cheerful. The new furnace at Arlington was giving trouble and already needed cleaning, Rooney was unhappy at Harvard and was spending too much money, and most worrisome of all, Mrs. Lee's health was not improving. Unlike his stern attitude of twenty years before when his wife had asked him to come home, Colonel Lee now offered no advice about being cheerful in adversity. Instead he wrote that he felt tied to "a profession that debars all hope of domestic enjoyment, the duties of which cannot be performed without a sacrifice of personal & private relations."[55]

Among the gloomy letters he received was one cheerful one from Mildred, filled with news that she now weighed sixty pounds and that she liked her new piano teacher. "You must be a very great personage now," he replied. "Sixty pounds! Enormous. I wish I had you here in all your ponderosity."[56] As to the change in teachers, he admonished that "you will like neither the teacher or the subject unless you practice diligently & learn to play, *well.* . . . We are always *fond* of what we *do well.* . . . That is one reason that you like your chickens. You attend to them & succeed." Lee also had a special request for Mildred. "Try hard to be a truly good, as well as wise girl, & rigidly obey your parents & tutors. I hope you will be particularly attentive to your Mother. Now that she is in pain & trouble, it is more than ever your duty to assist & serve her, & on no account to add to her distress. . . . Perhaps God has thus afflicted her to try her children & give them an opportunity of showing their appreciation of all she has done for them."[57] It was an injunction she would try to live up to many times in the years to come.

Two months later, Mildred received from her father a less serious note, all about the cats he saw in Texas, one in San Antonio with pink and blue ribbons tied on its ears, another that was so overfed it died "of apoplexy. I foretold his end. Coffee & cream for breakfast. Pound cake for lunch. Turtles & oysters for dinner. Buttered toast for tea, & Mexican rats, taken raw, for supper! Cat nature could not stand so much luxury."[58]

In Staunton Agnes and Annie were working hard at their lessons, for this was their final semester at the institute. Agnes, having been humiliated in the fall with getting chicken pox, now contracted "roseola."[59] Perhaps because she had been in her room so much, she was especially eager for treats from home. "If there is any room in the trunk, which I scarcely suppose there will be, send me some cakes and biscuits or apples, etc." Sometimes the parcels from Arlington did not bring just what the girls had asked for. "Annie says she does not want the *old pink* lawn but her *purple* with the body," Agnes complained. "She wants the *new* pink piece to make a *highnecked* body to the dress; you know they are both *low* necked and so are not useful at school, particularly as it will not be warm here much of the time. . . . I believe I asked you to make my dress tucked with narrow tucks to the waist."[60]

During March a religious revival swept through the school and Annie wrote her mother that she had "found comfort & peace in believing."[61] Agnes, too, studying one of her textbooks, McIlvaine's *Evidences of Christianity*, was overwhelmed by her need for personal salvation and she asked permission to be confirmed. On Easter Sunday, the presiding bishop, who was in Staunton, confirmed Agnes. Afterwards she, along with Annie and the cousins, took communion for the first time.

The Girls' sincerity in religious matters was matched by their parents' approval. Mrs. Lee wrote to Agnes that "I cannot let another day pass without telling you the real happiness your letter afforded me . . . to hear that God had sent his spirit into your heart & drawn you to himself."[62] Their father, too, was pleased to learn of the spiritual pilgrimage. "I have great comfort in my reflections about Anne & Agnes," he wrote to his wife. "I hope they will continue in their present blessed resolutions, & acquire strength from heaven to enable them to carry them to perfection. If they can lead the life of pure & earnest Christians . . . they will realize the only true happiness in this world."[63]

Colonel and Mrs. Lee's pleasure in their girls was more than offset by their concern for Rooney, who continued to be rebellious and extravagant and was unable to see the relevance of his studies at Harvard. Sick with intermittent fever and still in debt, he decided to leave school before graduation and seek a direct army commission, asking his mother to intercede with her old friend, General Winfield Scott, general-in-chief of the army.

Reluctantly, Mrs. Lee made the request, though she worried over making such a move without her husband's counsel. "Oh, if you were only here to consult," she wrote him.[64] Before she could receive Lee's guarded reply,—"He is very young yet"—the appointment had been made, and Rooney was beside himself with joy.[65] Lee wrote a graceful letter of thanks to General Scott, acknowledging that he had hoped that Fitzhugh might have "graduated, & have made a useful citizen. But as you (used to) say, 'boys are only fit to be shot' & he seems to have had from infancy an ardent desire for this high privilege, perhaps the sooner it is done the better."[66] The words were unhappily prophetic, for of the three Lee sons, only Rooney was seriously wounded during the Civil War.

In May, two months before she was to graduate, Annie became ill, so sick the school authorities decided she had best return home. Mr. Phillips took her back to Arlington, where her condition was attributed to overwork at school and "a weak stomach."[67] In spite of being separated from Annie for the first time and filled with "frantic longings for home,"Agnes managed to finish her examinations, take part in the spring exhibition, and receive her diploma.[68] A certificate was also awarded to Annie, even though she could not complete her work or take final tests.

Before Agnes returned to Arlington, Rooney had come home, "a *lieutenant usa* at last. . . . as large as life," Annie wrote to Helen Bratt.[69] Mary Custis, too, returned after months away in Philadelphia and West Point. Lee had been considerably annoyed at Daughter's prolonged absence, for he believed her mother needed her, especially during the long visit of Lee's French brother-in-law, Edward Childe, and his daughter Mary. "Besides the addition she might have been to their entertainment," he wrote his wife, "I fear they may think she ought to have been there. She is naturally dilatory in her movements, & if she has to depend upon herself to return home, I do not know when she will reach there."[70] Mary Custis, after years of living in Baltimore and New York State, evidently found the rural atmosphere of Arlington less appealing than city life. Perhaps she enjoyed greater freedom as an attractive young female guest than as a dependent daughter at home.

Lee continued to worry about his wife's health, urging her to try a different medicinal spa. She agreed to the vacation, more concerned about Annie than about herself. "Annie does not improve as rapidly as I could desire, tho' she is better than when she came."[71] With Mary Custis now home to take care of Grandfather and the younger ones, she took

Annie to Berkeley Springs, Virginia, near the headwaters of the Potomac River, nearly one hundred miles west of Arlington.*

These temperate bubbling springs had been famous since Revolutionary times, George Washington himself having taken the cure there. By the time Mrs. Lee and Annie visited Berkeley—or "Bath" as it was sometimes called—the spa had become easily accessible by rail, and there was an elaborate four-hundred-room hotel in the village, which provided a large gentlemen's pool and a smaller "swimming bath" for ladies, complete with a hanging swing, poolside seats, and broad steps leading down into the water with its constant seventy-four-degree temperature.[72] Annie wrote to Helen Bratt that she liked the water—"so buoyant you have no idea how charming it is"—and she even thought she might learn to swim.[73]

Before long she and Mrs. Lee were joined by other members of the family, Agnes, Rooney, Custis on leave before going to California, and cousin Mary Childe. Annie wrote to her father that Custis had acquired a beard "all over his chin & mouth, more red than his hair," that Rooney was now taller than Custis, and that Agnes was "growing like Sister in appearance & manners," descriptions sure to please Lee, who had not seen his children for eighteen months.[74]

Though Annie professed to feel better from her stay, Mrs. Lee showed little improvement. So she, Annie, and Mary Childe moved on from Berkeley to a small, unnamed sulphur spring, "highly recommended," Annie wrote, "where we were told we could procure good plain accommodations in a farm house." Unfortunately, the girls' visions of "milking the cows churning & feeding sweet little chickens" were quickly dashed by a churly landlady, poor food, and bedbugs in their quarters.[75] They made a hasty getaway to a more traditional resort hotel at Jordan Springs, not far from Winchester.

Agnes, meantime, had gone back to Arlington to help Markie take care of Mr. Custis, now seventy-six years old. It was one of the few times that Agnes had spent quietly with her grandfather. "I, then, more than ever before, ministered to his wants, sought his comforts, & prized his companionship. And how much & how undeservedly he thanked me."[76] The others came back early in September, full of excitement over the news that Rooney had recently announced—he was engaged to be married to Charlotte Wickham, a distant cousin.

*Berkeley Springs became part of West Virginia in 1863.

Charlotte was an orphan who had been reared by her maternal grandmother at the Carter plantation at Shirley. The Lees had come to know her in 1855 and 1856 during visits to Baltimore, where Charlotte was attending school and living with Carter relatives near the Louis Marshalls. They all felt her to be "a sweet amiable girl," as Colonel Lee put it, but there was obvious concern among the adults over her age, Rooney's uncertain future, and Charlotte's frailty. Lee wrote to his wife that he feared that Charlotte was "ill calculated in health or . . . education to follow the drum over our Western Prairies. . . . They are both mere children & each requires some staid person to take care of them."[77]

He mentioned none of his misgivings, however, in a warm letter to the new fiancée. "I never thought my dear Charlotte when I held you . . . in my arms [as a baby during Lee's visits to Shirley] . . . that you would ever be nearer & dearer to me than then. But you are now united in my heart with one, who from infancy has been dearer to me than myself & whose welfare in manhood I value beyond my own. . . . I feel very sensibly your kindness in consenting to enter our family. I fear you will find us rough soldiers."[78]

Charlotte and Rooney were not the only ones with romantic ideas that summer. Orton Williams, Markie's younger brother, began spending more and more time at Arlington. As a child he had played with both Annie and Agnes, but now he took Agnes off alone for long horseback rides and walks. Markie recalled, years later, that "it was always — where are Agnes & Orton?" She remembered one day in particular when the couple came back from a long ride, Agnes with a "glowing face & streaming hair," Orton beside her with "admiring glances."[79]

Far away, Colonel Lee probably knew little of this romance. He was more concerned about Annie, whose health did not improve as quickly as the family would have wished. "Perhaps it is only the sight of your venerable papa that is wanting?" he wrote her. "Pack up your trunk, come to New Orleans, & take the steamer to Indianola. . . . I will promise you a cordial welcome & . . . a pony & blanket . . . to accompany me on the plains." Suddenly turning serious, he added a poignant hope. "I wish you to be very good, very wise, very healthy, & very happy."[80]

In spite of his worry over the health of his wife and daughter, Colonel Lee did not anticipate an early return to Virginia. In October, however, he received unexpected news that Mr. Custis had died after a brief illness, influenza complicated by pneumonia. As executor of his father-in-law's estate, Lee felt obliged to ask for a short furlough and immediately began the long trip home.

Unlike the funeral services for Mrs. Custis, the final ceremony for George Washington Parke Custis was a large, public affair. The morning of October 13 was clear and bright as a brass band from the Washington Light Infantry led mourners up the hill from Arlington House to the gravesite beside Mrs. Custis'. In addition to family members, there were government officials; priests and students from Georgetown College; neighboring plantation owners; "Survivors of the War of 1812"; a group from the "Jamestown Society of the District of Columbia"; and an official "delegation of the officers of the President's Mounted Guards."[81] The crowds would have pleased Mr. Custis, but to Agnes, "it was a sad, sad day."[82] Speaking for the whole family, she wrote, "None can ever fill his place. So kind he was, so indulgent, loving us so fondly, humouring our childish caprices, grateful for our little kindnesses."[83]

When Colonel Lee arrived home nearly a month later, he discovered that the problems awaiting him were far more serious than he had anticipated. Mr. Custis' will, prepared without the help of a lawyer, was complicated and in places contradictory. The plantation at Arlington and the other properties were in serious financial disarray. Most troubling of all, Colonel Lee found his wife terribly aged by her illness and pathetically crippled. Though he had known from the beginning of her pain and discomfort, he was not prepared to see her gray and drawn at the age of only forty-nine, her hands and feet gnarled and swollen. On good days she was able to hobble about with cane or crutches, but during periods of great suffering she was virtually chair-bound or confined to bed. It was a shock for which her letters had not prepared him. "I almost dread him seeing me in this crippled state," she had written to a friend.[84]

Even if he had been able to have Mr. Custis' will probated quickly, Lee realized that his wife was physically unable to handle the estate by herself. The two older boys were away, Rob was only fourteen, and the girls were untrained to supervise slipshod or absentee overseers. There seemed no alternative but to request a full year's leave of absence from his post to work out details of the will and attempt to bring some sort of financial stability.

Mr. Custis had left Arlington to his daughter for use during her lifetime, but at her death the estate was to go to Custis, along with "the Mount Vernon plate [and] every article I possess relating to Washington and that came from Mt. Vernon."[85] To his other grandsons, Rooney and Rob, he left his two principal holdings on the Pamunkey River in Tidewater Virginia, one a plantation called the White House, where

Martha Custis and George Washington had been married, the other, Romancoke, a less cultivated farm a few miles downstream. To his four granddaughters Mr. Custis willed $10,000 apiece, money which was to be accumulated through the sale of additional property and profits from the Pamunkey holdings. Unfortunately, the old gentleman died $10,000 in debt, Arlington had not been profitable for years, and the other two plantations were being poorly managed. All three estates had become "slave-poor," as Mr. Custis owned 196 slaves at the time of his death, many more than could efficiently work the farms.[86] An additional complicating stipulation in the will provided for freeing all the slaves within five years.

Though Colonel Lee had never farmed, he began at once to tackle the problems at Arlington. Roofs on the big house and stables needed replacing, and outbuildings had to be repaired and painted. Though most of the family were home, it was a subdued Christmas. Even the cats seemed to sense that Mr. Custis was gone. Writing her final entry in the diary she had kept for five years, Agnes was suddenly weighed down by adult cares. "I am no longer the free thoughtless child at sixteen," she noted. "I am but truly commencing the *battle of life*."[87] To prepare herself for the struggle, she made four New Year's resolutions: to rise early each morning, to be gentler in her manner, to keep her good intentions, and to read her Bible regularly.

Perhaps sensing her depression, Colonel and Mrs. Lee urged Agnes to spend the remainder of the winter and spring in Baltimore with the Marshalls, studying "in various branches" with her French cousin Mary Childe. It was a move Agnes was not altogether enthusiastic about, though she was fond of Mary and looked forward to being near Charlotte Wickham. "Dear dear Arlington," she wrote, "I can not bear to leave it."[88] Perhaps she found it hard, too, to leave the company of Orton Williams, who was now spending so much time at Arlington that Lee began calling his sons' bedroom "Orton's room."[89]

Annie was lonely without Agnes, though she kept busy giving music lessons to Mildred and handling housekeeping chores for her mother. She was delighted when Rooney came home for one last furlough before leaving for Utah to help subdue polygamous Mormons. "He is a very dear brother," she wrote Helen Bratt. In order to find time for letter writing, she found that she had to get up early. At daybreak one winter morning, she watched the sun climb over a bank of dark clouds. "The Sun is struggling up," she wrote with obvious appreciation of the scene, "tinging with gold the heavy clouds which oppose its progress, &

throwing its reflection full upon the water beneath, leaving it like a sheet of fire." Across the Potomac, "the mist still hangs over Washington, & the rest of the river, is tossed about by the wind, its waves instead of gently flowing on, as blue as the sky, have a greenish angry appearance & are all crested with foam." Suddenly the breakfast bell broke the spell of gold and green. "What a termination to so beautiful a scene," she concluded.[90]

Her father, too, found that he needed to arise early to accomplish all that had to be done. With debts "pouring in on me, not in large amounts, but sufficient to absorb my available funds," Colonel Lee felt unable to see much progress.[91] He shared his frustrations and concerns with Custis, even though his letters took weeks and even months to reach the West Coast. Custis had already made application for a transfer to Washington, so that he might assume management of the estate and relieve his father, but reassignment took a long time. Increasingly aware of the high costs of maintenance and repair, Lee wrote only partly in jest when he urged his eldest son to "pick up in California some bags of gold, or marry some nice young woman with enough for both." Only with independent means could Custis hope to "live the life of a country gentleman."[92]

Though on leave, Colonel Lee was still subject to temporary duties, one of which was to serve on courts-martial. Such a responsibility came in April, when he was ordered to Kentucky for a few weeks. On the way home he stopped in Baltimore to see the Marshalls and Agnes. She and Mary Childe were so busy helping a friend with wedding plans that they scarcely had time to visit with him. "There was a great rage for matrimony in B——," he wrote to Mrs. Lee's aunt, Mrs. Fitzhugh, "& the fever seemed to be contagious. . . . It made me anxious to extricate Agnes."[93]

Warm weather brought little relief to Mrs. Lee, but she was not to be outdone when the rest of the family stayed so busy. Even before her father's death, she had begun compiling his sketches and the articles that he had written for newspapers and other periodicals. Her plan was to publish these, augmented by a biographical memoir of Mr. Custis that she herself would write. To assist her with editing and publishing, she turned to Benson Lossing, the journalist who had spent a week at Arlington in the spring of 1853 and had written so admiringly of her father. "I shall be most truly indebted to you for your advice & supervision," she wrote Lossing. "From your long experience & success as an author & your friendship for my Father I am sure you would take an interest in the work that no one else could."[94] The project took longer than she had anticipated, but it finally appeared in 1860 under an impressive title: *Recollections and Private Memoirs of Washington, by his Adopted Son, George Washington Parke Custis, with a Memoir of the Author, by his Daughter.*

By summer Lee was still so concerned about his wife's and Annie's continued poor health that he decided to leave his supervision of the plantation and take them himself to Hot Springs, Virginia, to try those waters. Rob, Mildred, and Agnes were to stay at Ravensworth, and Mary Custis was already in Baltimore. Annie made her own traveling dress for the eighteen-hour journey, "much to my pride & satisfaction," she wrote to Helen Bratt. It was a tiring but scenic trip by stagecoach, with the road winding "round the mountains, & the little streams instead of rushing & leaping as they do at the Point [West Point] . . . running, gurgling over the stones, the last rays of light as they lit up the clouds & mountains were very beautiful."[95]

The village of Hot Springs, nestled at the base of Warm Springs Mountain, had grown up around twenty natural hot pools. Here a well-known hotel, The Homestead, catered to invalids and summer tourists, offering cottages, bathhouses, fine food, and pleasant weather. Annie found the one-hundred-degree water to be "very hot . . . which they say works wonders," but she decided the accommodations were not as pleasant as Berkeley's. When not taking the waters, she spent her time reading a new book, *Two Millions*, by William Allen Butler, written in iambic pentameter, which satirized the *nouveaux riches* and women's rights groups. Annie considered it "quite pretty."[96]

September found the family back at Arlington, Lee busy with harvest and most of the travelers improved in health and spirits. Mary Custis, however, returned from Baltimore sick and "as knowing and opinion-ated as her Aunt Anne" Marshall, Lee wrote to his son. "All the experi-ence of others is lost on her."[97] Fortunately, the autumn days were long and pleasant, "cool enough to be comfortable, and warm enough to sit out doors and talk," according to a Washington visitor.[98] At night a spectacular comet lit up the sky.

Early in December Colonel Lee was sent to West Point for another session of court-martial duty, and both Agnes and Annie took the opportunity to send long letters to Helen Bratt. Annie was hoping that Christmas at Arlington would be more like the Christmases of old, which "used to be so very bright and joyous that we wished Christmas would come all the time . . . [T]he night before [we were] so excited that we could hardly be got to bed, and then the next morning [we would] spring up by the first faint light, pattering along in our little bare feet to the chimney where hung our stockings, how eagerly they were opened and one by one our presents displayed to our admiring eyes." The servants also looked forward to the day, she wrote, eager to compete with the children at the traditional "Christmas gift" game, in which the first person to shout the phrase on Christmas morning won a prize. "Their great desire was to catch us Christmas gift which we generally let them do, so that we might have the pleasure of bestowing a bright bandanna or ribbon."[99]

Unfortunately, the holiday was not as pleasant as she had hoped for, as Colonel Lee did not return in time for the celebration, the weather was wretched, and she herself was sick in bed, so ill that Mrs. Lee summoned the doctor, a red-haired physician "with a dried up visage, long legs, immense feet, [and] a very sharp voice." She had recovered by the time her father returned, bringing watches for Mary Custis and Agnes, games for Mildred, and for herself "a gold thimble, some pins and a beautiful set of balls for my hair."[100]

In January Rooney sent word that he was leaving San Francisco, where he had been sent after the Utah expedition. He was ready to resign his commission, marry Charlotte, and begin farming at the White House. A few weeks later, Annie was awakened early one cold morning by a commotion downstairs, followed by a knock on her door and Mary Custis' announcement that "Roon had come." Putting on her dressing gown, Annie hurried to the head of the stairs to be "clasped in the arms of a tall creature, with a great deal of beard & a most shaggy outlandish coat." Bathed and combed, Rooney looked more like himself, "a very fine looking officer," Annie pronounced him.[101]

Heavy rains kept everyone inside, testing the efficiency of the new roofs over house and stable and giving the family plenty of time to make plans for the wedding, which was set for March. Mrs. Lee was not well enough to make the journey down to Shirley, and so Agnes and Annie accompanied their father, along with numerous Stuart and Carter cousins, for the nuptial festivities, which lasted two weeks. They returned with the bride and groom, who remained at Arlington for several months while the farmhouse on the White House plantation was readied for occupancy.

During the winter Rooney and Custis had been stationed near each other in California, thus enabling them to renew the closeness that they had always felt for one another. Realizing how much it would have meant to Custis to have attended his brother's wedding, Agnes wrote him a detailed letter about the happy fortnight. He replied in May,

thanking her for her "long and very interesting letter." He had not heard
from home for a long time, he said, but he had received a "very kind and
affectionate letter from Cousin Markie," who spoke of "having some
flowers which my 'sweet Sister Agnes' had sent her by Orton." Still
uncertain about his return to Virginia, Custis concluded by sending
"quantities of love to Pa', Ma', Sister, Annie, Mr. & Mrs. Rooney, Mildred,
Rob, . . . and to other relations, and believe me your affectionate brother,
Custis."[102]

Spring brought the usual abundance of flowers at Arlington, and
Annie decided it was time to begin gardening in earnest. "I am devoted
to my flowers," she wrote to Helen at West Point, "& have 24 little
geraniums of my own raising, plenty of Parmese violets, heliotropes, &
callas."[103] As for Mildred, she was finding less and less space each year
for flowers in her tiny plot because of the graves of all the family cats
buried there—"'Thomas Chalmers,' 'Thomas Aquinas,' etc. Ah, the
burning tears I have dropped upon those graves."[104] This year Agnes
was not well enough to work in the garden, for she had been having
pains in her eyes and face for several months. The doctors diagnosed
her affliction as rheumatism. Still struggling to bring order to the
plantation, Lee wrote to Custis in discouragement about Mrs. Lee's
continuing poor health, Agnes' ailments, and the neuralgia that bothered Markie from time to time. "You see what a suffering set we are," he
concluded. "Annie is never very strong, & Precious Life is the only well
one of our womankind."[105] Mary Custis, as usual, was away visiting.

This summer Mrs. Lee decided to try the waters at Capon Springs,
twenty miles west of Winchester. Agnes went with her, hoping to find
relief in the spa's alkaloidal springs. While they were away, Mildred
visited Peter relatives in Georgetown, leaving Annie, Rob, and Sister the
only young people at Arlington to welcome Jeb Stuart, on leave in
Virginia, who came by the house several times to renew his old friendship with Mary Custis.

Perhaps because they were so concerned with family problems of
health and finances, the Lees devoted little attention in their letters to
the two volatile issues that in 1859 gripped the country: slavery and
states' rights. Their papers were filled with accounts of the acrimonious
disputes in Congress, but it was not until the Lees were touched
personally by two incidents that the seriousness of the country's problems became real to the women of the family.

The first had to do with the disappearance and later return of three
slaves from the Arlington plantation. Northern agitators had begun to

visit the slave quarters behind the great house after the death of Mr. Custis. These abolitionists—"miscreants," Mrs. Lee called them—stirred up some of the servants, "making them discontented and impertinent" and finally "enticing off 3 of the most valuable," Mrs. Lee wrote to a friend. The family was especially hurt that one of these was Mrs. Lee's chamber "*maid* who fared as well as my daughters & whose *wardrobe* & *hoops* was [sic] equally extensive."[106] No advertisement for their return was published, but the runaways were captured before they had gotten far and were returned. In order to prevent further dissension, Lee sent the three offenders down to the Pamunkey estates along with a number of other servants to supplement the work force on those lower plantations.

The matter might have been forgotten except for two letters that appeared in the *New York Tribune* late in June of 1859, purportedly written by neighbors of the Lees, accusing Colonel Lee of keeping Mr. Custis' slaves in bondage beyond the date of their supposed freedom, of beating the malcontents, and of breaking up slave families by sending them to southside Virginia. The tone of the letters and their innuendos infuriated the Lee ladies, "telling lies so atrocious that they scarcely deserved a reply," Mrs. Lee felt.[107] Lee merely commented to Custis, "The *N. Y. Tribune* has attacked me for my treatment of your grandfather's slaves, but I shall not reply. He has left me an unpleasant legacy."[108]

Colonel Lee's plan for fulfilling that portion of Mr. Custis' will was to provide freedom within five years, in accordance with his father-in-law's instructions, after the debts had been paid off and the girls' legacies accumulated.* Mrs. Lee would have preferred a speedier manumission. "It will be a great relief to me when they are all gone," she wrote, "for they are much trouble and no profit."[109]

The second incident that made abolition seem very real to the family involved Colonel Lee himself. Early in the morning of October 17, Jeb Stuart appeared on the Arlington portico, carrying orders for Lee to

---

*Though the debts were not fully paid and his daughters' legacies still incomplete, Robert E. Lee did his best in the latter months of 1862 to give the Custis slaves their freedom officially. Despite his own involvement leading Confederate troops in battle around Fredericksburg, Lee managed to compile the complete list of Custis slaves, and he filed an official deed of manumission on December 29, 1862 in Spotsylvania County, Virginia. Though by the second year of the war many of the servants had already left Arlington or the Pamunkey plantations, Lee sent papers of manumission to all whose locations he knew about (Douglas Southall Freeman, *R. E. Lee* [New York: Charles Scribner's Sons, 1934], IV:385; Clifford Dowdey, *Lee* [Boston: Little, Brown & Co., 1965], 331).

report at once to the secretary of war. Without taking time to change into uniform, Lee hurried to Washington and on to Harper's Ferry, leaving the family unaware of the momentous drama unfolding at the arsenal eighty miles away. For the next twenty-four hours, he was commanding officer of all Federal forces at the site, with responsibility for quelling the bizarre insurrection of John "Osawatomie" Brown, taking back the building that Brown had captured, freeing hostages, and restoring order.

Four days later he was home again, commending Jeb Stuart's courage and the bravery of Mrs. Lee's cousin, Lewis Washington, who was one of the hostages, and dismissing the incident as the work of a madman, a troublemaker who had tried in vain to incite a slave rebellion. His daughters no doubt took their cue from him, grateful that father and friend had returned unharmed from a dangerous situation and seeing no special national significance in the uprising. Along with many other moderate Southerners, they were dismayed and surprised to find that when Brown was hanged in early December, he suddenly became a hero among Northern abolitionists, who held prayer meetings and rang church bells at the hour of his execution. It seemed to Mrs. Lee an almost unbelievable transformation from common criminal to abolitionist saint.

In the meantime, Custis finally received his transfer to Washington, with the accompanying opportunity to live at home. Now Colonel Lee should have been free to rejoin his regiment, but he was delayed once more, till after Christmas, to testify at the official hearing on the John Brown uprising. While he waited, he wrote a long letter of recommendation for Orton Williams, who was trying to obtain an army commission. Lee was genuinely fond of his wife's young cousin who had spent so much time at Arlington, but he must have been aware of some of Orton's less admirable traits—a quick temper and a tendency to drink heavily. His letter of recommendation mentioned none of these shortcomings, however, but dwelt on those qualities he could honestly endorse—the young man's heritage, his draftsmanship, mathematical ability, and knowledge of engineering and surveying, as well as an "inventive turn of mind, & . . . ingenuity." "Without . . . having had an opportunity of acquiring military knowledge," Colonel Lee asserted, "he possesses those acquirements & qualities necessary to a soldier & always required in the military service."[110]

Lee began his journey back to Texas on February 10, 1860, almost two years after he had been called home. Though he was glad to be returning to his professional duties, he found that the farther he traveled from home, the more he missed the family. "I thought of you, when I got in my blankets," he wrote to Annie from Laredo, "& knew you were happy for you were asleep, with Agnes by your side." The girls had houseguests and he wished them all "a jolly time. You must all be happy & agreable [*sic*] to each other. Youth is so fleeting & life so short."[111]

He always liked to think about the whole family being together, and it irritated him that Mary Custis should enjoy being away from home so much. With thinly veiled sarcasm, he wrote that he was "glad Daughter is with Miss Carrie [Stuart of Cedar Grove]. I suppose that is the reason she has not written to me."[112]

In March Mrs. Lee felt well enough to undertake the long trip to New Kent County for a visit with Rooney and Charlotte. She left Custis in charge of the girls, but gave Annie specific instructions about housekeeping. With spring-cleaning under way, Annie was to take down the heavy curtains and roll up the rugs for storage in the attic, as well as supervise the yearly application of walnut stain on bare floors. Several of the servants had been sick when the mistress left and Annie was to continue administering home remedies.

It had been thirty-five years since Mrs. Lee had been to the Pamunkey White House, and she especially enjoyed seeing the familiar scenery in early spring. She was still with Rooney and his wife when Charlotte gave birth to their first child, a boy named Robert Edward Lee for his grandfather. Lee was touched that the young couple had named the boy for him. "You must kiss his dear mother for me," Lee wrote to Rooney, "[and] tell her I have thought much of her & long to see you both & your little treasure."[113]

The weather in Texas grew unbearably hot. "The thermometer ranges daily from 95° to 110° F.," Lee told Annie. He hoped she would eat "plenty of strawberries for me ... & raspberries with cold cream."[114] In a series of homesick letters, he sent special messages to all the family and commended Ephraim, the gardener, who was beginning to harvest a bumper crop from the family vegetable garden. He even teased Agnes about a possible suitor, one Lieutenant Eagle, who was just leaving the 2nd Cavalry for duty near Washington. "By the intervention of that fine back, & an afternoon ride, something might be accomplished for the ladies of Arlington," he wrote.[115] The comment was all in jest, for Lee was in no hurry to marry off his daughters. "As to your impression about its being time for a wedding in our family," he counseled his wife, "I

must refer you to Cousin Charlotte & the young people themselves.
Whenever they think it is time, it is time."[116]

Having tried most of the healing springs in Virginia without success,
Mrs. Lee decided this summer to travel the long distance to St.
Catharine's Well in Canada, a spa just north of Niagara Falls. Taking Agnes
and Markie Williams with her and accompanied by Custis as an escort,
she set out on the long journey via Baltimore, New York City, and Elmira
to the city of Niagara. Mrs. Lee wrote home that she was disappointed by
the commercialism of the great falls, feeling that the "workshops & mills
down to [the] very edge" of the waterfall had "mar[red] its sublimity. . . .
How grand it must have been when the Indians first wandered on its
shore."[117] St. Catharine's was a community of seven thousand persons,
four miles from Lake Ontario and only twelve miles from Niagara. Its
plank sidewalks were lined with hotels and boardinghouses for invalids
coming to try the salty mineral waters of the famous spring. The Lee
party stayed in one of the boardinghouses, "a sweet little vine covered
cottage."[118]

From Texas Colonel Lee wrote that he hoped the spa and "its sainted
waters has [*sic*] caused some amelioration."[119] The travelers, however,
scarcely mentioned health in their early letters, but spoke instead of the
large numbers of runaway slaves they saw living on the edge of town
under miserable conditions. "I am told," Mrs. Lee wrote home, "they
suffer a great deal here in the long cold winters. After enticing them over
here, the white people will not let their children go to the same schools
or treat them as equals." She added that she did not recognize any black
faces: "Tell Nurse . . . I have not met with any acquaintance." On Sundays
the family attended St. George's English Church, where they were
amused to find themselves praying for "the sovereign lady Queen
Victoria."[120]

Before she left for Canada, Mrs. Lee had enrolled Mildred in a small
girls' school in Winchester for the fall term. Both Colonel and Mrs. Lee
had been concerned that the haphazard instruction by her sisters had
not been disciplined enough, and they began looking for an academy
where Mildred could "*learn & improve* herself." Lee even wanted her to
have the opportunity to learn to dance, to "give her a good carriage, of
which she is in need."[121]

Sometimes referred to simply as "Mrs. Powell's school" or "Mrs.
Selina Powell's academy," the new school, which opened in 1856, had
already attracted a number of Alexandria girls and several Lee cousins.
Cassius Lee, a first cousin of Robert Lee, was listed among its trustees. A

brochure about the school emphasized the seminary's "advantageous location in the town of Winchester . . . enjoying the healthful breezes from the mountains which encircle it, with a refined and intelligent society, and happy social and moral influences."[122]

Since the travelers would not be returning to Arlington until late in the summer, Annie found herself responsible not only for the general housekeeping at Arlington, but also for getting her youngest sister ready for boarding school. Writing to Annie from St. Catharine's, Mrs. Lee hoped that Mildred would be "reasonable about her clothes," requiring only a few new dresses and willing to use any cast-off outfits from "you or your sister . . . that will do for her." Annie should concentrate on getting an adequate supply of new undergarments made for Mildred from "*everlasting* cotton which is *thick*. . . . [at the cost of] 12 1/2 cts. per yd. . . . Let Mical [one of the servants] pay for it out of the market money."[123] In addition to instructions from her mother, Annie received information from Mrs. Powell that "each pupil must bring with her a list of her clothing, which must be marked with her name in full; half a dozen towels, also marked; over-shoes and an umbrella."[124]

Not only did Mrs. Lee give advice about Mildred's school preparations; she also sent careful messages to Annie about housekeeping details. Billy and Ephraim were to wash the newly shorn wool, with Nurse to oversee its drying and storing until "Sally & Patsey . . . can pick it." Abundant tomatoes could be canned, but "not . . . so many as I did last year," with extra quantities used for catsup. Late-maturing vegetables would need special watering (Rob's responsibility), while Daniel was to haul manure for Ephraim's strawberry bed. Finally, Annie must remember to keep close watch on the cellar, "as the wine there is a tempting article."[125]

Though the water at St. Catharine's Well helped Mrs. Lee's arthritis, she worried about giving so much responsibility to Annie and she wanted to be home to say good-bye to Mildred. So, leaving Markie and Agnes in New York City, she traveled all night by train to reach Arlington before Mildred's expected departure, only to find that the enterprising fourteen-year-old had made arrangements to get herself to Winchester. "Perhaps it [is] as well," her mother wrote wistfully, "that you went under such a good escort & I am glad you are so much pleased."[126]

Mrs. Lee may well have had a less obvious reason for wanting to leave New York early. As a moderate Southern slaveholder, she must have been acutely uncomfortable in the increasingly polarized atmosphere of Northern cities. How could she read without anger of the acclaim

given to John Brown when her own husband had risked his life to
capture the anarchist, or listen without rancor when her newfound
acquaintances mimicked Thoreau and Emerson in a blanket condemna-
tion of all slave owners? At the same time, as the great-granddaughter of
George Washington, she was appalled that extremists from the deep
South were calling for secession if Lincoln were elected.

Neither Agnes nor Markie Williams seemed in any hurry to get south
of the Mason-Dixon line, perhaps because they were less politically
sensitive than Mrs. Lee. Agnes remained in New York State throughout
October, attending a ball in New York City in honor of "His Royal
Highness, the Prince of Wales."[127] She also visited West Point and
Morrisania and offered to come home, Mrs. Lee reported, only "if she is
wanted."[128] Meanwhile, Markie made plans to stay with an aunt in New
York City all winter, so that she might study painting at Cooper Institute.
Colonel Lee began to be anxious about his outspoken daughter. "If
Agnes has not returned yet," he wrote Custis, "I fear she will be captured
by the Abolitionists, especially if she has been expressing any opinions
inimical to their theories."[129] Fortunately, no such crisis occurred, and
Agnes reached Arlington without incident, writing her father all about
the visits she had made and the old friends she had seen.

Lee also had encouraging news from Mildred and Rob, both of whom
were happy at school, Rob at the University of Virginia at Charlottesville,
Mildred in Winchester, at that time a community of more than four
thousand. Mrs. Powell's school was located near the center of town in a
large brick structure which accommodated fifty pupils with classroom
and dormitory space. In addition to Mr. and Mrs. Powell, the teachers
included Professor E. Falk, who taught music, and Mademoiselle
Vaucher, "a French lady, who will reside in the family of the Principal,
and converse with her pupils in her native language." Mr. Falk not only
taught piano lessons, but also offered "instruction in pure Musical
Composition and Thorough Bass" to advanced music students. All these
benefits, along with the opportunity to achieve "harmonious develop-
ment of all the faculties of the mind," cost $200 for a ten-month session,
including room and board, with additional fees for Latin, French,
drawing, and music. Laundry was $1.25 extra per month as long as the
number of dresses washed for each pupil did not exceed twelve.[130]

From the few letters sent back to Arlington or written to her father,
one may surmise that Mildred adjusted rapidly and enjoyed herself
immensely, although she admitted to being homesick for the latest Tom
kitten at Arlington. "I am glad that you are comfortably located," her

father replied to one of her letters, "& that the prospects before you are so pleasant." He urged her to learn to play the piano "*well. . . . well enough to take pleasure in your own performance . . . & to impart true pleasure to those who hear you. . . .* I want you to grow in size, strength, & wisdom, & at the same time to be an accomplished & useful woman." As to her longing for the cat, he replied that he had no friends to play with and was probably lonelier than "you are without Tom."[131]

With Christmas approaching, Mildred asked for permission to travel home for the holidays. Her mother replied that because of "the cold season, the difficulty of finding a good escort," and the suddenly troubled national situation, she would not advise the journey. "Still," Mrs. Lee continued, "I will not say you *must not come*, if there should be any good opportunity & if your holiday should be long enough to justify it."[132] That was all the encouragement Mildred needed. She found herself an escort and arrived home in time for Christmas. It was to be the last Christmas any of the family would spend at Arlington.

The weather was bitterly cold, with heavy snow. But more disturbing than the unseasonable temperature was the unhappy state of the country. South Carolina had seceded on December 20, and other states were considering secession. In spite of their concerns, the family attempted to have as normal a holiday as possible. In addition to the four girls and Custis, there were Carter and Stuart cousins at the great house. Lee was grateful that Mildred could be at home. "She will feel better for her visit the balance of the session. . . . You did not tell me whether she had grown."[133]

Between snowstorms Mildred returned to Winchester, notifying her mother at once of her safe arrival. "I was glad to hear, my dear little Millie," Mrs. Lee replied, "that you got safely back to your school. You could not have chosen a more propitious day. It has been raining & snowing ever since." With Mississippi, Florida, Alabama, and Georgia having seceded within the week, she added, "I do not feel much in heart to go anywhere viewing constantly the sad state of my country. We must be more earnest in supplication to that Almighty Power who alone can save us. That is all we poor women can do."[134]

February rains followed the winter snows, making "the roads almost impassable."[135] Still, the family at Arlington tried to follow their usual routine, attending church in Alexandria each Sunday and even crossing the river for the annual parade in honor of Washington's birthday. Benson Lossing paid a visit, presumably in connection with the promotion of Mr. Custis' *Recollections*, and the girls had a pleasant evening with

Charles Francis Adams and his brother, Henry, the latter a classmate of Rooney's at Harvard. Charles Francis Adams wrote that he found Agnes "extremely attractive."[136] Rooney and Charlotte came for a visit, and Grandmother Lee enjoyed a happy interlude tending little Robert while his parents made a quick trip to Baltimore.

No one in the family planned to attend the inauguration of Abraham Lincoln, though Lees and Custises traditionally had taken part in inaugural ceremonies. Mrs. Lee, like many Southerners, felt that Lincoln should have resigned before taking office, "if [he] had consulted his own happiness and had been a true and disinterested patriot. Nothing he can do now will meet with any favour from the South."[137]

By now Virginia was under heavy pressure from already-seceded states to leave the Union and join the new Confederacy. With pro-Union and anti-Union forces jockeying for control of the Commonwealth, banks and other commercial ventures closed their doors. "I hope you will be able to get along with what I have sent you," Mrs. Lee wrote to Mildred on February 25, "as times are very hard & the Banks are all suspending payment." The girl had evidently written that her dresses were not warm enough for the cold Winchester climate, and Mrs. Lee made a few suggestions. "You could wear your calicoes when the weather is *not severe* with a *josey* over them—& if your arms are cold it is well just to pin up under your sleeves the legs of stockings."[138] Except for practical matters, the mother had no enthusiasm for correspondence, as it was "with a sad heavy heart, my dear child, I write for the prospects before us are sad indeed . . . as I think both parties are in the wrong in this fratricidal war. . . . I see no *right* in the matter."[139]

The atmosphere was becoming so tense that when Custis found he had to be away for several days, he asked Orton Williams to remain at Arlington "to protect us lone feminines," Mrs. Lee explained, "though I am not the least afraid."[140] Orton was delighted with the opportunity to spend more time than usual at the great house. Though his army duties were in General Scott's office in Washington, Orton was already looking forward to becoming an officer in "the Army of the Southern Republic," and he urged Custis to join him in applying for a Confederate captaincy. Such talk angered him, Colonel Lee wrote, and "recalls my grief at the condition of our country."[141]

By the time his stinging letter of rebuke reached Virginia, Lee was already on his way home, summoned by direct orders from the Department of War. He reached Arlington on March 1, three days before Lincoln's inaugural. Deeply disturbed by the seemingly irreparable divisions within the country, he remained for the next month quietly at home, except for an occasional visit to Alexandria and several trips to Washington for long, off-the-record conversations with Army Secretary Scott. On March 28, he was promoted to full colonel, the commission being signed by President Lincoln. But Lee scarcely mentioned his career or his apprehensions about the future to Mildred, for he was too concerned about "the state of the country. . . . to give my thoughts in a letter." Instead, he commended her on her improved handwriting, acknowledged her request to take Latin the following school year, and filled up the letter with descriptions of the latest Arlington pets. Tom, the newest kitten, he told Mildred, was "the delight of the house. I fear he will be ruined by indulgence. He is so petted by your sisters and Miss Helen Peters [a friend of Mary Custis, visiting at Arlington]. The latter wants to put him in ruffles. . . . Your sisters never array him in collars, believing that . . . they would cloud his verdant eyes."[142] Lee himself spent more time with the new Newfoundland puppy, who was his constant companion. "He is very belligerent & carries on perpetual combats with the wild cats," he wrote. "His face is much scarred & he begins to look like a veteran."[143]

Mrs. Lee, too, avoided open talk of approaching conflict, writing instead to Mildred about a new bonnet which Helen Peters was trimming for the schoolgirl. The new chapeau, her mother suggested, should be saved for special occasions. In these troubled times, finery ought to be cherished and old garments refurbished. "Clean up your black silk . . . with coffee & have it smoothed on the *wrong* side."[144]

In spite of their attempts to sound cheerful, the family at Arlington realized that each day the national news seemed more ominous. On Saturday morning, April 13, Virginians learned in their newspapers of the attack on Fort Sumter by General P. G. T. Beauregard and the Confederate forces under his command. War now seemed unavoidable, especially after Lincoln's call for 75,000 troops. A perceptive Southern diarist, Elizabeth Lindsay Lomax, who lived in Washington and was a friend of the Lees, spoke for all moderate Virginians when she wrote in her diary that night, "The news from the South makes me wretched— God help us!"[145]

Five days later Colonel Lee was called to Washington, where he was officially invited to take command of Union forces. The offer was one he had hoped would never materialize, for such leadership would inevitably involve him in battle against friends and kinspeople. Without hesitation he refused the position, explaining to General Scott and later to his family that "though opposed to secession and deprecating war, I could take no part in an invasion of the Southern States."[146] Deeply troubled, he stopped to discuss the situation with his brother Smith, who was still in the Federal navy and stationed in Washington. Both men, after years of military service, were torn by conflicting loyalties—adherence to profession and country on the one hand, and loyalty to home, family, and the Commonwealth on the other. Both knew that Virginia's special session of the General Assembly was meeting on the matter of secession, but they parted with the hope that somehow, if Virginia should stay in the Union, they might not have to resign immediately.

The following morning was cool but clear enough for Agnes and Helen Peters to go outdoors for a long walk. On the way back to the house, they learned that the General Assembly had voted for secession.* "I cannot yet realize it," Agnes wrote later in the day to Mildred. "It seems so dreadful. But [Virginia] had to take one side or the other & truly I hope she has chosen the right one. It is a very solemn step & I fear we will have to go through a great deal of suffering."[147]

By afternoon, as news of secession spread, friends and relatives began to gather in the Arlington parlor to discuss the stirring events, the fall of Fort Sumter a few days before, and the imminence of war. "Nothing here is talked or thought of," Agnes told Mildred, "except our troubles."[148] Early in the evening, Colonel Lee excused himself to make his final decision upstairs alone. It was after midnight when he returned to Mrs. Lee's room. "Well, Mary," he said, "the question is settled. Here is my letter of resignation and a letter I have written to General Scott."[149]

The family retired for a few hours of restless sleep, but Lee was up again early Saturday morning to draft letters to his sister, Anne Marshall, a loyal Unionist, and to Smith Lee. The message to Smith ended with the hope that Lee might stay quietly at home as "a private citizen. . . . Save in defense of my native state, I have no desire ever again to draw my sword."[150]

In midafternoon Rooney Lee arrived, surprising the family with his sudden visit to consult his father about future plans. Both Rooney and Custis were appalled by Virginia's secession and the sudden euphoria that gripped Alexandria. Custis would have preferred to "call it revolu-

---

*The order of secession was subject to ratification by Virginia's voters, the vote to be held on May 23, 1861. It was ratified by an overwhelming majority.

tion and order at once the seizing and fortifying of Arlington Heights," while Rooney felt only "deep depression with the prevalent elation and jubilancy" of the crowds he saw at the Alexandria depot. "The people," he told the family, "had lost their senses and had no conception of what a terrible mistake they were making." In contrast to the town's excitement, the mood at Arlington was somber and hushed, almost "as if there had been a death."[151] The sense of foreboding was deepened Saturday afternoon by receipt of the day's *Alexandria Gazette*, its lead editorial urging the Commonwealth to request that Colonel Lee undertake Virginia's defense, "to head our forces and lead our army."[152]

The following morning, Sunday, Lee made plans as usual to attend Christ Church in Alexandria, though he had no desire to fuel speculation or appear publicly. One of his daughters, probably Mary Custis, rode with him to church.* After the service, friends and fellow parishioners stood about in the churchyard, talking and watching for a signal from Colonel Lee. A group of strangers came up to talk, keeping him so long that his daughter and some of her friends grew restless. One of the girls, who lived only a few doors from the church, invited her to wait there. A friend remembered Mary Custis sitting at the upstairs window of the Lloyds' house, sharing the "suspense and uncertainty" that they were all feeling and wondering "what detained her father so long with these gentlemen."[153] Finally, Lee knocked at the Lloyds' door, and in an attempt to lighten the mood of the group, he asked for a kiss from his young hostess. He was nonplussed when she refused unless he promised to take command of Virginia's defenses. He could not promise, he said, for he had not been officially made such an offer. Without receiving his kiss, he and Mary Custis returned to Arlington.

In the evening a messenger arrived with a terse request that Lee travel as soon as possible to Richmond for an important meeting with Governor Letcher. The message did not specifically indicate the nature of the meeting, but Lee felt confident enough of his future to leave a note at the Lloyds' next morning assuring the daughter of the house that he would come back and "claim that kiss from my dear cousin."[154]

---

*Neither of the accounts of this interlude indicates which of the girls went with her father to church. Annie was away visiting Rooney's family at the White House; Mildred was away at school. Agnes was most often the family nurse, and Mary Custis was the most ardent member of the parish among family members. So it seems safe to presume that the story revolved around Mary Custis.

There is no record as to whether Agnes or Mary Custis rose early to bid their father farewell. The events of the past two days had been so emotionally wearing that they could be forgiven if they had slept late. But if they did get up in time to stand on the portico to wave good-bye, it was the last time they would ever see Lee ride down the familiar winding path to the river road, turning his course southward toward Alexandria, Richmond, and the Confederacy. His historic journey was to mark the end of the first phase of their lives, an abrupt break from the happy existence that had revolved around Arlington. The girls did not fully realize it on that morning of April 22, 1861, but their father understood full well what his refusal to accept Union command, his resignation from the army, and his trip to Richmond would mean. "To take sides with Virginia was to give up Arlington to its fate."[155]

4

The Broken Circle

1861–1862

ROBERT E. LEE had made his decision. Now the choices were up to the rest of the family, how best to achieve personal safety and, at the same time, protect home and property.

At first life resumed an eerie normalcy. Traffic moved as usual across Long Bridge, enabling Custis to leave each morning for his army engineering duties in Washington and offering Orton Williams, still on General Scott's staff, the opportunity to cross over frequently for visits. Trains ran on schedule and letters from Annie, now at the White House, arrived without difficulty. There was one correspondent, however, from whom the girls no longer heard. Helen Bratt had married a Union quartermaster named Beekman DuBarry, a man who finished at the academy five years before Custis.[1] With father and husband so completely allied with the Federal cause, Helen must have felt it necessary to terminate her long correspondence with Agnes and Annie.

As if to emphasize the orderly changing of seasons, the late spring burst out in a riot of color and scent, with tulips, daffodils, lilacs, and jasmine all blooming together. Roses budded beside the house, and down by the river the apple orchard was snowy with blossoms. "I never saw the country more beautiful," Mrs. Lee wrote to her husband in Richmond, "perfectly *radiant*. The yellow jasmine [is] in full bloom & perfuming all the air."[2]

Could it be, they wondered, that their fears of war and potential destruction had been exaggerated? Could a normal life at Arlington still be possible, even though Virginia had seceded? As the girls and their mother looked anxiously across the broad river toward Washington, they saw no unusual activity, only a "death like stillness."3

Writing from the pastoral isolation of the Pamunkey River plantation, Annie found it hard to believe that they might really have to abandon Arlington. "Are you really getting ready to leave," she asked Agnes in a letter written on May 2, "and who is staying?"4 Mildred, too, seemed to have little appreciation of the wrenching decisions that would have to be made at home. Answering a letter in which Mildred had complained about her inadequate wardrobe, Mrs. Lee replied sharply that she was "both hurt & mortified that a *daughter* of *mine* at a time when her Father's life is in peril, her home in danger of being trampled over by a lawless foe should allow a disappointment about a *bonnet* to be so deep in her mind."5

In Richmond, General Lee knew that both sides were calling up volunteers, tightening defenses, and assessing the other's strengths and weaknesses. It could be only a matter of time till the Federals would cross to Virginia, with Arlington a prime target. "You *have to move*," he wrote his wife on April 26, adding that "the Mt. Vernon plate & pictures ought to be secured."6 A week later, when the family showed no signs of evacuating, he wrote them urgently to "prepare all things for removal . . . & be prepared at any moment. There is no prospect or intention of the government to propose a truce—Do not be deceived by it."7

Ultimately, it was not her husband's letters but a dramatic visit from Orton Williams that startled them all into making preparations. One afternoon, as Mrs. Lee sat quietly in her room copying a portrait of Rob, Orton burst in with the frightening news that Federal troops would occupy Arlington the next morning. Breathlessly, he urged her to pack and send away her most valuable possessions immediately. Though he did not specifically say so, she was convinced that her young cousin had been sent as a personal messenger from General Scott to alert them.

Next morning he appeared again, this time to announce that troop movements had been changed and the occupation was delayed. He warned, however, that occupation was inevitable and preparations must be made. Now thoroughly alarmed, the women decided that they should dismantle the house as quickly as possible, grateful for the delay which would give them time to pack more carefully.

First they placed the Custis and Lee silver in two heavy wooden chests to be sent to Richmond along with General Lee's personal papers and irreplaceable Washington and Custis documents.* After dispatching these two precious cartons to the Alexandria train depot, they removed family portraits from the walls, took off the frames, and packed them for storage at Ravensworth. In the past, they had always rolled up carpets and curtains and put them away for the summer, but this year they stored, with unusual care, the heavy rugs and drapes, including one especially handsome damask set that had belonged to Martha Washington. Books from the parlor were placed in closets, which were then locked. Other volumes and engravings went into the small room off the staircase on the second-floor landing. The rest of the Mount Vernon mementos, including George Washington's punch bowl and the Cincinnati china, were securely nailed in wooden boxes and locked in the cellar, the key being entrusted to Selina Grey, Mrs. Lee's personal maid. Most of the large furniture was left in place.

"We have packed up a good many things," Agnes wrote to Annie, "but it is hard to tell where they will be safest. . . . It is *so so* sad to leave home." In her letter she spoke of Custis' resignation from the army on May 2, but Orton, she reported, was still on duty on General Scott's staff. "We see him very often. He will probably resign in a day or two."[8]

On the eighth of May, Agnes and Mary Custis bundled all the boxes and barrels into carriages and open wagons, along with the household wine supplies, foodstuffs, and the family piano, for the ten-mile ride to Ravensworth. Just before she left, Agnes handed Mildred's kitten, Tom Titta, to old "Uncle George," one of the house servants, for safekeeping.

After the confusion of the past few days, the girls found Ravensworth serene and quiet, and they tried to respond to Aunt Maria Fitzhugh's cordiality. However, by the time Custis and Mrs. Lee joined them, Agnes was beginning to fret about the safety of Orton Williams, who had not come to bid them farewell. He had been arrested, she learned, when he tried to submit his resignation from the army, for Federal authorities believed he knew too much about Union troop movements. To prevent him from passing on important military information to the Confederates, the government sent him as a prisoner to Governor's Island, New York. Agnes feared that his friendship with the Lee family would compound his punishment. "We it seems are considered the *Rebel* influence

---

*On May 11, General Lee sent the silver and the family documents to Lexington, Virginia, for safekeeping (REL to Mrs. REL, 11 May 1861, VHS).

that induced him to take his course," she wrote to Annie, "though it has been just the contrary."[9] Fortunately, the young officer was quickly paroled on his personal promise not to cross into Confederate territory for a month.

Not long after their arrival at Ravensworth, Agnes heard from Markie Williams, who was still studying art in New York City. Though she remained loyal to the Union throughout the war, Markie never forgot her ties to Arlington and the Lees. "I have seen Helen Peters & bitterly wept," she wrote, "over the account she gives me of the last days at dear, dear Arlington. I could imagine so entirely how you all felt. . . . Are the peaceful happy days when we culled those flowers to-gether, my dear Cousin, forever gone?" She had received only sketchy information from a mutual friend about the evacuation, and she was worried about her own possessions at the now abandoned house. "Please dear Agnes write as soon as you get my letter & tell me all about yourselves & of the fate of our treasures. . . . Give much love to your Father, dear Agnes. God bless you all."[10]

For two weeks Arlington stood empty, with only servants in attendance. Then, on the moonlit night of May 23, more than 13,000 Federal troops, including scarlet-uniformed Zouave battalions, marched silently across Long Bridge to occupy the bluffs and wharf of the plantation. Agnes had written with bitter wit to Annie about Union troops enjoying "cool airy rooms . . . for summer quarters on 'Arlington heights,'" but at first the soldiers stayed away from the mansion on strict orders from General Irving McDowell, though they pitched their tents on the lawn and cut down quantities of trees.[11] Before long, however, the restless men began to harass Arlington's overseer, who hastened over to Ravensworth to complain. He "was so nervous," Mrs. Lee wrote, "that he could scarcely refrain from tears."[12] Indignant over his treatment and irritated that she could not return to Arlington whenever she wished, Mrs. Lee sent a strongly worded protest to General Charles W. Sandford, the officer in charge of occupying forces.

> It never occurred to me Gen'l Sanford [*sic*] that *I* could be forced to sue for permission to enter my *own house* & that such an outrage as its military occupation to the exclusion of me & my children could ever have been perpetrated. . . . I implore you by the courtesy due to any woman & which no brave soldier could deny, to

allow my old coachman by whom I send this letter to get his clothes, to give some letters to my manager relative to the farm etc. [and] to give my market man a pass that will enable him to go & return from Washington as usual where his family resides. My gardener Ephraim also has a wife in Washington & is accustomed to go over every Saturday & return on Monday. . . . [A]llow my boy Billy whom I only left at home to complete some work in the garden to come to me with his clothes . . . [and] permit my maid Marcellina to send me some small articles that I did not bring away. She & the woman in the yard Selina can get what I want out of the House. I will not trouble you with any further requests.[13]

So distraught that she could not "trust my pen to write what I feel," Mrs. Lee marveled at how calm and uncomplaining Custis remained.[14] "He never indulges in invective or a word of reflection on the cruel course of the administration," she wrote to her husband. "He leaves all that to his Mamma & sisters."[15] Custis stayed at Ravensworth for less than a month before leaving for Richmond and a position in the Confederate engineering corps. Rooney was already in the cavalry, along with Fitz Lee, while Rob, still at the University of Virginia, was asking eagerly for permission to enlist.

Though Ravensworth, with its broad lawns and leafy catalpa trees, seemed quiet and safe, General Lee was concerned about his wife and two daughters there alone with Mrs. Fitzhugh and a handful of servants. If the Federals should take over her home, it would be an embarrassment to her to be harboring the Lee family. Perhaps, he suggested, they should go "to the upper country."[16] Not much caring where she was since she could not be at Arlington, Mrs. Lee dutifully moved west, accompanied by Mary Custis, first to Chantilly near Fairfax Court House, the home of Stuart relatives, then to a Randolph home, Eastern View, and finally to Kinloch, the Turner estate in Fauquier County where she had spent a happy summer holiday with the children in 1839. Agnes, meantime, had taken the train to Richmond on her way to the White House to be with Annie, Charlotte, and the baby. Mildred would join her mother after school was out.

The cooler hill country around Kinloch soothed Mrs. Lee's agitation, but the girls found it difficult to adjust to refugeeing with few books, no schedules, and a lack of familiar chores and duties to perform. Mary Custis was soon off for a visit at Manassas, and after a few weeks at the White House, Agnes began making plans to visit Cedar Grove and the homes of cousins near Richmond. Their father was not pleased with their interest in"'pleasant times.'. . . . [I]n my opinion these are serious times & our chief pleasure must be what is necessary & proper for the occasion."[17] Later, he again stressed that "I wish they were all at some quiet & safe place."[18]

He did have cheerful news about Orton Williams, however, who had traveled to Richmond at the end of his parole period. Aware that placing Orton on his own staff might renew the "accusations . . . of the Northern press . . . [concerning] his intended betrayal of Gen. Scott's plans," Lee made sure that the young man was sent to Tennessee to serve with General L. Polk.[19]

In Winchester Mildred was finishing her school term, sometimes enjoying more excitement in the community than in the classroom, for Winchester was infected with wartime enthusiasm. Pretty girls waved to the soldiers parading through the streets on their way to Harper's Ferry, flags flew from every balcony, and townspeople entertained the gallant young warriors with fetes and dances. Everyone assumed that after a battle or two, the Yankees would ask for peace. Her father was grateful that Precious Life had the opportunity to complete one full year of boarding school. "Whatever may happen," he wrote her, "continue your studies, alone if necessary, & commence with them a system of reading which will be very beneficial. . . . These are calamitous times, & we must conform to them & make the most of the opportunities afforded us." Knowing how much she worried about the kitten left at Arlington, he reassured her that Tom Titta was a resilient little cat, who "no doubt lords it in a high manner over the British [sic] at Arlington. He will have strange things to tell when you next see him."[20]

Early in July, Mildred packed all her schoolbooks in a large box marked with her name and stored it at Mrs. Powell's. The rest of her belongings, "winter as well as summer clothes," she carried with her to Kinloch. "As we know not what may happen," her mother had advised her, "it is best to be prepared for any emergency."[21]

She was already with her mother and Mary Custis when they received a long, heart-wrenching letter from Markie, who had returned to Georgetown with permission from General Scott to retrieve her personal things from Arlington. Driving up to the Heights, Markie wrote, there were "soldiers . . . everywhere. I was blinded with tears & choked with sorrow. . . . The poor House looked so desolate." She had hurried upstairs to the room she used to share with Mary Custis and closed the door for a long cry alone before packing her trunk. On her way to the attic to rescue some letters stored there, she opened the door to be greeted by Tom Titta, who "rubbed his little head against my dress in the most affectionate way." The sight of the lonely kitten brought another flood of tears. "I took him up, covered him with tears & kisses. Oh! how many fond associations of the past did that poor little cat bring up. He looked so pitiful there in his lonely garret home." As Markie left the house, several of the servants, including Selina, David, and Ephraim, came up to greet her. "All asked after you all with interest. . . . Oh! who in their wildest dreams could have conjectured all this last summer," she concluded. "It was but one year ago that we were all there, so happy & so peaceful."[22]

Although Markie's letter was sad, the family was grateful to have any news at all from Arlington, for mails had been stopped and the printing presses of the Alexandria *Gazette* confiscated by Federal troops. Writing to a friend near Fairfax Court House, Mrs. Lee asked for a Washington paper, "if you have one," for she and the girls had heard rumors of "marches & countermarches," and she felt sure that "some crisis is approaching."[23]

Their sources of information had been correct, for only forty miles from Kinloch, Northern and Southern troops were massing for the first major battle of the war at Manassas. On July 21, a "warm, bright, quiet . . . midsummer . . . Sabbath," the Lee women could hear, faintly but distinctly, the sound of cannonading.[24] By day's end they learned of the decisive Confederate victory, a triumph made sweeter for them by the knowledge that none of their relatives had been in the thick of fighting. The next morning, however, the full impact of the bloody victory burst upon them as the first ambulances rolled into Fauquier County amid torrential rain. A makeshift hospital was set up at Blantyre, a large private estate near Kinloch, and Mary Custis and Mildred were among the many women who came to nurse the horribly maimed and suffering soldiers. One of the volunteer nurses at Blantyre, Margaret Elizabeth Clewell, remembered years later how attractive and wholesome Mildred had seemed, in contrast to the filth and stench of the hospital. She was "dressed in a blue riding habit," Clewell recalled, "very pretty, and so fresh and fair." Someone asked her if she had family in the army, and she modestly replied that she was concerned about her father who was in the service but was more "uneasy about my brother." At that point in the conversation, another volunteer interposed with the information that "her father is General Lee."[25]

Lee was not at the battle of First Manassas because he had been requested by President Davis to remain in Richmond, in spite of the fact that much of the strategy was his and many of the soldiers involved were technically under his command. He had found his first months of service to the Confederacy frustrating and far from glamorous after a hearty initial welcome by the new government, which had bestowed on him the rank of brigadier general as "commander of the military and naval forces of Virginia." Working from an office in Richmond with numerous inspections of trouble spots, he organized 40,000 Virginians into disciplined fighting units, collected arms, ammunition, and rolling stock to supply them, and made the first tactical plans for the defense of his native state. Grateful for the "glorious victory" at Manassas and generous in his praise of Generals Beauregard and Joseph E. Johnston, he privately admitted to Mrs. Lee that he had "wished to partake in the ... struggle, & am mortified at my absence."[26]

Soon after Manassas, General Lee left Richmond for western Virginia to coordinate the struggle of Confederate troops against Federal forces threatening to invade the Shenandoah Valley from the west. Though he was hundreds of miles from them as he traveled across Virginia, he thought constantly of his family. When the train stopped at Staunton, now filled with "ragged men, hungry men, the sick and the road-worn," he found it difficult to believe it was the same community Agnes and Annie had written about in their letters six years before.[27] Later, as he rode horseback to Monterey, he remembered that this was the identical route he had taken toward St. Louis in 1840, just after Annie's birth. "If any one had then told me that the next time I travelled that road would have been on my present errand," he wrote to Mrs. Lee, "I should have supposed him insane."[28] His next letters were less reminiscent and far less cheerful, as he faced the unhappy task of melding raw recruits and demoralized battalions into one fighting unit, while at the same time struggling against wretched weather, rocky terrain, and an epidemic of measles which decimated his troops. Fortunately, Rooney was stationed near him and he was able to report to the rest of the family that the young cavalry officer was healthy, cheerful, and in no immediate danger.

Feeling that they had stayed with the Turners long enough, Mrs. Lee, Mildred, and Mary Custis moved on to Audley, a country home near Berryville in Clarke County that had belonged to Mrs. Lee's aunt, the beautiful Nelly Custis Lewis. The estate was only a few miles from

Winchester, still in Confederate hands but under constant threat from Federal forces just across the Potomac at Harper's Ferry. As fall approached, Mrs. Lee began to wonder whether she should risk sending Mildred back to Mrs. Powell's if the school reopened or send her farther south, perhaps to Raleigh. Too busy with his impossible campaign to give advice, Lee wrote his wife to do "as you think best about Mildred. I am unable to help you, even about your own movements. . . . Every thing within the seat of war must be uncertain."[29]

Precious Life did go back to the Winchester school when it began its fall term late in September with a small enrollment and a saddened faculty. The Powells' second son, who had enlisted in the Confederate army only a few weeks before the battle of Manassas, had been killed in that bloody conflict along with many other Winchester men. But in spite of the subdued atmosphere and the Federal threats, Mildred seemed glad to be back in school with her friends, and her only regret was that the summer had passed without her seeing the Girls. Agnes, too, was disappointed that the vacation time was over and they had not been together. She and Annie were staying temporarily at Laburnum, Agnes wrote, "a pretty country place about two miles from Richmond." Her principal concern was the failing health of little Rob, Charlotte and Rooney's baby. "You would hardly know our precious little nephew," Agnes lamented, "he looks so badly."[30]

Heavy rains in August as well as continued inactivity had made Mrs. Lee's arthritic condition more acute. Now, with Mildred back in school, Mary Custis and her mother had to decide whether or not to seek remedial treatment before the long, cold winter. In September the pair made the decision to travel to Hot Springs, Virginia, accompanied by young Rob, still on vacation between semesters at college. General Lee worried that the resort was only fifty miles from enemy lines, but the others showed little fear of capture. "Ma & Sister are in search of health," Rob wrote to Mildred, "& myself in search of Pleasure."[31] Mrs. Lee was disappointed that Annie and Agnes did not join them, but she was relieved that their remaining near Richmond did not signal her grandson's worsening health. "I feared you had been detained by the death of my little darling," she wrote to the Girls. "It is good news to hear that he is better."[32]

After several weeks of treatment in the hot waters, Mrs. Lee was well enough to journey east to Richmond and on to the White House, so that Charlotte, lonely and still concerned about her baby's health, would have an older family member she could "*depend* upon," as Mrs. Lee put it.[33] Rob traveled part of the way with his mother and Mary Custis, turning aside at Charlottesville for a reluctant third year at the university. Since their mother was to stay with Charlotte, Annie and Agnes now felt free to visit the Stuarts in King George County and to make a short excursion to nearby Stratford, their father's birthplace.

General Lee, too, had moved, reassigned from western Virginia to the piney woods and salt coves of South Carolina. From Charleston he wrote long letters to his girls at Winchester and Clydale, the Stuarts' summer home. He acknowledged to Mildred his discouragement over the failure of the West Virginia campaign and he feared that his new work, improving coastal defenses, would prove to be just "another forlorn hope expedition. Worse than western Virginia." But he attempted to be cheerful and wished Life a happy and useful year at Mrs. Powell's. "You must labour at your books & gain knowledge & wisdom," he told her. As for himself he had grown a beard, "a beautiful white beard. It is much admired. At least much remarked on."[34]

To Annie and Agnes he apologized for the infrequency of his letters— "I am so pressed with business"—but he was delighted to receive theirs, especially the one describing their trip to Stratford. "Stratford . . . is endeared to me by many memories," he told them. "The horse chestnut you mention was planted by my mother. I am sorry the vault is so dilapidated. You did not mention the spring, one of the objects of my earliest recollections." Now that Arlington had been "so foully polluted," he wondered if he might someday purchase Stratford for a family home.[35]

While Agnes and Annie lingered with the Stuarts, Mary Custis traveled north from Richmond for a sojourn at Kinloch and an unsuccessful attempt to visit Ravensworth, now occupied by Federal troops. Turned away from that destination, she stopped by Jeb Stuart's winter headquarters at Camp Qui Vive, near Fairfax Court House, to renew her friendship with the dashing cavalry general. "Miss Mary Lee spent a few days down [at our camp] the other day, during a fine spell of weather," Stuart wrote to his wife, Flora. "She came down to try to visit Ravensworth but found it too risky & ended her trip at Machen's where many of her Army friends visited her. Poor Gen Ewell is desperately but hopelessly smitten." *Stuart continued, "I hope you will make her acquaintance as she is a dear friend of mine."[36]

---

*General Richard S. Ewell, at the time a division commander under Stonewall Jackson, an eccentric bachelor, and a West Point graduate, class of 1840.

Before Christmas the family received news about Arlington when Mrs. Lee happened to see a stray copy of *Harper's Magazine* with an illustrated article about the estate. A sketch of the mansion showed the house to be intact, but the article indicated that most of the fine old oak trees in the forest had been felled for soldiers' campfires. More cheerful word came from "Aunt Brit" Kennon, who had received permission to remove the family's curtains and carpets to Tudor Place for safekeeping. That salvaging had come just in time, for Jeb Stuart's scouts revealed that the cellar at Arlington had been broken into sometime during the fall and Washington's punch bowl and other valuables had been stolen. A tearful Selina Grey, realizing that she could not prevent looting, had relinquished her basement key to General McDowell and begged his protection. Georgetown relatives urged the Union general to permit removal of all the remaining mementos to Tudor Place, but General McDowell decided to send the relics to the United States Patent Office in Washington, where they remained until finally restored to the Lee descendants in 1901, after years of litigation.

Though his wife and the girls still clung to the hope of returning someday to Arlington, General Lee was less sanguine. "It is better to make up our minds to a general loss," he counseled. "They cannot take away the remembrances of the spot, & the memories of those that to us rendered it sacred. That will remain to us as long as life will last & that we can preserve."[37]

As Christmas approached, Mrs. Lee tried to gather the family together. Rob, who had been "studying so many languages that I can hardly write English properly," traveled from Charlottesville to join his mother, Annie, Agnes, Custis, Charlotte, and little Rob at the White House in a concerted effort to celebrate the holiday.[38] How different this December, with its "chilling rains and frequent . . . melting . . . snows," must have seemed from the many cheerful vacations they had all spent at Arlington.[39] Mildred remained at Winchester, studying so hard, she apparently feared, that her hair was falling out. Agnes urged her to cut her hair short, as she had done. "It waves & twists itself up; some say it is very becoming," Agnes wrote. "It is quite fashionable now."[40] Realizing that this was the first year she had spent Christmas away from the family, Rob took time to write Mildred a long letter about the family's activities, describing the Pamunkey plantation and their holiday schedule.

Agnes, too, turned to letter writing that winter, sending a concerned letter to Orton Williams, from whom she had heard nothing.

> White House
> Dec. 1, 1861

> I have been hoping, dear Orton, ever since I sent my
> last long letter written the 29th of Sept. from Clydale, to
> have a response in due time. But "hope told a flattering
> tale" this time sure enough. I have been tempted to
> believe you have forgotten your old Virginia friends
> generally, me in particular, but ashamed of this skepti-
> cism in regard to "our brave defenders" I am going to
> do what I rarely ever do—write again.

After a few paragraphs describing her various visits with cousins
whom he knew, Agnes confessed that she was at a loss to know how to
proceed, for she had no idea whether he had been in battle, or been
sick, or even wounded. "In fact, Orton, I know nothing about you & am
writing in perfect mental darkness." Her only news of him came from
Custis, who had heard a rumor that Orton might return to Virginia. "I
wish indeed you could come," she wrote. When he saw her, she told
him, he would see a more mature person than the carefree young
woman who had ridden in the woods with him less than a year ago.
"How differently Orton we will pass this winter from last. I can hardly
realize sometimes I am the same girl." At the end of the letter, her old
worries about him surfaced again.

> Remember to take care of yourself. . . . I pray daily
> dear O His blessing may be upon you, & how I wish
> your own voice may ascend as often for yourself.

> Your friend
> Agnes L[41]

On Christmas Day General Lee, still in South Carolina, sent a holiday
letter to the assembled family at the White House, and he wrote a
separate message to Mary Custis, who was staying in Richmond at the
home of Mr. and Mrs. James Caskie. In his letter to Daughter, Lee
enclosed some pressed flowers from a South Carolina garden, "sweet
violets, that I gathered for you this morning while covered with dense

white frost." He continued, "God guard and preserve you for me, my dear daughter. In my absence from you, I have thought of you often, and regretted that I could do nothing for your comfort. Your old home, if not destroyed by our enemies, has been so desecrated that I cannot bear to think of it. . . . In your houseless condition, I hope you can make yourself contented and useful. Occupy yourself in aiding those more helpless than yourself."[42]

Mary Custis remained in Richmond throughout that winter and spring, occupying a spare bedroom in the Caskie home. She and Mrs. Lee had met the hospitable Richmond couple at Hot Springs in October, and they and their daughter Norvell, a young woman about Agnes' age, had urged the Lees to use their home whenever they were in the capital. Mary Custis probably attended President Jefferson Davis' inaugural on February 22 in the pouring rain, and she witnessed the first real invasion scare that engulfed the city, as the initial refugees—"fugees," the natives called them—poured into Richmond from occupied Norfolk and other communities in the Tidewater.

Not long after sending his Christmas messages, Lee wrote a birthday letter to Mildred, for she had just turned sixteen.

> Are you really sweet sixteen? That is charming, and I want to see you more than ever. But, when that will be, my darling child, I have no idea. I hope, after the war, that we may again all be united, and I may have some pleasant years with my dear children, that they may cheer the remnant of my days.
>
> I am very glad to hear that you are progressing so well in your studies, and that your reports are so favorable. Your mother wrote me about them. . . . It has been a long time since I have seen you, and you must have grown a great deal. Rob says he is told that you are a young woman. . . . But I love you just as much as ever, and you know how great a love that is.[43]

Mildred had hardly had time to receive his letter before she had to make a hasty departure from Winchester. General T. J. "Stonewall" Jackson withdrew from the city, and the Powells, overwhelmed by their responsibility for so many young women, dismissed the school with little warning. With characteristic self-reliance, the girl made her way to join Mrs. Lee at the White House.

Though her father had very much hoped that Precious Life could continue at school "to the end of the session," he now enjoyed picturing the three younger girls together again.[44] "In the busy hours of the day & the silent hours of the night . . . in which my anxious thoughts drive away sleep," he thought about each one and their reunion. Frustrated with his task of preventing Union ships from entering Carolina waterways, he envisioned Annie and Agnes asleep in one bed, "sound & happy," quite oblivious to "where the blockaders are, or what their progress is in the river." He hoped the girls would use their free time to learn to sew, dividing their responsibilities like a military campaign. "Enter . . . into domestic manufactures," he counseled. "Take separate departments & prepare fabric."[45]

By the time spring arrived in Virginia with "a sudden glory of green leaves, magnolia blooms, and flowers among the grass," General Lee was back in Richmond, where he had numerous opportunities to see Mary Custis.[46] One day he offered her a ride on his new horse, Traveller, whom most riders found difficult to become accustomed to, for none of the mount's gaits was "very easy . . . save his walk & canter." But Lee proudly reported that Daughter, an excellent horsewoman, was "charmed" by the handsome gray stallion and "thinks she never rode a more pleasant goer."[47]

The ride on Traveller was not the only unexpected pleasure Mary Custis enjoyed that spring. One day a mysterious parcel was delivered to the Caskies' door, containing an old copybook of hers into which as a young girl she had transcribed poems, songs, and homilies. Inside the cover she had written many years before that the book was "given me when a little girl at Arlington by my Greataunt, Eleanor Parke Custis Lewis."[48] When she leafed through the pages she discovered, in different handwriting, two new pieces of poetry on previously blank pages, verses that explained the mystery of the long-lost copybook and its surprising recovery.

Jeb Stuart, now a major general and the chief cavalry officer in the Army of Northern Virginia, and her own cousin Fitzhugh Lee, a lieutenant colonel on Stuart's staff, had been out on bivouac in northern Virginia, wandering in and around Federal positions. They had evidently stopped by Kinloch, where they either discovered the book or were given it by a family member to return to Mary Custis. By the light of their campfire, they had glanced through its pages and then composed their own poems of explanation.

Fitz Lee's versification was dated March 20, 1862 and was addressed to "Sweet flower." With typical cousinly frankness, "Chudie" Lee poked gentle fun at Mary Custis' outspoken ways and her unwillingness to be "bossed."

> Sweet flower! for by that name at last
> When all my reveries are past
> I call thee, and to that cleave fast;
> Sweet *silent* creature!
>
> That breath'st with me in sun and air
> Do thou, as thou art wont, repair
> My heart with gladness, and a share
> Of thy *meek* nature.
>
> I am your husband, if you will marry me
> If not, I'll die your slave. To be your master
> You may deny me; but I'll be your "devoted"
> Whether you will or no.

In the fourth unrhymed stanza, Fitz Lee incorporated the famous lines that their grandfather, "Light Horse Harry" Lee, had used to describe George Washington.

> From one who like the "Father
> of his Country" is "first in war
> first in peace," first in the
> heart of his country cousin.
> —& her first cousin.
>
> Fitz.
>
> Cavalry Bivouac
> Warrenton Junction
> Yankees around
> March 20th 1862[49]

Stuart's poem was longer and more polished. He loved to write verse and had a reputation for using hyperbole, even in his military orders. General Lee once commented dryly that "the Genl deals in the flowery style."[50] Written the night before Fitz Lee's doggerel, Stuart's poem was addressed "To Marielle," the romantic name Mary Custis had used during her years at Pelham Priory and West Point, when Jeb had first met her.

It chanced to-night on outpost duty—
I found an album with thy name in:
So full of gems of love and beauty
I looked it o'er till lo! there came in—
My muse—so long forgot—neglected—
A form I least of all expected.

In the gay old days—the *West Point* days,
She led me o'er its sweet romance—
Where Hudson, foaming tribute pays
To mountain-crag and highland haunts—
We parted there, the cause untold—
My muse & I will ne'er unfold.

In gazing on this precious token—
Fond mem'ry links a chain of pleasure
Back to those youthful days, unbroken;
Each page discloses some dear treasure—
Love-off'rings to the darling one—
That graced West Point and Arlington.

Snatched from the foul invader's touch—
Restored, unsullied to Marielle!
Be thou, pure page,—I beg this much—
A still reminder, some day to tell—
That one too true to be discreet—
Here laid his off'ring at her feet!

Jeb

Cavalry Bivouac
Fauquier. Mar 19th 1862[51]

The old notebook, and even more the verses written in by cousin and friend, were carefully treasured by Mary Custis Lee. To be sure, she could not take seriously the sentiments suggested by Jeb Stuart's doggerel, for she knew that he flirted with every pretty girl in the Confederacy, much to the annoyance of his staid wife, Flora. But he was "the idol of the hour," and to receive such a message from the dashing hero must have been heartwarming.[52] She cared enough about the book and its handwritten verses to keep it for the rest of her long life, though she destroyed almost all her other correspondence. Two years later, near Jeb Stuart's sentimental poem, she pasted a newspaper obituary of his death in May of 1864.

Grateful as he was for the chance to see something of Daughter, General Lee was more concerned about the welfare of other family members, especially Mrs. Lee, Annie, and Mildred, still in residence at the White House beside the Pamunkey River. On April 1, 1862, General George McClellan, in command of twelve divisions of troops, had joined other Union soldiers at Fort Monroe, preparatory to a sustained drive toward Richmond. Lee worried that within days 100,000 Federals might be deployed by ship up the York River. "Should they select that [route]," he wrote to Mrs. Lee on the fourth of April, "their whole army etc. will land at the White House. To be enveloped in it would be extremely annoying & embarrassing. . . . No one can say what place will be perfectly safe or even quiet, but I think a locality within the route of an invading army will be least so."[53]

While Lee worried over her safety and that of their daughters, Mrs. Lee viewed her stay at the White House from a different perspective. She wanted to remain on the property to protect it; if the plantation were taken, she and the girls might by their presence dissuade Federal troops from desecrating Rooney's home as they had the empty house at Arlington. In deference to her husband's wishes, she did move from the more conspicuous farmhouse near the river to a smaller dwelling nearby.

But McClellan did not move as Lee had conjectured. Instead of using the water route, the Union general chose to direct his vast Army of the Potomac slowly up the peninsula between the James and York rivers, laying siege to Yorktown, and then pressing on toward Norfolk, Williamsburg, and Portsmouth. But neither the land movements of the Union army nor Mrs. Lee's change in location eased General Lee's mind, though he acknowledged that her temporary dwelling was "more retired from the line of the enemy than the W. H., though by no means removed."[54] Had she really considered all the consequences of capture, he asked—harassment, danger, and the loss of buying power? Under Federal occupation, her Confederate currency would be valueless.

Finally, on May 11, with advance units of enemy troops only a few miles away, Mrs. Lee and the girls abandoned the White House property altogether. Before she drove away in a carriage, Mrs. Lee tacked a defiant note to the front door of the old Custis home.

> Northern soldiers who profess to reverence Washington, forbear to desecrate the home of his first married life, the property of his wife, now owned by her descendants.
>
>   A Grand-daughter of Mrs. Washington[55]

Moving not far away to a house called Criss Cross, she and the girls watched enemy troops come into the area on May 18. Later that same day, a Union search party insisted on examining her shelter and speaking with the women. Mrs. Lee made sure they knew who she was and were aware that she did not appreciate the humiliation being forced upon her. Years later one of the Federal officers wrote of the interview:

> By orders from general headquarters, General Porter sent Captain Kirkland, of his staff, and myself, to make sure that she [Mrs. Lee] was properly protected. Upon arrival our reception was not very gracious. Being informed by Kirkland that he was the bearer of a communication from General Porter and his desire to assure her proper care and protection . . . she complained bitterly of the indignity of being confined to her house, and her movements watched by sentinels, and, especially, of General Porter's part in the matter, he having been formerly a favored guest at Arlington. . . . The visit was finally terminated with much more of courtesy on her part than our reception promised.[56]

Perhaps because of her defiant attitude or her invalid condition, Mrs. Lee and the girls were permitted to move a few days later farther up the

Pamunkey River to the home of Edmund Ruffin, the Virginia agriculturalist and patriot who had fired the first shot at Fort Sumter. But the tide of battle caught up with them there, too, and this time they were placed under house arrest. Lee, still in Richmond, learned of their capture a few days later. "It is true," he wrote to Agnes on May 29, "that your mother, Annie, & Mildred are in the hands of the enemy. The house was surrounded by a body of the enemy's Cav." He was, he confided to Agnes, "very anxious about them."[57]

It was a time of anxiety for all Virginians. After the fall of Norfolk and Portsmouth, there seemed to be no way to stop Federal forces from occupying the capital itself. Congress adjourned in haste, President Davis' wife and children fled to Raleigh, and ordinary Richmond citizens panicked, "leaving by hundreds in all directions, and in all manner of conveyances. Baggage-wagons, heaped up with trunks, boxes and baskets were constantly rattling through the streets."[58] Union soldiers and Confederate troops battled only miles from the outskirts of Richmond. On May 31, after General Joseph E. Johnston was wounded at the battle of Seven Pines, President Jefferson Davis named Lee to be commander of all Confederate forces before Richmond.

As he rallied his troops and planned strategy for the series of engagements that came to be known as the Seven Days' campaign, Lee received word that his wife had requested an exchange. Under a flag of truce, his emissaries got in touch with General McClellan, who graciously issued a pass, assisted Mrs. Lee and the two young ladies into the carriage that Lee had sent over the line, and watched them cross into Confederate territory on June 10, where they were warmly welcomed by General Lee himself.

They went at once to the Caskies' home, where the hospitable family made them comfortable. For the next month, however, Richmond seemed no safer than the White House, as Union forces came so close to the city that townspeople could hear cannonading and see bursts of musket fire. Casualties were so heavy that the 5,000 wounded men overflowed established medical facilities, forcing many to be housed in private homes. Busy with nursing the wounded, rolling bandages, and scraping lint, the Lee girls nonetheless found time occasionally to see their father when he made short trips to town from the battlefield. They also were treated to visits from Custis and Rob, who since late spring had been serving as a private in the Stonewall Brigade. His unit had been called from the Valley of Virginia to reinforce troops defending Richmond, and now he was on leave in the city, staying with Custis and several fellow officers at a house on Franklin Street, which they nick-named "The Mess." Only a few blocks from the Caskies', both young men came over frequently to see their mother and sisters, read the latest letters from General Lee and Rooney, and share their concern over the tide of battle. With the rest of Richmond, they rejoiced when McClellan and his troops moved away from the Pamunkey River toward Harrison's Landing early in July. The fate of their White House property was still unknown.

For some time Charlotte Lee, Rooney's wife, staying at Hickory Hill with little Rob and Agnes, had been eager to get away from the summer heat, the danger of malaria, and the persistent threat of enemy occupa-tion. The baby was sick, and she herself was five months' pregnant. Because the mountains and spas of western Virginia were too close to enemy lines, she chose a smaller healing spring near Warrenton, North Carolina, which was owned by a distant cousin of the Lees, William Duke Jones.

Together with Annie, Agnes, and Mildred, she and young Rob took the train from Richmond south across the Carolina border to Warren Plains, a depot near the village of Warrenton. From there an omnibus trans-ported passengers to the two resorts catering to summer tourists, Shockoe Springs and Jones Springs. The Jones Springs hotel, built beside sulphur chalybeate springs, could accommodate 350 guests, and here the four young women settled in, eager to bring the sickly little boy back to robust health. It was the first time that any of the four had been in North Carolina, and they were pleased with their new surroundings. "This is [a] nice clean comfortable place, fine for children I should think," Annie wrote to her mother, who was planning to join them later. "Mr. Jones says it is perfectly healthy here."[59] Lee, too, was informed of the party's safe arrival, and he replied with an encouraging letter to Charlotte, ending with the request to "kiss your sweet boy for me."[60]

In spite of their high hopes and the promise of a healthy environ-ment, however, the child did not improve, but instead took a bad cold that quickly developed into terminal bronchitis or pneumonia. The doctors called it gangrene or affection of the lungs.* Heartbroken, Charlotte returned alone to Virginia to bury her firstborn in Richmond's

---

*Margaret Sanborn quotes the doctor's diagnosis as "gangrene of the lungs" (*Robert E. Lee* [Philadelphia: J. B. Lippincott Co., 1966–67], 2:58). The notice in Shockoe Cemetery lists the cause of death as "affection of the lungs."

brick-walled Shockoe Cemetery on July 5, 1862, in a tiny grave beside her parents and grandparents. Rooney, on active duty with his cavalry unit, was unable to attend the short service.

There was a great deal of sickness in Richmond that summer, caused in part by excessive heat and humidity and intensified by the presence of so many wounded soldiers, casualties from the bloody Seven Days' campaign. One resident described the city as "one immense hospital" where citizens "breathed the vapors of the charnel house."[61] Custis Lee was among the many seriously ill, and both Mrs. Lee and Mary Custis ministered to him devotedly, prevented by their nursing duties from going at once to be with the grieving Charlotte. As soon as Custis was well enough to be left and the area was safely in Confederate hands, Mrs. Lee made the twenty-mile trip to the Wickham plantation at Hickory Hill, outside Ashland. While there she received another long letter from Markie Williams, bringing the latest sad news from Arlington. With a wagon, Markie had been out to the plantation, hoping to retrieve some of her own furniture, but the commanding general had been away, and she left downcast and empty-handed. She had made an inventory, however, of all that remained in the house.

> My Dearest Cousin Mary, what a sad, sad visit it was—so changed, so changed & yet so like itself, is the dear place. Where once, peace & love dwelt, now, all the insignia of war is arrayed. Mrs. Whipple [wife of the occupying general] occupies *your* room, down stairs, as the parlor. In it, is all the parlor furnature [sic]. . . . It presents a strange appearance & yet the surroundings are so familiar. . . . The garden is enclosed with a white washed fence & the roses & white jasmine were blooming as they used to do in the happy days gone bye. Poor old Ephraim who tells me he has had "typer" fever . . . escorted us around the garden with the flower sissors [sic]. I walked in & with tearful eyes, gathered a bouquet.

Markie pressed and enclosed in her letter one "little leaf," which "came from the garden at A——." Just before her departure, Uncle Ephraim had told her, "in an unusually loud tone, 'Miss Martha, when you write to Miss Mary please give my best love to her & all the family &

tell her we miss them all very much indeed—these people does the best
they can for us, but it ain't like those we all been raised with.' I saw the
sentinel smile, and tears rolled down my cheeks as I bid the poor old
man good bye."[62]

Mrs. Lee must have wept, too, as she read the letter, but at least
Arlington was still standing, unlike the White House which had burned
to the ground, fired against McClellan's orders by Union troops. Now
only two blackened chimneys remained of the frame structure where
Martha Custis had married George Washington and where Rooney and
Charlotte had begun housekeeping. Not far away, the Shirley plantation
had been plundered by 12,000 Federal soldiers, who shot or ate all the
horses, mules, oxen, hogs, and sheep, broke the wheels of the wagons,
and destroyed the cradles used to harvest wheat. Among the Union
officers who invaded Virginia was Louis Marshall, the Lee girls' first
cousin from Baltimore, who was serving under General John Pope.
Young Rob had been sent down the peninsula with the rest of the
Stonewall Brigade to head off Pope's forces, and Lee hoped that his
youngest son might capture Marshall. Writing to Mrs. Lee, General Lee
indicated that he could "forgive [Louis] fighting against us, but not his
joining such a miscreant as Pope."[63]

In August Custis wrote a long letter to Annie and Agnes, still at Jones
Springs. "Pa," he wrote, was at Gordonsville, with Rooney and their
cousin, "Fitzy" Lee, who had just been promoted to the rank of "Brig.
Gen. of Cavalry." His mother was "enjoying herself at Hickory Hill and
does not express the least intention . . . [of] going to Jones!" Mary Custis,
after helping Custis to regain his health, had then nursed Mrs. Caskie
through a serious illness. "Sister . . . was made sick herself," Custis
informed them. He acknowledged that both he and Mary Custis were a
"little pulled down by . . . all the hot weather." Since Richmond was
rumored to have so little food and fuel for the coming winter, he urged
his sisters to consider staying in the South.[64]

For a year General Lee had been urging Mildred to consider attending St. Mary's Academy at Raleigh, the largest church-related seminary
for girls in antebellum America. But Mildred was hesitant to enter a
large boarding school where she had no friends or relatives. Finally, in
September of 1862, Annie wrote from North Carolina that Life had
agreed to try St. Mary's.

"I wish Mildred had made her decision about school *earlier*," her
mother replied on September 21. Because Mrs. Lee was at Hickory Hill,
Agnes and Annie would have to collect a wardrobe for the girl as best

they could. Did Mildred have a pair of "India rubbers," her mother wondered? Perhaps one of her sisters could spare a "black silk mantilla" to send along to Raleigh. Mrs. Lee certainly did not want Mildred to travel by herself. "One of you might go *with Mildred*," she suggested, "& place her there or send her by any *reliable* person."[65] As Annie had been complaining of "constant headache & dizziness" since August, it is likely that neither girl went with Mildred.[66] Instead, a chaperone from the resort accompanied Life to the depot at Warren Springs for the trip via the Raleigh and Gaston Railroad to the state capital. At the Raleigh station they were met by a hack, probably driven by the hackdriver noted for cheerfully offering to drive young students to "the cemetery," meaning "seminary."[67]

Though she had decided for herself that she would attend St. Mary's, Mildred came to this school with a very different frame of mind from the cheerful enthusiasm with which she had entered Mrs. Powell's. That academy had been small, and Mildred already had known a number of the pupils who were cousins, neighbors, or friends of friends. Here, she was coming into a school of several hundred girls she had never seen before, who had already had a chance to become acquainted because she was enrolling late.

For their part, the students at St. Mary's were reported to be in "quite a flutter" when they learned that General Lee's daughter was about to attend. The young ladies' apprehensions were quickly squelched by Miss Evertson, the stern matron of one of the dormitories and a long-time teacher at the school who, in addition to serving as housemother, taught botany, history, and mental philosophy. Scornful of her pupils' nervousness about the newcomer's imminent arrival, Miss Evertson suggested tartly that Mildred Lee was probably "no more than an ordinary mortal like the rest of us."[68] As the boarding students watched silently, Mildred and her chaperone got out of the hack and walked up the steps of the large central building, called "the brick house," and entered the office of the rector, or headmaster, the Reverend Aldert Smedes, a large man with gray beard and friendly eyes.

Later, in the dormitory room of the second floor of an adjacent building, West Rock, the girls had a chance to get a closer look at the new boarder. One of her nine roommates remembered Mildred as "a slender girl, with a prominent nose . . . [and] a good voice, sweet and clear."[69] Another student recalled years later that the girls never cared much for the new Virginian, feeling that she was too "strong-minded."[70]

Whatever they thought of one another, Mildred and the rest were soon caught up in the busy routine of school—breakfast, an hour's walk, chapel, morning classes, dinner at one o'clock, afternoon class sessions, tea, study hour, and bed at ten o'clock. The morning and afternoon recitations, five days a week, were in the usual subjects of French, Latin, biblical history, church catechism, music, and art. Most of the teachers were women, including Miss Eliza Evertson, who was lame and always wore a black lace cap; Miss Stella Shaw, the plump, cheerful piano teacher who it was rumored had been abandoned as a foundling on the school's doorstep; Miss Lizzie Liddell, the art teacher; Madame Gouyé, a French immigrant, whose health was so uncertain that she held classes in her bedroom; and Miss Hanson, a large, rather masculine German who taught voice. Male professors included Herr Hanson, chairman of the music department, and Dr. Smedes, who taught all subjects for which there was not a ready teacher.

In spite of her full schedule, Mildred was extremely lonely and ill at ease. She poured out her unhappiness in a letter to Agnes, who replied with sympathy.

Oct. 13, 1862

I am indeed sorry dear Mildred that you were so disappointed in "St. Mary's" though of course I make some little allowance for slight exaggeration just to make it more interesting you know. But it is really very forlorn to go all by yourself among so many strange girls after they have had time to know each other well. . . . I cannot *promise* to write every day, you know my laziness. . . . Write soon I am very anxious to hear from you.

Your attached sister,
Agnes[71]

A month later, Mildred was still unhappily reporting to Agnes about the students' unkindness. "I am sorry," Agnes replied, "[that] in your school too 'the girls don't speak,' & I hope you will have too much self respect to indulge in such nonsense."[72]

But the family had far greater concerns than Mildred's supposed slights. Soon after the first of October, Annie's chills and headaches worsened and she developed fever and intestinal discomfort. Though there were several cases of typhoid fever at the springs, neither Agnes nor Annie had any personal acquaintance with the illness, and they may have assumed that Annie merely had a kind of flu. Within a few days, however, her spiraling fever and extreme lassitude frightened Agnes, who notified her mother and requested that Dr. Patterson, the resident physician at the springs, come to see Annie. Her continuing high fever, rash, and dark red tongue enabled the doctor to make the definite diagnosis of typhoid.

The symptoms of typhoid fever, one of the four or five most common illnesses of the 1860s, had already been well documented. In addition to the debilitating fever, which could often rise to 106 degrees just before the characteristic rash appeared, a patient suffered aching and general weakness. If one were fortunate, the body's natural disease-fighting mechanism conquered the illness, and the patient recovered slowly. If sickness continued longer than ten days or two weeks, serious and often fatal complications could occur. Before the Civil War, standard treatment consisted of little more than alleviating the fever with cold cloths, offering plenty of liquids, and using sedatives in cases where the headache and stomach pains were severe. No attempt was made to isolate patients.

As soon as she learned of Annie's condition, Mrs. Lee hastened down to Jones Springs, accompanied by a cousin, Ella Carter. She had resisted when her husband urged her to find a safer location, for she felt that Charlotte needed her. But Annie's illness now became her first priority. Agnes served as the nurse during the daylight hours, Mrs. Lee at night, and between them they tried to let Mildred, Mary Custis, and General Lee know the progress of the sickness. At first Mrs. Lee was not especially worried, and she did not feel it was necessary for either Mildred or Mary Custis to come. After all, other guests at the springs had had typhoid, and they had all recovered. On October 13 Agnes wrote to Mildred that "Annie continues the same, very tired, & her fever still unbroken. Ella, Ma, & I keep up our nursing."[73] But five days later, even the usually sanguine mother was growing apprehensive. Annie was "much worse than when I came," she reported to Mary Custis, "more attenuated, & pulse higher. The disease must be at its crisis now. . . . She has been suffering today with pain in her stomach & bowels. . . . She is so deaf that she can scarcely hear a word."[74]*

---

*Annie's symptoms, deafness and severe stomach pains, suggest that she had the most serious complications of typhoid—spinal meningitis and a ruptured appendix.

The following morning, Mrs. Lee added an ominous postscript. "Annie passed a very uncomfortable night. . . . The Dr. considers her extremely ill."75 For much of the day Annie lay in a coma. Once she roused to ask for her hymnbook, but she was unable to read, and the volume slipped from her fingers. "Mamma thinks her hand rested on a hymn entitled 'In Extremety [*sic*],'" Agnes later wrote Mary Custis. That night "she said 'Lay me down, lay me down,' & afterwards 'I am ready to rise' which I feel now referred to what was to come. About three in the morning, Annie called, 'Where's Agnes?' & felt for me, I pressed my face to hers & I told her I was sleeping with her, she was content."76 At seven in the morning of October 20, 1862, "she breathed her last—very quietly & peacefully. O Mildred," Agnes agonized later that day, "I cannot realize it; it is too strange, too unnatural. I never had an idea of it, never felt she was even seriously ill until yesterday morning, nor until last night that she was to die. I wish you could have been with us so much, it would have been a comfort to be to-gether."77 Anne Carter Lee was twenty-three when she died.

Alone, the two women now had to decide where they should bury Annie. With no regular cemetery in Warrenton, property owners simply utilized a portion of their land for small individual grave sites. The Jones family kindly offered a plot in their family cemetery, a rose garden near the springs. Mrs. Lee wished to accept their offer, while Agnes was eager to take Annie's body back to Richmond for burial. If the grave were in Richmond, Agnes felt sure she could visit it often. During the hours of uncertainty, telegrams were sent to Custis and Daughter and Mrs. Lee wrote her husband a letter containing the sad news. Perhaps Custis would travel to the springs to lend support and see to details. But word came back that he was out of town, and he did not receive the message until after Annie had been buried. Without Custis' guidance, Agnes yielded to her mother's insistence that Annie be buried in North Carolina.

A black cabinetmaker from Warrenton, James M. Ransom, put together a simple pine coffin for the slender figure "with her black hair braided over her marble brow & covered with beautiful flowers."78 With Mrs. Lee, Agnes, and a few others in attendance, Dr. William Hodges, the Episcopal rector from Warrenton, read the service for the dead and in an impressive manner performed "the last sad duties at your sister's grave," Mrs. Lee wrote to Mary Custis. "She is placed in a lovely secluded spot."79

His wife's letter reached Lee a day or so after Annie's death, along with routine mail. He opened the letters privately, then summoned Walter H. Taylor, his chief of staff, for consultation about several military matters. There was no hint in his manner, Taylor later recalled, that in any way indicated sorrow or distress. "I then left him," the deputy continued, "but for some cause returned in a few moments, and with my accustomed freedom entered his tent without announcement or ceremony [and] I was startled and shocked to see him overcome with grief, an open letter in his hands."[80]

It was a bitter blow to Lee. He had known how very ill his "gentle Annie" was, but now "to know that I shall never see her again on earth, that her place in our circle, which I always hoped one day to enjoy, is forever vacant, is agonising [*sic*] in the extreme. But God in this, as in all things, has mingled mercy with the blow, in selecting that one best prepared to leave us." He wished he could offer some real comfort to his wife, but he had none except his personal belief that God had taken her "at the time and place when it is best for her to go. . . . May you be able to join me in saying, 'His will be done.'"[81]

Both Rooney and Rob were notified by their father of Annie's death. Rob, on duty in Clarke County near Berryville, had not even known of his sister's illness. He wrote to Mrs. Lee that "I could not then [when he learned the news] nor can I now realize that I shall never see her any more in this world. . . . I never even heard of poor Annie's illness until I heard she was dead."[82]

Together, Mrs. Lee and Agnes took the train back to Richmond, just as the weather turned cold and bleak. For Mrs. Lee, the loss of Annie meant more than the death of the tiny child she had cradled in her arms and nursed through illness and accident, the adolescent girl whose laughter had brightened the halls of Arlington. In recent years Annie had become the steady, dependable, capable mainstay of the household who had managed the plantation, taught her youngest sister, prepared Mildred's wardrobe for school, and performed unostentatiously the numerous chores that Mrs. Lee, in her invalidism, could no longer handle. For Agnes, Annie's death meant the loss of a sister as close as a twin. With her ready wit and lively imagination, Annie had been the instigator and leader of their games, the confidante of Agnes' hopes and dreams, and her closest friend. As the chill rain turned to snow and bitter winds blew across the city and about the chimneys at the Caskie house, Agnes re-echoed the sentiment she had shared with Mildred the day of Annie's death: "We will have to be more & more to each other now that Annie is taken away from me."[83]

Their despondency was not lightened by the premature arrival and frail condition of Charlotte's baby girl, who was evidently in such uncertain health that she was never christened. The baby survived only until the second week in December, when Agnes and Mrs. Lee accompanied the weeping Charlotte to Shockoe Cemetery once more, to lay the tiny girl beside her brother.

Somehow Markie Williams learned of Annie's death and she hastened to send condolences through the lines. "I long to see you all," she wrote Agnes, "& since I have heard of this deep affliction, have sometimes felt that I *must* go to you . . . but this cannot be." She added that it had been a long time since she had heard from Orton. Perhaps Agnes had had some word. "When you write Agnes, tell me if you hear from my dear dear Brother & how & where he is. Tell me everything you know of him. It has been more than a year since I have heard from him. . . . I wonder sometimes if he ever thinks of or cares for me. . . . Give much love to him & tell him I have written until I am tired of writing."[84]

Mrs. Lee and Agnes had expected to receive some comfort from Mary Custis, either through letters or from Daughter's return to Richmond to be with them. But Mary Custis suddenly found herself trapped behind enemy lines as Union forces, under General Ambrose Burnside, occupied Stuart's Landing, Acquia Creek, and the entire Northern Neck region from the "Rappahannock to the Potomac" as part of the Fredericksburg campaign. Lee had tried to warn Daughter that the Federals would soon be "in position to oppress our friends and citizens of the Northern Neck," but Mary Custis had delayed too long.[85]

All alone now in North Carolina, Mildred was still miserable at school, in spite of the teachers' attempts to put her at ease and Dr. Smedes' cheery greetings as he called each pupil by name. In her homesickness and grief over Annie, she wrote asking for permission to come to Virginia for Christmas. The first response to her request came from Agnes, who answered evasively, "Mama . . . will have to tell you about vacation."[86] But General Lee was quite firm on the matter. Concerned that yet another of his children might fall into enemy hands as she traveled back and forth, he decided without hesitation that Mildred should stay in Raleigh. "As regards Mildred," he wrote his wife, "no one can say with certainty as to her continuing within our lines. . . . I think she had better remain." After all, he continued, she was no longer a child needing to be home for the holiday, "but a young woman anxious to obtain wisdom."[87]

His words must have seemed so stern to Mrs. Lee that she added a softening postscript to his letter when she sent it on to Mildred. "My dear Mild. . . . You know how much pleasure it would give me to have you here but perhaps on the whole you had better remain. Things are so unsettled, & I have no home to offer you."[88] And so Mildred stayed at St. Mary's, where the Smedes did their best to make Christmas cheerful for the many girls who, like Precious Life, were unable to reach their own families. This experience, more than any other, probably made the girl feel more at ease, as the refugee group played parlor games together, stayed up late every night with special permission, and were treated to as bountiful a holiday dinner as the rector and his wife could manage with their limited supplies.

In many ways, Christmas was to be harder for the family in Virginia. Mrs. Lee and Agnes, making plans to join Charlotte at Hickory Hill, could not help remembering last year's Christmas at the Wickham plantation, with Annie, Rob, and Charlotte's son together with them. This year Annie and little Rob were dead, there seemed no prospect that General Lee or any of his sons could leave their winter quarters, and they could not even write to Mary Custis. "I can only hold oral communication with your sister," Lee explained to Agnes in December. "I have received one letter from her, but have forbidden the scouts to bring any writing, & have taken back some that I had given them for her. If caught, it would compromise them. They only convey messages. I learn in that way she is well & is profuse in speech."[89]

Lee's ban on letters, however, did not deter Jeb Stuart from making an attempt to rescue his good friend. Stuart dispatched two of his most successful scouts, "Honeybun" Hullihen and Thomas Turner, on a dangerous mission, to cross the Rappahannock River into the enemy's rear to rescue Mary Custis "marooned" at Cedar Grove.[90] The scouts found Mary and offered to carry her back to the "happy land of Dixie," but the independent young woman, "for some reason—doubtless a good one," declined their offer, and the two scouts had to return empty-handed.[91] Perhaps her hosts feared that if she were caught, the consequences would be more serious than if she remained where she was.

At Hickory Hill Agnes and Mrs. Lee tried hard to be cheerful and put themselves in a holiday mood, but their efforts were hampered by memories of Annie and by Charlotte's despair over the loss of two children in less than six months. Fortunately, there were other relatives in the house, including a young cousin of Charlotte's, Harry Wickham, and his sister, as well as the patriarch of the clan, old Mr. W. F. Wickham. In spite of her infirmities, Mrs. Lee offered to make a special holiday dessert one night, a confection that she knew the master especially liked. With wartime frugality, she put very little sugar in the pudding, much to Mr. Wickham's disgust. Even in the making and eating of Christmas desserts, they could not get away from the grim realities of war.

An unexpected guest at Hickory Hill that Christmas was Orton Williams, on furlough from a short assignment as a cavalry captain with the Army of Northern Virginia. In his uniform the young man was handsomer than ever, "tall, blond, erect, scrupulously groomed," wearing "kepi, hussar jacket, duck trousers, Wellington boots" and a "rattling saber" in his belt.[92] But in other ways, Orton Williams had changed. His finely chiseled features seemed to have coarsened, as if he had been drinking heavily. Prior to the battle of Shiloh, Tennessee, in the spring of 1862, his quick temper and insistence upon absolute military discipline had brought him into conflict with an independent-minded volunteer soldier, and in a flash of anger Orton had shot the man. No charges were pressed and he was commended for bravery in the ensuing battle, but Captain Williams became so unpopular with his own troops after this incident that he was transferred to service under General Braxton Bragg. When he reached his new command, he announced suddenly that his name was no longer William Orton Williams, but Lawrence Williams Orton, adopting his brother's given name, then his own surname, and his own middle name last. In a letter to Markie after more than a year's silence, he gave no reason for the change, merely a laconic comment, "I have changed my name."[93]

None of this erratic behavior was immediately visible, however, as Orton made himself agreeable to Agnes and the rest of the family at Hickory Hill. Young Harry Wickham and his sister found the dashing officer wonderfully "handsome and charming." Sensing a romance in the making, the youngsters stayed as close to Orton and Agnes as they could, watching the couple's horses saddled up each day for long rides in the woods and admiring the Christmas gifts he had brought to Agnes, "a pair of ladies' riding gauntlets and a riding whip." Many years later Harry Wickham wrote that in their childish eyes Orton had been the "Prince Charming and she the Sleeping Beauty that our fairy tale book had made us acquainted with, and we became excited partisans of Prince Charming."[94]

Plate 1

Arlington House, 1983

Photo by Clara Griffin   Courtesy of the Arlington House Collection, National Park Service

Plate 2

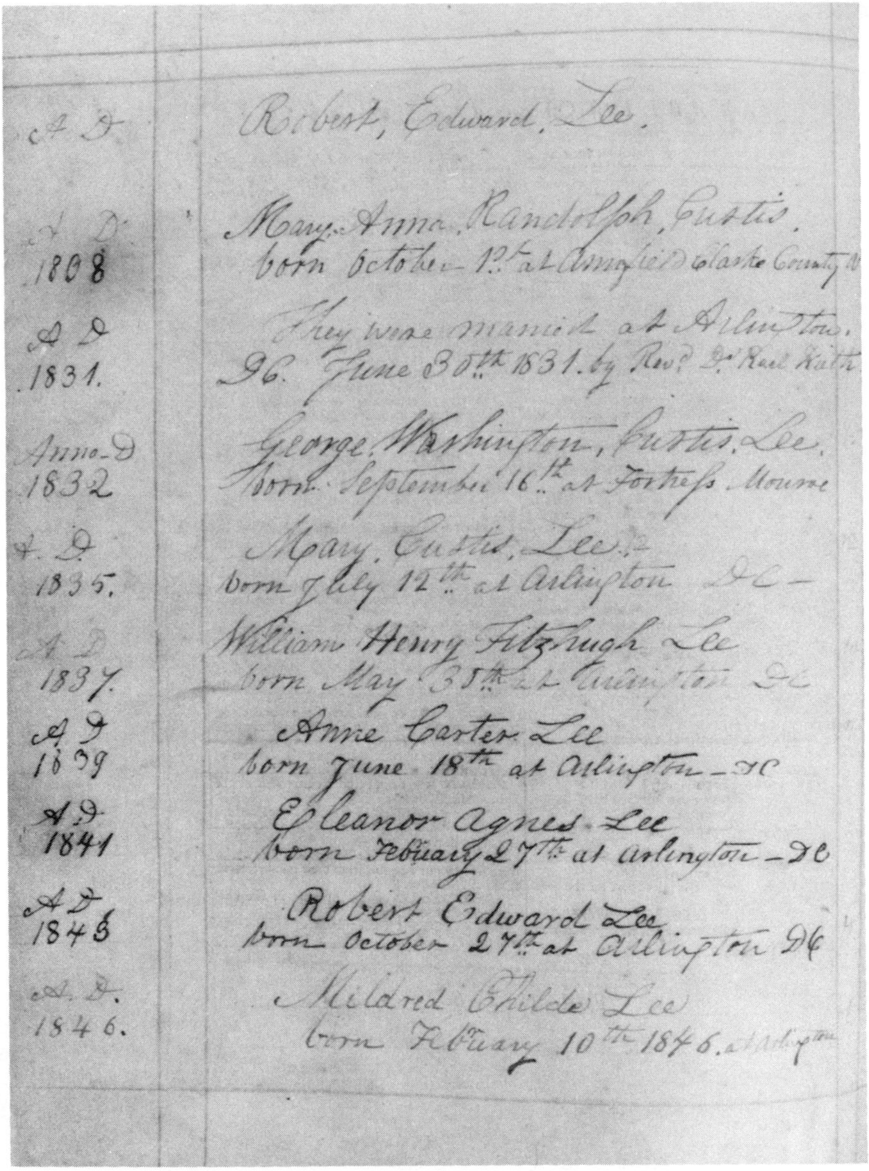

A. D. Robert, Edward, Lee.

A. D. 1808 Mary Anna Randolph, Custis.
born October 1st at Annefield Clarke County V

A. D. 1831. They were married at Arlington.
DC. June 30th 1831. by Revd Dr Reul Keith

Anno D 1832 George Washington, Custis Lee.
born September 16th at Fortress Monroe

A. D. 1835. Mary, Custis, Lee.
born July 12th at Arlington DC

A. D. 1837. William Henry Fitzhugh Lee
born May 31st at Arlington DC

A. D. 1839 Anne Carter Lee
born June 18th at Arlington DC

A. D. 1841 Eleanor Agnes Lee
born Febuary 27th at Arlington DC

A. D. 1843 Robert Edward Lee
born October 27th at Arlington DC

A. D. 1846. Mildred Childe Lee
born Febuary 10th 1846. at Arlington

A Page from the Custis Family Bible

Courtesy of Mrs. W. Hunter deButts and the Virginia Historical Society

Plate 3

Mary Custis Lee

On the back of the photograph are these words, dated 1917: "To Frances Weeks, from her affectionate friend Mary Custis Lee, as she *was*, when taken in Leamington, England, more than 30 yrs. ago! Time changes us all!"

Archives of Lee Chapel

Plate 4

Eleanor Agnes Lee, circa. 1861

Courtesy of the Virginia Historical Society

Plate 5

Mildred Childe Lee in 1870

Courtesy of the Virginia Historical Society

Plate 6

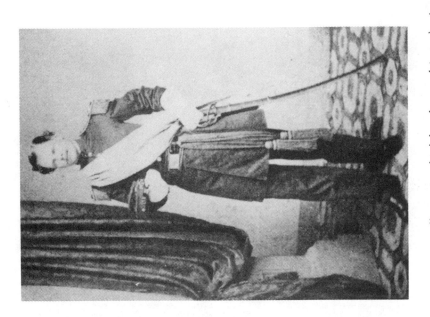

William Orton Williams, Markie's brother and Agnes' suitor

Courtesy of the Virginia Historical Society

Mildred Childe Lee at age four

Portrait by Ernst Fischer, 1850   Courtesy of Mrs. Frederick A. Zimmer, Jr.

Plate 7

Robert E. Lee as a lieutenant of engineers, United States Army

Portrait by William Edward West, 1838
Courtesy of the Washington-Custis-Lee Collection
Washington and Lee University

Mary Anna Randolph Custis Lee (Mrs. Robert E. Lee)

Portrait by William Edward West, 1838
Courtesy of the Washington-Custis-Lee Collection
Washington and Lee University

Plate 8

Robert E. Lee in Confederate uniform

Painted by Theodore Pine from photographs, 1904
Courtesy of Washington and Lee University

Plate 9

Mary Custis Lee in 1874

Courtesy of the Arlington House Collection, National Park Service

Plate 10

Eleanor Agnes Lee at Lexington

Courtesy of Mrs. W. Hunter deButts and the Virginia Historical Society

Plate 11

Mildred Childe Lee at Lexington

Courtesy of Mrs. W. Hunter deButts and the Virginia Historical Society

Plate 12

Robert E. Lee as president of Washington College in January of 1870,
the last year of his life

Courtesy of the Michael Miley Collection
Washington and Lee University

Plate 13

Mrs. Robert E. Lee near the end of her life

Courtesy of the Michael Miley Collection
Washington and Lee University

Plate 14

The president's house at Washington College, the Lees' last home
Courtesy of the Michael Miley Collection   Washington and Lee University

The interior of the president's house as it looked while the Lees resided there.
Here the Lee girls entertained friends and suitors.

Courtesy of the Michael Miley Collection   Washington and Lee University

Plate 15

The funeral of Robert E. Lee, 15 October 1870
The columns of the college buildings were draped with black ribbons.
Courtesy of the Michael Miley Collection   Washington and Lee University

The Lee Chapel in Lexington
General and Mrs. Lee and six of their children are buried here.
Courtesy of Washington and Lee University

Plate 16

Grave of Anne Carter Lee near Warrenton, North Carolina

Robert E. Lee and Agnes visited this "lovely secluded spot" in 1870, shortly before Lee's death.

Courtesy of the Warren Record, *Warrenton, North Carolina*

Much to their disappointment, the end of the visit was not a happy one. "We could not understand it at all," Wickham continued, "when after a long session in the parlor (from which we children had been warned to keep away) he came out, bade the family goodbye and rode away alone."[95] But if the Wickham children could not comprehend, later biographers can. Still aching from the loss of Annie, Agnes was not ready for the tempestuous kind of love Orton was offering. She had heard enough of the temper and passion of her step-uncle, "Black Horse Harry" Lee, to know that she might pay heavily for allowing herself to fall in love with a man of those traits. Most important of all, Orton no longer seemed the boy she had cared for, the young man whose welfare in the army she had prayed about. But in her heart Agnes Lee never forgot her childhood sweetheart. As valuable and handsome as his Christmas gifts were, she found she cared far more for the worn Testament he had given her in happier times. Ten years later, as she lay dying in Lexington, she spoke of Orton and the old Bible during the last hours of her life.[96]

5

The Streets of Richmond

1863–1865

WHEN AGNES RETURNED with her mother to the Caskies' a few weeks after New Year's, it marked the first time she had lived for any length of time in the Confederate capital. At the White House or Hickory Hill during the first months of the war, she had missed seeing Richmond transformed from a slow-moving Southern community of thirty-eight thousand into a bustling metropolis four times that size, overflowing with refugees, soldiers, congressmen, and government workers. She had still been away during much of 1862 when the early glitter of extravagant parties had given way to fear and panic at the frequent tolling of the tocsin—the warning bell—in Capitol Square and the frightening sound of Federal cannon less than ten miles away. Now, at the beginning of 1863, citizens were facing their third year of war full of renewed courage and patriotism, in spite of increasing privations, military uncertainties, and mounting casualties.

The elegant balls continued, but many Richmonders now attended "starvation parties" that provided music and dancing but no refreshments, and the famous soirées of President Davis' wife featured, at least part of the time, coffee made from chestnuts and chicory along with cakes baked with molasses. Theaters, concert halls, and variety shows offered solace for weary soldiers, but the large numbers of hospitals within the city limits reminded people that the war was already old and far from over.

One soldier on leave remarked that there had never been "so many pretty girls to the square inch as there are now in Richmond,"[1] and Agnes knew most of them—Constance Cary and her cousins from Baltimore, Hettie and Jennie, who had brought with them the stirring Confederate song,"Maryland, My Maryland"; Sally Warwick, the charming coquette who at one time was engaged to Custis Lee; the Triplett girls; the Haxall sisters; Sally Corbett, who married General George Pickett; Mrs. Davis' sister, Margaret Howell; and of course Norvell Caskie, her young hostess and contemporary. Agnes saw them all at church, visited with them as they walked to and from the shops of Richmond, ate ice cream with them at Pizzini's confectioners on Broad Street, and occasionally attended a fete or costume party with them. But for the most part she and her mother, in mourning for Annie and Charlotte's two children, made "no conspicuous appearance in society," as Constance Cary put it. Since General Lee was sleeping in a tent in winter quarters near Fredericksburg, struggling with cold, mud, and scant rations, they felt it would be poor taste to indulge in "any entertainments of a social sort."[2] Instead they devoted their time to knitting for the soldiers, an occupation which Mrs. Lee had begun early in the war and in which she and Agnes now engaged nearly full-time.

Though she spent her days quietly for the most part, Agnes undoubtedly met numbers of young men, friends of Custis' and staff officers of her father's on leave in Richmond. She still played the piano and may well have helped to entertain groups of young people in the Caskie parlor or in the homes of friends, as soldiers and belles alike sang the popular war ballads of the day: "Lorena," "When the Great War Is Over," and "My Southern Soldier Boy."[3] At least one soldier was so smitten by her reserve and ethereal beauty that he wrote a poem which she pasted in her album, a volume much like Mary Custis' copybook. Dated May 17, 1863, the stanzas were dedicated "To Miss Agnes."

> When genius, wealth, & fashion, bow in homage at thy feet,
> When youth and beauty smile in all thy happy glances greet—
> When I shall pitch, beneath the sky, my bivouac on the lea,
> I ask not then for 'twould be vain that thou wouldst think of me.

When music's soft enrapt'ring spell delights thy listening ear
When Zephyrs whisper "all is well" and all thou lov'st
are near—
When skies are bright and thou art all that thou couldst
wish to be
I dare not ask—'twould be in vain—that thou couldst
think of me.

But when misfortune frowns upon that fair and radiant
face
And o'er the past thy mem'ry's dove can find no resting
place,
When friends are *false*, save *one* whose *heart* still faithful proves to thee,
'Tis *then* I ask that thou wouldst turn confidingly to
me.

K. G. S.

Richmond Va
May 17th 1863

In pencil below the poem Agnes made a notation—"written
on my *knee*."[4] The verses may have had as little romantic significance as
Jeb Stuart's and Fitz Lee's had had for Mary Custis, but they do suggest
that at least one young man was intrigued by Agnes' reticence and
possibly the rumor of a mysterious love affair.

The weather was wretched the entire winter, with bitter cold, rain,
snow, and mud until the middle of March, "the dreariest, coldest,
wettest, saddest winter . . . within the memory of man," wrote one
refugee.[5] Agnes had planned to visit her father in his winter camp, but
weather or personal reasons prevented the trip. He was disappointed,
for he had hoped to have her in his tent to "sit by this little stove, look
out at the rain & keep yourself dry."[6] But two weeks later he was grateful
she had not attempted to come, for "a heavy storm of three days, snow,
sleet, & rain" had completely soaked his shelter.[7]

Throughout these trying months both Mrs. Lee and Agnes were in
poor health. Mrs. Lee's arthritis had become more acute because of the
severe cold and dampness, and Agnes suffered from pains in her face
and neck which the doctors diagnosed as neuralgia. Always thin, she

had lost so much weight that her father suggested that she could easily make a bed out of "three stools in the corner of my tent. . . . I will lend her some warm blankets."[8] In March Lee himself became ill with a heavy chest cold and sore throat. The doctors "have been tapping me all over like an old steam boiler before condemning it," he wrote to his wife, but he was sure his ailments were "a mixture of your's [*sic*] & Agnes' diseases."[9] If only Agnes could have gotten up to see him, he said, she "could have taken all my pills, etc. & kept the doctors off me."[10] Though uncomfortable, he continued to be more concerned about his daughter's health than his own, fearing Agnes' pains might spread to her arms and legs. "I hope her little propellers are not becoming afflicted, too."[11] He urged her to "keep in the open air—take all the exercise" available.[12]

Anxious as he was about Agnes and Mrs. Lee in Richmond, General Lee was even more concerned about Mary Custis, still at Cedar Grove behind enemy lines, for Union troops remained in that area after the battle of Fredericksburg. Sometimes an oral message came through a scout, and in May he received a letter directly from her. Rob, stationed near the Rappahannock River, managed to see Mary Custis one day while he was out on patrol. She was, he reported, "delighted seemingly with her hostess . . . & seems to be enjoying herself very much."[13] Mary Custis was probably making the best of a difficult situation, for families in King George County were constantly harassed by Yankee troops who searched houses at will and stole chickens, horses, and food supplies.[14]

The coming of a late spring brightened the spirits of Richmond residents, but sunny skies and drier roads meant that both Yankee and Confederate forces could now begin preparations for battle. The city's four newspapers carried regular columns about troop movements around Fredericksburg, while Northern dailies from Baltimore, New York, and Philadelphia, available for perusal in Richmond's Confederate Reading Room, contained editorials vilifying General Joseph Hooker for his inaction. During the first week in May, heavy fighting began west of Fredericksburg near Chancellorsville. The bloody battle brought victory to Lee's troops, but it also resulted in the fatal wounding of General Thomas J. "Stonewall" Jackson. Richmond learned of the death of the brilliant general on May 11, and suddenly the city was plunged into mourning, as stores closed, church bells tolled, and flags flew at half-mast. The following day a long funeral procession wound through the streets near the capitol, several blocks from the Caskies' home. Even if they did not leave the house, Agnes and her mother must have heard the dirges of the three brass bands that led the plumed hearse and riderless horse past silent crowds, who wept with such emotion that one observer wrote that it was as if "every person in the City of Richmond had today buried their [sic] nearest and dearest friend."[15]

The death of General Lee's most capable officer, as well as the daily peril of her own loved ones, moved Agnes to write an unhappy letter to her father in which she longed for the day when war would end and the family could be together again. Lee replied that he, too, wished "the war was over & that we could all be once more united," but he reminded Agnes and her sisters that they had no time to be gloomy, for "you have a sacred charge, the care of your poor mother."[16] He may have felt that Agnes was anticipating trouble, for Rooney, Rob, and their cousin Fitz Lee had all escaped serious injury. Rooney had been bruised in a fall from a horse, and General Lee himself had fallen the previous summer and broken bones in his hand, but all of them had gone unscathed through enemy fire, even though they had fought in every major battle in which the Army of Northern Virginia had participated. Custis was secure from attack, though he remained miserable at his desk assignment in Richmond. From Orton Williams the family heard nothing.

Meanwhile, in North Carolina, Mildred must have felt very far removed from the scenes of war and destruction, for the occasional Federal raiding parties ventured no farther into the Piedmont than fifty miles east of Raleigh. She was studying with more enthusiasm this term and enjoying a new subject, astronomy, which was taught by the rector, Dr. Smedes. "The report of her studies . . . embraces a large area," her father commented drily. "I hope she may understand them all."[17] He anticipated that "she will derive the pleasure I enjoyed in the study of Astronomy. I think it afforded me more pleasure than any other branch of study."[18] He was pleased by a letter from Dr. Smedes, who wrote favorably about Mildred's adjustment—"a very complimentary letter," Lee proudly told his wife. "I have been extremely gratified at his account of her progress & deportment."[19]

Though her classwork was easier, Mildred still found it hard to adjust to the lack of privacy at school. The large room on the second floor of West Rock housed ten girls, who were each assigned a tiny alcove which had a window and only enough space for a trunk, closet, and simple wooden shelf holding a brown pottery bowl and pitcher for bathing. All ten of the plain wooden beds were lined up in the center of the room. Flimsy curtains, separating the beds from the alcoves, were drawn back during the day to allow for inspection.

Fortunately, St. Mary's girls did not spend much of their weekday time in their rooms. On Saturdays, however, after a special breakfast of "hash and hominy," they returned to their sleeping quarters for "mending hour," a time set aside for repairing worn clothes and blacking boots.[20] One day the matron, Miss Evertson, discovered Mildred reading a book instead of sewing. Reprimanded, Mildred replied that she had only one dress that needed repair and she had no material with which to patch it. A piece of coarse muslin was found, and she proceeded to appliqué yellow hearts, diamonds, and stars onto her fine white cambric dress.

She must have told her family about her needlework, for in April General Lee wrote, concerned about "poor little Life's wardrobe. . . . What can be done for her?" He could offer her, he said, "some socks" and "a long pair of boots that cover up a great deal of space," or if none of these would do, perhaps she would feel less conspicuous joining him at camp near Fredericksburg. The soldiers, he suggested, were "accustomed to short commons every way & scant wardrobes are fashionable."[21] In spite of his worries, Mildred had no need of new outfits, since most of her friends dressed with wartime simplicity. Hoop skirts, if worn at all, were smaller than antebellum petticoats, and dresses were often remade from old silks and cambrics. Many girls wove their own sunbonnets and tied their high-topped shoes with string that they had dyed in black ink. Because of the blockade, hairpins were almost nonexistent, so most of the students used hair nets to keep their heavy chignons in place.

On Saturday afternoons the girls were allowed to walk about the school grounds or take chaperoned trips into Raleigh, where they spent their time staring through shop windows at expensive foods and imported goods that had been "run" through the blockade—leather shoes, ladies' corsets, and linen handkerchiefs. Saturday evenings were usually spent reading, an occupation that appealed to Mildred, who dearly loved a novel. Dr. Smedes encouraged his pupils to browse freely in his large library on the second floor of Old Main, where he kept, in addition to Dickens, Cooper, Thackeray, and Irving, several complete sets of Scott.

In spite of their restrictions, the St. Mary's girls managed to stay in touch with army friends and family members through letters, occasional visits by soldiers on leave, and not infrequent serenades by regimental bands stationed nearby. On such occasions the strict regimen of study would be relaxed and the girls were allowed to sit on the upstairs porch to listen to brass renditions of "Take Me Home," "Dixie,"

and "Carry Me Back to Old Virginny."[22] Mildred did her share of
knitting socks and gloves for the army, but judging by messages to her
from General Lee and Rob, she was not as diligent in her letter writing to
them as she might have been.

Throughout the winter and spring of 1863, Lee wrote frequently to
Agnes, expressing tenderness and affection. Yet not one of his letters
mentioned the name of Orton Williams, though Lee must have known
about—and possibly had a deciding voice in—her rejection of her
cousin, and he must have been aware that Orton had returned to
Tennessee as a cavalry officer under General Bragg. Though Orton's
name was never referred to, Agnes surely thought about him a great
deal during that long winter. Every day as she went out for her walks or
visited with friends, she saw dozens of young men in gray uniforms and
leather boots to remind her of the handsome officer who had ridden
away in anger from Hickory Hill. And in the quiet nights when she lay
awake suffering from her aching face and neck, she must have wondered where Orton was, if he was safe, and whether or not she had done
the right thing in sending him away.

But in her most exaggerated worries and fears she could not have
imagined the tragic news that appeared on the front page of the *Daily
Richmond Examiner* on June 13, 1863. A Union dispatch from
Murfreesboro, Tennessee, dated June 9, reported that Orton was dead,
having been arrested by Federal troops near Franklin and hanged as a
spy after a drumhead trial.

> Colonel Lawrence Williams Orton, formerly Law-
> rence Williams of the Second United States Cavalry, one
> time on General Scott's staff, and later General Bragg's
> chief of artillery, and Lieutenant Dunlop, of the rebel
> army, were arrested and hung as spies last night, at
> Franklin, under the following circumstances.
>
> They made their appearance at Franklin in full
> Federal uniform, horses and equipment of Colonel and
> Major, and, presenting themselves as inspectors of the
> United States Army, having orders from Assistant Adju-
> tant General R. A. Townsend, and countersigned by
> General Rosecrans, to inspect the fortifications of this
> Department. Colonel Watson grew suspicious of them,
> and communicated his doubts to Colonel Baird who

telegraphed to Rosecrans if any such persons held positions in the army. General Rosecrans replied in the negative. Documents of a treasonable nature and contraband information were found on them. General Rosecrans ordered a court martial, and this morning they were hung. Colonel Baird telegraphs that they were spies of no ordinary character. Orton was cousin to General Robert E. Lee, and was brother of Williams, late of McClellan's staff.

Suspicious of Federal dispatches, the editors of the Richmond paper added a postscript that the "atrocious act of hanging" had been confirmed "by official dispatches received at Washington from Rosecrans himself."[23]

General Lee learned of the news on the same day, and though some of the details were in error, he feared that the story was essentially correct. He was particularly disturbed over the death penalty meted out to Orton, for it was common practice in both North and South to place spies in prison with the possibility of parole. "I read in the papers yesterday," he wrote to Mrs. Lee on June 14, "an account of the death of Orton Williams, which I can hardly believe; & yet it is given with such circumstantiality, & is in such accordance with the spirit of our enemies that I fear it is. . . . I see no necessity for his death except to gratify the evil passions of those whom he offended by leaving Genl. Scott." He added, with little conviction, that possibly the whole story had been fabricated, "to gratify their vengeful feelings & to torture the feelings of his friends."[24]

Later newspaper accounts and letters from Markie, however, verified the essential truth of the account and filled in additional details about Orton Williams' disastrous misadventure. About dusk on June 8, two young men in the uniforms of Union officers had ridden into the Yankee command post of the 85th Indiana Regiment near Franklin, Tennessee. The senior officer on duty, Colonel J. B. Baird, was much taken with the visitors, who claimed they were Federal inspectors whose money and servants had been stolen in a Confederate ambush. Fortunately, they said, they had managed to retain their credentials, which Baird examined carefully. Lending the young colonel fifty dollars, he urged the pair to spend the night at camp, but they demurred, saying they needed to hurry on to Nashville. After they had left, another officer on Baird's staff, somewhat suspicious of the two men, wondered aloud if the signatures on their papers might have been forgeries. The horrified Baird sent a soldier rushing after them in the fog.

Placing the suspicious strangers under guard this time, Baird tried to communicate with his superior officer in Triune by means of signal flares, but the thickening mist was too dense for torches to be seen. So at 11:30 that night, Baird telegraphed to Brigadier General James A. Garfield, Rosecrans' chief of staff, to verify his prisoners' identities. An ominous message came back by wire a few minutes later: "There are no such men as Inspector General Lawrence Orton, colonel U. S. Army, and assistant Major Dunlop, in this army, nor in any army, so far as we know. Why do you ask?"[25]

Even before Garfield's telegram arrived, several Union officers had already found incriminating evidence on the two men, including their real names and Confederate rank clearly marked in their hatbands, more than one thousand dollars in Confederate money hidden on Williams' clothing, and his name and rank carved on his saber. The pair admitted to being Orton Williams (or Lawrence Orton) and his young cousin, Walter Gibson Peter, both Confederate officers. Baird telegraphed again to Murfreesboro, asking what he should do with his prisoners. In less than an hour, the reply was in his hands. "The two men are no doubt spies. Call a drum-head court-martial to-night, and if they are found to be spies, hang them before morning, without fail."[26]

Daylight was only a few hours away, so Colonel Baird reluctantly sent a messenger to the silent tents to rouse enough men to serve on the court-martial. By three o'clock, four sleepy officers had been assembled, their rank ranging from full colonel to captain, and a lieutenant had been sworn in to act as judge advocate. The trial took less than an hour, with the court handing down a verdict of "guilty of the charge of being spies." Colonel Baird wired General Garfield once more. "Must I hang him?" Baird queried. "If you can direct me to send him to hang somewhere else, I would like it; but if not, or I do not hear from you, they will be executed." The grim word came back shortly. "The general . . . directs that the two spies, if found guilty, be hung at once."[27]

By now a chaplain from the 78th Illinois Regiment had arrived to talk to the prisoners and give them communion. Both men asked for paper and pens, and Orton wrote several letters, including one to Markie which ended, "Do not believe that I am a spy; with my dying breath I deny the charge."[28] As infantry and cavalry troops stood at attention,

Orton Williams and Walter Peter were escorted to the scaffold. By nine-thirty in the morning of June 9, 1863, it was all over. Orton was dead at the age of twenty-four.

For weeks both Southern and Northern newspapers continued to carry stories about the trial and hanging, questioning the severity and speed of the sentences and speculating upon the true mission of the young Confederates. The *Richmond Examiner* of July 3 called the harsh sentence "murder," suggesting that officers of their rank would not "have undertaken the dishonorable office of spies in the enemy's camp."[29] Perhaps, the paper continued, the pair were merely trying to slip through enemy lines to travel to Europe to visit friends. Northern editors, less extreme in their views, were nonetheless concerned about the trial and questioned its validity with enough persistence to force Secretary of War Edwin M. Stanton to commend General Rosecrans publicly for his insistence on speedy death to the spies. "Your prompt action," Stanton wired, "is approved."[30]

No satisfactory motive for the mission has ever been discovered, in spite of the theories of journalists and amateur sleuths from 1863 to the present. As early as July 1863, the *Richmond Examiner* confirmed that "none of our commanders in Tennessee are aware of any such mission being undertaken by these officers,"[31] while the *Chattanooga Rebel* assured its readers that Williams' "expedition . . . was undertaken on his account and was unknown to his brother officers."[32] The war correspondent of the *New York Herald* believed the two men were on some kind of special secret mission, possibly to "the copperheads of the North," since only a major assignment "could have induced two officers of their rank and character to undertake so hazardous an enterprise."[33] His assessment was echoed by a reporter for the *Detroit Free Press*, who had interviewed both Williams and Peter and found Williams to be "as fine a looking man as I have ever seen . . . [and] one of the most intellectual and accomplished men that I have ever known."[34] Confederate intelligence headquarters in Richmond, which might have confirmed or denied all the rumors, admitted nothing. To this day, the purpose of Orton Williams' strange escapade remains a mystery.

But for Agnes the enigmas surrounding the death of Orton and the validity of his sentence must have mattered far less than the private reasons for his extraordinary behavior. Again and again she must have wondered whether her refusal of him the previous Christmas had propelled him toward such a daring, death-defying scheme. Or was she vindicated now, recognizing in the altered Orton a man whose impet-

uosity readied him for such an adventure? There is no question that
Orton's death affected Agnes deeply. Harry Wickham, who saw her a few
days after the news had appeared in the Richmond paper and who also
lived near her several years thereafter, maintained that she was changed
forever. "The terrible death of Orton Williams," Wickham wrote, "was a
shock to Agnes from which she never recovered. She became very quiet
and pensive in after life. I do not recall hearing her laugh, and when she
smiled it seemed to me that she was looking beyond."[35]

Circumstances, however, did not allow Agnes time to dwell on her
grief. On the day that Orton was hanged, Rooney was seriously wounded
in the battle of Brandy Station. Catching a glimpse of his son "on the
field as they were bringing him from the front," Lee at once assigned
Rob to escort Rooney back to Hickory Hill for recuperation.[36] As soon as
the family learned of Rooney's condition, Mrs. Lee, Charlotte, and Agnes
hurried to the Wickham estate, accompanied by Mildred, who had
returned to Virginia on vacation from school.

Before he was wounded, Rooney had been unusually strong and
robust, a great bear of a man, and in two weeks of convalescence he
made considerable progress, attended by his wife and sisters during the
day and Rob acting as night nurse in a small outbuilding on the plantation. The family believed that he had received a bullet from a Spencer
carbine, a new type of rifle just issued to Union cavalrymen, which
discharged a cartridge whose zinc cap detached from the rest of the
bullet when it struck, remaining in the wound to cause infection and
gangrene. Fortunately, Rooney had been shot from such close range that
both parts of the missile had passed through, leaving him with three
jagged but relatively clean wounds—one where the bullet had entered,
two where the pieces had been expelled.

Happy with their patient's improvement, the family had just finished
breakfast on the clear, quiet morning of June 26 when, stepping outside
to sit on the front porch for a few minutes, they heard gunfire in the
woods. Suddenly several Federal officers on horseback appeared at the
edge of the clearing. Rob ducked quickly out of sight and hurried to
warn his brother. Too ill to consider escape, Rooney urged Rob to get
away if possible. The Union raiding party had been sent specifically to
capture Rooney, a mission they quickly accomplished by removing him
from his sickroom on a mattress, placing him in the Hickory Hill
carriage, and driving off to the White House landing dock a few miles
downstream on the Pamunkey River. Rooney's exasperation at being
captured and forced to leave his weeping wife and invalid mother must

have been compounded by seeing the charred remains of his home as he passed the ruined White House on his way to the wharf.

Mrs. Lee managed to keep her composure through the harrowing incident, Harry Wickham reported, but as soon as Rooney was out of sight, Charlotte broke down completely. She had lost her children and her home; now her wounded husband was snatched from her, bound for prison. She was sure that if the rough journey did not kill him, a Union prison would. It must have taken all the ingenuity of both Agnes and Mildred to calm her agitation and restore some degree of tranquillity. As soon as he was sure the 1,500 Federal troops had left, Rob crept back from his hiding place in the woods to assess the situation. In addition to capturing Rooney, the soldiers had burned bridges, raided neighboring plantations, and severely beaten old Mr. Williams Wickham, Lee's uncle, who had rented them the row house in Baltimore years before. Hot with indignation, the girls and Mrs. Lee wrote to the general about Rooney's capture and the brutal treatment accorded his eighty-year-old uncle. But Lee was already on his way to Maryland and Pennsylvania, leading Confederate forces on a wide sweep into Federal territory that would culminate in the decisive battle of Gettysburg in July of 1863. He learned of Rooney's capture weeks later.

At first the news of the Confederate advance across the Potomac was cheerful, but soon after the Fourth of July the family realized the enormity of the disaster that had overcome Lee's army. One unexpected benefit from the expedition, however, was that Mary Custis found herself free at last to join her mother and sisters, when Union forces were withdrawn from the Northern Neck to meet the dangers of Confederate pressure against Washington. Daughter appeared to be little affected by her long period of enforced subjugation, in spite of the "restraint and ill usage by our enemies."[37]

Even Mary Custis' return failed to raise Charlotte's spirits, as the young woman worried herself into a decline, in spite of the word from various sources that Rooney's condition had not deteriorated during his unpleasant journey and that he was reasonably comfortable in a prison hospital at Fort Monroe. After returning from Gettysburg, Lee wrote reassuringly to Charlotte, confident that old friends among Union army surgeons would quickly restore Rooney's health. She must not pine away during her husband's absence, he counseled. "Nothing would do him more harm than for him to learn that you were sick & sad," he wrote, and how then "could he get well?" In words reminiscent of his remarks to Mrs. Lee twenty years before, he urged Charlotte to "cheer up & prove your fortitude & patriotism. . . . [T]hink of F. & love him as much as you please, but do not grieve over him or grow sad."[38]

But Charlotte seemed unable to follow her father-in-law's injunctions, and she grew more feeble and depressed day by day. Partly to divert her and take her to cooler air, Mrs. Lee and the girls decided to visit Hot Springs, which Charlotte had expressed an interest in seeing. A boxcar was fitted up with bed and chairs, so that Mrs. Lee could journey by rail with relative comfort. Agnes, Mary Custis, and Charlotte accompanied her on the overnight journey to the familiar spa, all of them hoping for improved health. Agnes was still bothered with facial neuralgia, Mrs. Lee could now move about very little even on her crutches, and the drooping Charlotte longed for new scenes to blot out the nightmare of Rooney's capture. Though she was tense and nervous, Mary Custis was the healthiest of the group.

Mildred did not go west with the others, for she had decided reluctantly to return to St. Mary's. This year she arrived in time for the opening of classes, which began the last week in July. The campus was especially attractive in midsummer, with "multiflora roses . . . over the covered way" that connected the two dormitories with Old Main, and "cloth of gold" vines clambering over "the old grey rocks" of the two-storied building. In front of the school, "little gardens . . . were gay with flowers."[39] Not only was the physical appearance of the boarding school more appealing this year, but Mildred found that she was welcomed back by old classmates as well as by a number of new girls whom she had known during her short sojourn at Warrenton and Jones Springs.

Tuition and board at St. Mary's were costlier this session, having risen from $115 to $300 for a five-month term, as recorded in a circular letter from Dr. Smedes, dated July 11, 1863.

> It is with great reluctance that I sit down to pen what will follow. I have had such a horror of extortion, that, ever since these troublous times, I have advertised rates of charging that have proved inadequate to meet the continually increasing cost of the necessaries of life.

Apologetically, Dr. Smedes also explained that "our laundresses insist that at the present cost of fuel, starch and soap, they cannot wash for less than $25 the Term." Because the Union blockade kept new books and supplies from reaching Raleigh, the rector requested that pupils bring "with them Music of their elder sisters, Slates, Atlases, Lead Pencils, Pen-Holders, etc."[40]

Soon after her return to school, Lee wrote Mildred a long letter from his headquarters near Culpeper, expressing regret that he had not seen her during her summer vacation and hoping that she would have a happy term.

> I have heard my precious daughter that you have returned to your school. . . . I had looked forward to your vacation with so much pleasure . . . in the hope of seeing you a little while at least. . . . I wanted to see how you were, how you looked, & whom you resembled. Have you no photograph of yourself that you could send me?[41]

In spite of his disappointment, he was grateful that she had decided to return to Raleigh. "I think it is the best course you could have pursued. I hope you will be able to learn a great deal this year & by the next that there will be peace over the land." He had seen some of her former classmates from Mrs. Powell's, he wrote, as he had passed through Winchester on his way to Pennsylvania. "Poor Winchester has been terribly devastated, & the inhabitants plundered of all they possessed." Now he hoped she would write him about her new friends, as well as her studies. "All that concerns you will be interesting to me. . . . May God bless you, my dear daughter, strew your path in this world with every happiness, & finally gather you & all of us to His mansions of bliss in heaven, is my daily and hourly prayer."[42]

After a wearing journey, Mrs. Lee and her companions arrived at Hot Springs, where the spa was still operating under a curtailed wartime regime. In spite of the change of scene and the cool mountain air, Charlotte did not improve. Rather, her condition deteriorated to such an extent that the family called in a physician. She seemed so frail and listless that one observer commented on the "sad, delicate lineaments of her young face."[43] When the steaming waters of the "Hot" did not help, the group decided to move on, Mrs. Lee, Agnes, and Mary Custis journeying a few miles up the pike to Warm Springs, Charlotte and a cousin going to Bath Alum, a small resort farther east. Rooney had been stationed at Bath Alum during the first campaigns of 1861, and perhaps Charlotte felt that being so close to where he had been would give her comfort.

While they were in western Virginia, they learned from Rob the surprising news that Custis, the "confirmed bachelor" of the family, had become engaged to Sally Warwick, one of the large group of Agnes' acquaintances in Richmond.[44] Possibly the wartime mania for marriage had infected even the reticent Custis. More likely, young Sally, a charming girl and inveterate flirt, had temporarily bewitched the shy young general, now more unhappy than ever at being held at desk duty in Richmond while his father and brother shared dangers and professional opportunities on the battlefield and Rooney languished in prison. When the wedding date was postponed again and again, Lee decided that the marriage might never take place. "You have no immediate prospects of acquiring any new daughters," he wrote his wife on August 9, so "you must take good care of your old ones."[45] He reported that he himself was in poor health, suffering from rheumatism in the back, with such uncomfortable lotions prescribed by his doctors that he wished in jest that other family members could share his medications. "I wish I had daughter's back here to apply it to, it might do it service."[46]

He also mentioned that he had received an unexpected letter from Markie Williams, his first direct communication from her since the beginning of the war. She had heard, erroneously, that "two Federal officers were in prison in Richmond & were to be executed in retaliation for the death of Orton," and she begged him to intercede for the threatened soldiers.[47] Lee asked his wife to reply to Markie, assuring her that there was nothing to the story, but only a vicious rumor. Markie had enclosed a copy of Orton's last message to her, which Lee forwarded without comment to his wife and Agnes.

Mrs. Lee found Warm Springs a pleasant resort, and their cottage, near the bathhouse, was "covered with beautiful vines & roses & looking upon a meadow full of haycocks & a clear stream running thro' it."[48] But by the end of August, the travelers felt it was time to turn back toward Richmond, even though Charlotte was still far from well. She became so sick on the way that they had to leave her behind in Charlottesville to be near doctors who could treat her "indisposition."[49] The others went on to Liberty, a small town at the foot of the Peaks of Otter in Bedford County. There they took rooms for several weeks with a Captain Buford, who ran a farm and took in boarders.

Soon after his wife and the other two girls had settled at Liberty, Lee wrote another long letter to Mildred, in response to a rambling, contemplative one from her. "I am glad to hear of the progress made in your studies," he wrote, "& feel assured that you will continue to improve by diligent application. . . . [T]he more you learn the more you are conscious of your ignorance. . . . You will find all the days of your life that there is much to learn & much to do." Precious Life had indicated that she found it hard sometimes to do what she knew to be right. By practice, he replied, such appropriate actions would become easier, and she could begin to "enjoy in the midst of your trials, the pleasure of an approving conscience. That will be worth every thing else."[50] It was a philosophy by which he was living during the grim days after Gettysburg.

At the end of her letter, Mildred had requested permission to leave school at the end of the fall term. She had found that, with no set examinations or fixed standards of course work, most St. Mary's girls left school at the age of seventeen or eighteen when they were "thought to *know enough* for social requirements."[51] Her father was willing now to be flexible. "You can leave at the end of the present session or continue, as you think best," he wrote. But he did urge her, as long as she was at St. Mary's, to "learn all you can. You will find, in after life, you cannot know too much."[52]

After more than a month enjoying the fresh vegetables, thick cream, and mountain air at Liberty, Mary Custis, Agnes, and Mrs. Lee returned to Richmond, probably traveling by packet boat along the James River and Kanawha Canal. Once back in the city, they managed with the help of friends to rent a tiny house on Leigh Street, a few blocks northwest of the Caskie home, on the edge of the fashionable residential area. Unfortunately, there was space enough for only three of them, and propriety forbade one of the single girls—Agnes or Mary Custis—to live by herself among strangers, so Charlotte, sick as she was, had to board elsewhere. Lee was deeply troubled about his daughter-in-law, who by now was so ill that she was bedridden. He had not forgotten that in his welcoming letter to her in 1859 he had promised to take as good care of her as of his own daughters. Perhaps, he suggested, she would come and share his tent on the Rappahannock, if she promised to get well. "Only old people can be allowed to be sick," he wrote.[53]

The new house was furnished with makeshift belongings from friends, for the Lees had no furniture of their own. Even glassware, china, and eating utensils had to be borrowed. Agnes, serving as housekeeper, took satisfaction that there were "enough glasses to go around" when visitors came to call.[54] As inflation and shortages made prices skyrocket, the planning of meals and shopping for groceries became increasingly difficult. The cost of potatoes was twelve dollars a bushel, tea twenty-five dollars a pound, and sugar almost nonexistent. Coffee was so difficult to obtain that many families tried roasting their own combinations of part coffee, part corn. But these very problems may have made life more interesting for both Agnes and Mary Custis, who for the first time since they left Arlington had some responsibilities. In addition to caring for their mother, making frequent visits to see Charlotte, and supervising the housekeeping, they also felt a new impetus to knit huge quantities of socks, gloves, and scarfs for the ragtag Army of Northern Virginia, which faced a bitter winter. Agnes, whose father was always urging her to sew, spent some time remaking an old dress into a more fashionable "domestic . . . in the garibaldi style . . . very close around the neck."[55] In the evening, after the day's duties had been finished, the two young women read Victor Hugo's latest novel, *Les Miserables*, which had just been smuggled into Richmond. Along with their friends, they affectionately changed the book's title to "Lee's Miserables," in honor of their father's cold, underclad troops in winter quarters near Culpeper.

Charlotte's condition and Rooney's imprisonment were never far from their minds, and they kept hoping that some sort of special appeal might be made for their brother's release. General Lee counseled against any such request, fearing that an attempt to have the prisoner exchanged might bring additional retaliation. For a few weeks in November Charlotte seemed better, even well enough to leave her rented room to spend hours at a time in the Leigh Street house. Shortly before Christmas, however, her condition suddenly worsened. Rooney, now imprisoned at Fort Lafayette in New York harbor, requested a forty-eight hour pass to visit his dying wife. Custis volunteered to take his brother's place in the cell block. But Federal officials refused even the short parole, and with no hope of seeing her husband again, Charlotte seemed to give up completely. She died on December 24, silently slipping into unconsciousness, her hands clasped upon her breast. Family letters do not indicate the cause of her death (possibly tuberculosis or complications from her two pregnancies), but Lee, notified at camp, was sure that his daughter-in-law had died of a broken heart. In her five and a half years of marriage, Charlotte had thought about and cared for little else besides Rooney. Lee's only consolation was that she had now "joined her little cherubs & our angel Annie in heaven!"[56] She was buried in the Wickham plot in Shockoe Cemetery, where, a friend wrote, "the two little graves [of her children] look less lonely now."[57]

Not long after that sad Christmas, Agnes received a letter from Markie. Though it indicated Markie's continued affection and her acknowledgment that Orton and Agnes had been childhood sweethearts, the letter contained strange and disturbing news about a young woman who claimed to have become engaged to Orton shortly before his disastrous escapade. Markie and her brother Lawrence had met the woman soon after Orton's death and were convinced that she was "deranged," but she had received one of the letters Orton had written just before his death in Franklin, in which he spoke of his hope to meet and marry her in Canada or Europe. Markie believed the woman really had cared for Orton, even though at the time of her supposed "engagement" she was married to another man who subsequently was killed in action.

Turning to her own heartache, Markie continued:

> I go on in my routine of daily duties without allowing myself time to think. Yes, I can easily imagine the interest you feel in all connected with him. You were children together. In my mind's eye I can see you now. You & our darling Annie & he, sitting around the nursery fender telling fairy tales. But then when you had grown up, it was always—"where are Agnes & Orton?" Those forest shades could tell. . . .
>
> You are very dear to me dear Agnes—and ever will be. You seem like my little sister. Our beautiful home! What sorrow the memory of it brings to my heart. I have never been to Georgetown or Washington since my great grief. I feel as if I never could go again. Every place there is associated with him—especially dear A[rlington].[58]

It was a bittersweet letter, and Agnes must have been grateful for Markie's loving concern. But what was she to make of the news about the woman whom Orton had planned to marry, a woman who was still married at the time? The mystery and the pain only grew deeper.

After Christmas the family left the tiny house on Leigh Street to move several blocks nearer to the Caskies, only a few minutes' walk from Capitol Square and St. Paul's Church. The large brick house, affectionately dubbed "The Mess," had been rented by Custis and several of his fellow staff officers from a Richmond family named Stewart. General Lee was not happy about Mrs. Lee and the girls moving into the house, for he feared they would displace Custis and his friends. But the move seemed to work out well for both groups. The girls loved it, Mrs. Lee was more comfortable, and the young men now had a warm, friendly woman who listened to their concerns and sympathized with them. Mrs. Lee took over a room on the first floor of the ample house, which had wide halls, big windows, fine walnut woodwork, and best of all, two-story porches at the rear. Mrs. Lee's quarters opened out onto one of these verandas, from which she could see roses, periwinkle, crepe myrtle, and jasmine in spring and summer.

The family were just becoming reconciled to Charlotte's death when they received a new blow, word that Arlington had been officially confiscated by the Federal government. A year earlier, General and Mrs. Lee had been notified that they owed taxes of $92.07 on the occupied Arlington estate, money which had to be paid in person, according to recently passed statutes. General Lee's cousin, Philip Fendell, attempted to pay in their stead, but his offer was refused, and the property was put up for sale. On a bitterly cold day in January, the United States government purchased the entire eleven hundred acres and mansion house for less than three-fourths of its assessed value. Officials quickly established a freedman's village on the heights, with many frame houses, a school, and a home for the elderly. Six months later, the first Union soldiers were buried near Arlington's portico.

Mildred had returned from St. Mary's before Christmas, and by the time she and the others moved to the Franklin Street house, she had already taken up knitting as a full-time occupation. The Confederate commissary furnished Mrs. Lee with needles, and she had "yarn scouts" all over the South sending her worsted. Friends who came to call were ushered into the downstairs bedroom, where women scraped lint, rolled bandages, and knitted. One visitor compared the room to "an industrial school, with everybody so busy."[59] Lee was especially pleased that Mildred was making her share of wool garments. "Tell Life my reliance is on her," he wrote. "I think I hear her needles rattle as they fly through the meshes."[60] And later, "I have given out that my daughter just from a celebrated school is at work & the expectations of the soldiers are raised."[61] He did wish, however, that she would learn to knit double heels.

Month after month, the family kept up their work, counted out their quantities, and sent the socks off to Lee, who distributed them to his neediest soldiers. He often found, though, that their numbers did not jibe with his own, and he jokingly suggested a solution. "Get one of the girls to count them accurately & set down the number."[62] The very next week their tally agreed with his own. "The number . . . stated by you was correct," he wrote delightedly, "30 prs. good & true. I am glad to find there is arithmetic enough in my family to count 30. I thought if you placed your daughter at work all would go right."[63]

In addition to helping out with knitting and mathematics, Mildred, perhaps without realizing it, was slowly assuming the role of cheerful catalyst in the family circle, a place that had been left empty by Annie's death. Now seeking to be "Life" in reality as well as in name, Mildred decided that what the household really needed was a pet, since all the family's cats, dogs, and chickens had been left at Arlington. The only small animal she could find was a squirrel, which she tried over a period of months to domesticate, with questionable results. She named it Custis Morgan—*Custis* for her own brother and *Morgan* for General John Hunt Morgan, who in 1863 had escaped from Federal captors and made his way to Richmond. Mrs. Lee explained to a friend that the squirrel had been so named "because he will not stay in his cage," but instead "runs all over the house jumps on my head & pulls off my cap & shawl & is in all kinds of mischief." A more serious offense was the squirrel's habit of biting, "very hard sometimes especially strangers."[64]

Though General Lee often wrote his daughters about the progress of the war, Southern strategy, and his concerns about battle results, the girls preferred to write in their letters about more trivial matters in an attempt to keep up his morale. After Custis Morgan joined the household, the squirrel became a central theme in family correspondence, as Mrs. Lee and the girls described the pet's escapades, and the general replied with a variety of playful suggestions as to how best to dispose of the temperamental creature. In March he proposed that Agnes and Mary Custis enjoy a hearty soup for dinner one night, "squirrel soup thickened with peanuts. Custis Morgan in such an exit from the stage would cover himself with glory."[65] The following month, after the squirrel had bitten Mrs. Lee's doctor, he again suggested "squirrel soup for your disease."[66] Surely the small animal would be willing "to be converted into nutricious [*sic*] aliment."[67] After the squirrel had invaded the

Tripletts' house two doors away, Lee urged Life to "restore Custis Morgan to his native woods," though he admired the pet's "taste in going to see Miss Mary Triplett," a close friend of Mildred's and a great favorite with Lee.[68]

As the months passed, Lee became more serious about ridding "The Mess" of the still-wild creature. Fearing that the squirrel might inflict a truly dangerous bite on a family member or friend, he urged Mildred to "immerse his head under the water for five minutes in one of his daily baths."[69] But Life did not have to resort to such drastic measures, for in July Custis Morgan slipped out of the house and disappeared. "I was much pleased," Lee wrote with relief, to hear "that Custis Morgan was . . . among the missing. I think the farther he gets from you the better you will be."[70] In spite of his wild ways, however, the squirrel had provided the Lees with an innocuous nonmilitary subject to discuss in their letters for nearly six months, during a period when the general was fighting bloody battles and the Richmond family was trying to cope with food shortages, Federal encroachment, and war weariness.

In March of 1864 Rooney was exchanged, returning to Richmond along with a trainload of other prisoners. Custis, Rob, and the girls were at the station to greet the gaunt, subdued young giant as he swung down from the cars. Lee managed to get away from the front for a brief welcome, though he admitted that his heart was too full for speech when he saw his son. After resting at "The Mess" for a few days, Rooney became restless and quickly rejoined his old cavalry unit.

With the coming of spring, Lee found himself facing a new and more formidable enemy than the Union's war strategists of earlier years—General Ulysses S. Grant. Taking the offensive, Federal troops now concentrated their efforts not so much on taking Richmond as on destroying the far smaller Confederate Army of Northern Virginia. Through unfamiliar territory and drenching rains, they battled from May to early June, with appalling casualties on both sides. But by June 15, 1864, the Confederates had not been beaten, Richmond was still in Southern hands, and General Grant had shifted his tactics from frontal assault north and east of the capital to wearying siege at Petersburg, twenty miles to the south.

Since the major battles of these months—the Wilderness, Spotsylvania, North Anna, and Cold Harbor—had all been fought within earshot of Richmond, Mrs. Lee and her daughters had become inured to incessant booming of cannon and bursts of musket fire. More distressing were the thousands of wounded men who poured into the city, overflowing hospitals and pressing every available woman into nursing service. Hospital conditions had improved since the war began, but facilities were still primitive, with few anesthetics, little hygiene, rats in the walls, and more men dying of infection and disease than from bullet wounds. The intense heat of Richmond's summer added to the miseries of the injured, whose tempers were often short and their manners as crude as their surroundings. When one of the Lee girls waited patiently on a surly soldier, he was so rude that another volunteer tried to shame him by revealing the name of his nurse. "Lee, Lee?" the Mississippi man drawled. "There are some Lees down in Mississippi who keep a tavern there. Is she one of them Lees?"[71]

Rooney had been with his cavalry unit only a short while when his commanding officer, Jeb Stuart, was mortally wounded at the battle of Yellow Tavern, seven miles north of Richmond. Still living, but aware that he could not survive, Stuart was brought to Richmond to the home of his brother-in-law, a few blocks from "The Mess." Lee family letters do not indicate whether Mary Custis saw her old friend before his death or even whether she attended his elaborate funeral. But she carefully clipped his obituary from the Richmond paper and pasted it in her copybook near the verses he had written her in 1862.

In spite of the dangers of leaving Richmond with enemy soldiers so close, Mildred managed during May to take a quick trip to Shirley. While there, she was cut off by the sudden arrival of Federal troops. Some of the Yankee officers had known her father in the old army, and they came to the great house to ask to see her. Her host, Hill Carter, was incensed at the request, but Mildred merely shrugged and went outside to talk for a few minutes with a Federal cavalryman about his service under General Lee in Texas and Mexico. When Lee heard of the adventure, he was amused but relieved that she had returned to Richmond safely. He wrote to his wife that he was "glad you have got Precious Life back. You had all better keep together & go somewhere where you can get peace & quiet."[72]

Apprehensive as they were about the safety of brothers, father, and friends, and exposed daily to the sight of death and suffering, all three girls found real solace in regular attendance at St. Paul's Episcopal Church, one block from the Franklin Street house. Frequently they worshiped at early service, especially during Lent, and on one occasion two of the girls slipped in late, quickly finding a seat in pew 67, which was usually reserved for President Jefferson Davis and his family. Mrs. Davis' sister, Margaret Howell, also trying to reach her seat hastily, saw two unfamiliar figures in the Davis pew and requested the usher to remove them. When they rose to move, Miss Howell discovered to her distinct embarrassment that the occupants were personal friends of hers and members of General Lee's family. The incident might have been forgotten except that enemies of the Davises circulated the story for many weeks with considerable embellishment.[73]

The month of June, often so pleasant, was unusually hot and dry that summer, with "the very woods . . . full of dust . . . [that] settles over the garden & fields as if they were public roads," complained one diarist.[74] In addition to the heat, Richmonders were plagued by a lack of fresh food because farmers from surrounding counties were fearful of traveling into the capital lest they be caught in skirmishes. Many a dinner in Richmond that summer consisted of "dried Indian peas, rice and salt bacon, and pork."[75] Lee worried how his wife, Custis, three girls, and two servants "can live long on 1/4 lb. of bacon and 1 1/2 pt. of meal."[76] With their limited diet and the heat, it is not surprising that both Mary Custis and Mrs. Lee became ill with "typhoid diarrhea."[77] The general urged them to leave Richmond for a cooler spot where they could "find security & food. Richmond is not the place for you."[78] But getting away would not be a simple task. Mrs. Lee and Mary Custis first had to recover sufficiently to travel, and discovering a safe haven was far more difficult than it had been in previous years. Their last vacation spot, Liberty, had been raided by enemy troops, and farther away in the valley, Staunton and Lexington had both been sacked by General David Hunter. Even homes along the James River east of Lynchburg had been attacked.

While they waited for the two patients to recover, Mildred spent her days shopping in vain for fresh fruits and vegetables to tempt the convalescents' appetites. She wrote to her father to see if he could procure lemons, as she had been unable to find any. From his headquarters near the sweltering trenches of Petersburg Lee replied on July 5.

> My precious Life:
>
> I received this morning by your brother your note of the 3rd & am very glad to hear that your mother is better. I sent out immediately to try & find some lemons, but could only procure two, sent to me by a kind lady. . . . These were gathered from her own trees. There are none to be purchased. I found one in my valise, dried

up, which I also send as it may prove of some value. I also put up some early apples which you can roast for your mother & one pear. This is all the fruit I can get. You must go to market every morning & see if you cannot find some fruit for her. . . . Tell her lemonade is not as palatable or digestible as buttermilk. Try & get some good buttermilk for her. With ice it is delicious & very nutritious. I hope she will continue to improve & be soon well & leave that heated city. It must be roasting now. . . .

Tell her I can only think of her & pray for her recovery. I wish I could be with her to nurse her & care for her. . . . Give much love to precious Agnes. I am glad your dear sister [Mary Custis] is well enough to be out. Tell her she must get strong & take care of your mother. . . . I think of you, long for you, pray for you. It is all I can do. Think sometimes of your devoted father

R E Lee[79]

Mildred's nursing must have been effective, for before the end of July Mrs. Lee was well enough to undertake an eighty-mile journey by canalboat to Bremo, an estate of fifteen hundred acres west of Richmond. The handsome house belonged to friends of the Lees, Dr. Charles Cocke and his family, who gladly welcomed Mrs. Lee, Mildred, and Agnes. Mary Custis stayed behind in the capital to regain strength and weight. She was in Richmond on July 30, when an enormous explosion rocked Petersburg as an underground mine set by Federal troops blew up many of the Confederate trenches. Though the force of the blast created a hole thirty feet deep, the sound of the explosion may not have been heard in Richmond. But like other citizens, Mary Custis was shocked and appalled by the reports of hundreds of Confederate troops blown to bits by the detonation, and the slaughter of thousands of Union soldiers who attempted to cross the gaping crater only to be mowed down by Confederate artillery, muskets, and bayonets.

By the time news of the crater reached Bremo, Mrs. Lee was just beginning to feel stronger. Her newfound health was short-lived, however, for less than a week later she suffered a painful accident. "Unfortunately," she wrote to a friend, "a few days after my arrival I had a severe fall from my crutches slipping on the polished floor . . . & the prospect of walking seems as far off as ever."[80] The doctors prescribed three weeks of bed rest, but Mrs. Lee ignored their orders and was soon up, insistent that she needed to make the general some badly needed undergarments. Lee was grateful for the clothes, but he chided her on getting up too soon. Besides, he wrote, "your daughters you know have very nimble fingers & my Agnes considers herself a great cutter & fitter. Why did you not let her try her hand upon some masculine garments. It is time she was learning, for my hopes in a certain quarter are not yet relinquished."[81] This remark was as close as General Lee ever came to suggesting that he still had hopes of Agnes' marrying.

Mary Custis lingered on in Richmond, where her father saw her during a quick trip to the capital in August. She was much better but still thin, her father reported, and she obviously wanted to stay in town. "I think she prefers it," Lee observed. "She sees more people."[82] But with the heat wave continuing into September, Daughter suddenly changed her mind and took the packet boat upriver to join her mother and sisters at Bremo. Lee hoped that she would "fatten up now under the generous feeding which Robt describes as practiced at Bremo & that Precious Life will find the means of assuaging her appetite."[83] He urged them all to continue their knitting.

Mildred wrote her father that she spent much of her time in the country practicing the piano and reading. As soon as they returned to Richmond at the end of October, Agnes sent off to Lee her own description of their summer adventures. In his reply, he told her that he had read her welcome letter over and over again, for it "brought me pleasant thoughts in our struggle, & softened the asperities of the day."[84] But he feared that, with enemy lines so close to his own, her communication might stray into Federal hands, so reluctantly he had torn it to pieces. Now that Mrs. Lee and Daughter were much healthier, he hoped they would try to remain so. His recipe for good health was to "keep well, not talk too much, & go to bed early."[85]

Sleep was a luxury he did not often enjoy, for during month after weary month Petersburg was subjected to "constant cannonade and continuous rattle of musketry," as Grant's troops kept up the pressure on Confederate lines.[86] Occasionally, Lee got away to Richmond on official business, and then he would visit "The Mess" for a few hours or a weekend, but he was not in the city on Christmas Day, which fell that year on a Sunday. The girls no doubt walked over to St. Paul's to join the congregation of subdued worshipers. Like other Richmond families, they decorated their house with cedar and holly and sat down to a plain holiday dinner, grateful enough for any food in a period when many families could afford only two meals a day.

The new year blew in with snow, then rain, and finally sleet, weather as chilling and capricious as the mood of many Virginians, who vacillated between despair and a kind of reckless bravado. Aware that General William T. Sherman was sweeping north from Savannah through the Carolinas and that General Philip H. Sheridan was devastating the Valley of Virginia, while Lee's own troops faced starvation, thoughtful people began to speak openly of "submission, surrender, subjugation [and] reconstruction."[87] Others tried to hide their worries by attending elaborate dinners and dances. But neither fear nor frivolity penetrated the studied normalcy of the Lee household. Each morning the women gathered in Mrs. Lee's room, with its view of the frozen garden and the bare branches of the ailanthus trees, to knit with greater intensity, as they thought about the hungry, ragged troops in open trenches only thirty miles away. Later each day, Mildred ventured downtown to pay exorbitant prices for any sort of food that might add variety to their meager diet, while Agnes and Mary Custis stayed home with their mother, visiting with neighbors and friends in the parlor. Among the guests that strange, unreal winter was Lancy Blackford, a young soldier who had served with Rob in the Rockbridge Artillery. In his diary Lancy noted how much he had enjoyed the relaxed atmosphere of the Lee home. Agnes was beautiful, he commented, but he found "her older sister more agreeable."[88] In February Custis left the household, for he was finally given field command over a motley collection of troops, including thirteen hundred men of the Home Guard, whose still-clean uniforms were characterized by "scarlet caps with trim."[89] Unfortunately, neither their careful training by Custis nor their elaborate regalia could change ill-prepared government clerks into adequate defense forces.

Surprisingly, the calmest person in the Franklin Street house that winter was Mrs. Lee, who seemed to grow in courage and tranquillity as news from the front grew worse. The bitterness, self-pity, and indecisiveness she had shown in early years of the war disappeared and were replaced by a contagious poise and inner repose. "No. 707 [Franklin Street] became a common meeting place," one young neighbor, Sally Robins, wrote years later. "People came here to talk of victory or sorrow. . . . They gathered here to work, the disheartened came for comfort."

Mrs. Lee "listened, and strengthened, and smiled even when her own heart ached. . . . The brightness of her nature, amidst uncertainty and pain, was wonderful."[90] The daughters, taking their cue from her tranquillity, made every effort to appear unafraid and hopeful, although in February their father warned them that he might soon have to withdraw from Petersburg and thereby abandon Richmond.

In spite of her father's concerns, Agnes decided late in March to accept a long-standing invitation to visit friends, the Meade family in Petersburg. Lee feared that she had "put off your visit too late," but perhaps Agnes felt that if her hosts had courage enough to ask her, she should match their spirit with her own.[91] Whatever her reasons, bravery or bravado, she left the Richmond train station on March 29, only three days before General Grant threw 50,000 troops against Lee's faltering line, a thrust that broke the defenses of Petersburg and led, a few weeks later, to the surrender at Appomattox.

But the first day of Agnes' truncated visit proved to be surprisingly pleasant. Petersburg citizens, used to constant bombardment, paid little heed to flying cannonballs, walking about the streets casually, "shopping and attending to usual occupations . . . laughing and talking."[92] That night a regimental band serenaded the Meade home, and Agnes tossed fresh roses to the gallant musicians. The following day she tried to see her father, who was quartered in a farmhouse near the Richmond-Petersburg pike, but she missed him, for in spite of heavy rain he had ridden toward the west to view for himself the ominous concentration of Union troops. The next morning he found time to write her a hasty note.

> My precious little Agnes:
>
> I was so sorry I was not here to see you yesterday. I might have persuaded you to have remained with me. If you had have staid [*sic*] or come out at 4 o'clock this morning I could have seen you with my weary sleepy eyes. Now I . . . do not know when I shall have the pleasure of seeing you.[93]

At home in Richmond, Mrs. Lee, Mildred, and Mary Custis were making plans to entertain two refugee cadets from the Virginia Military

Institute for Sunday dinner on April 2. Mrs. Lee had written to Colonel Francis Smith, superintendent of the institute, which had taken up temporary headquarters in Richmond after General Hunter had burned the barracks in Lexington.

> I write to beg the favour of you to allow my two young friends Peyton Skipwith & John Cocke of Bremo . . . to visit us sometime on Sunday, being the only day when we dine sufficiently early for them to return in time to the Institute. I will take care that they attend church. . . .
>
> Yrs. most truly & respectfully
>
> M. C. Lee[94]

On Saturday night General Grant ordered a massive bombardment of the Confederate lines before Petersburg. Custis Lee's officers, stationed at Chaffin's Bluff seven miles below Richmond, noticed a low murmur, almost like distant thunder, coming from the south, coupled with a "faint red glare," which their experienced ears recognized as cannonading.[95] If Mary Custis and Mildred kept their second-story windows open that night at "The Mess," they too may have heard or seen the telltale signals of approaching battle. But whether or not they were aware of the firing, they must surely have been apprehensive about Agnes, as they remembered their father's words of warning to her: "It would be very dreadful if you should be caught in a battle when the road would have to be used for military purposes & you cut off."[96] Fortunately, General Lee's quick action prevented her from being trapped, for during the evening, as shells rained down on his troops, he hastily dispatched a paroled officer named Jimmy Clark to fetch Agnes from the Meade home and take her to the train station. She and Clark managed to leave Petersburg on one of the last trains out of the city.[97] At two o'clock on Sunday morning, Clark delivered Agnes to the house on Franklin Street, much to the relief of Mrs. Lee, Mildred, and Mary Custis. As the girls crept back to their beds, their concerns now turned to their father and brothers under Grant's blistering attack. Their apprehensions were not lessened by the noisy clamor of the tocsin in Capitol Square, which started ringing incessantly not long after daybreak.

After days of rain Sunday, April 2, dawned clear and warm, "one of those unusually lovely days that the Spring sometimes brings," one woman remembered.[98] Another resident of the city called that Sabbath morning "as perfect a day as Richmond had ever seen; the budding trees, the flowers of spring, the balmy atmosphere, the clear sky, bright sunshine, all combining to make a spring day of unsurpassed loveliness."[99] Church bells rang out in the quiet air, and worshipers strolled along the silent streets.

Having had so little rest, the Lee girls might have missed church except that their mother had promised that they would take Cadets Skipwith and Cocke to the eleven o'clock service. It was Communion Sunday at old St. Paul's, and the church was filling up rapidly when the girls greeted the cadets and took their seats not far from where President Davis was already seated, an impressive, erect figure in gray trousers and Prince Albert coat. St. Paul's rector, Dr. Charles Minnegerode, had just begun his communion meditation when the church sexton walked silently down the center aisle, touched President Davis on the shoulder, and whispered in his ear. With no change of expression, the president rose and walked quickly down the aisle and out of the sanctuary, followed soon afterwards by other important military and governmental figures. As leader after leader left hurriedly, an audible murmur of apprehension rose among the worshipers. Sensing their distress, white-haired Dr. Minnegerode paused, spread his arms as if to embrace his parishioners, and urged people to stay in their seats till the end of the communion service. Though they must have guessed at least some of the calamitous news that summoned President Davis away, the girls probably remained with the two hundred or more worshipers till after the benediction. If their cadet escorts stayed with them, the boys surely excused themselves from their anticipated dinner and rushed off to report for any duty to which they might be assigned.

Small knots of people gathered after church to discuss the morning's events, and the dreaded news spread quickly—Lee's line had been broken, and Richmond was to be abandoned. There had been threats before, but now even the scoffers were silenced when they saw congressmen's belongings being packed in haste and long wagon lines queued up in front of government buildings to carry off gold bullion and state documents.

Two months earlier, Lee had urged his family to make contingency plans for evacuation. But Mrs. Lee and the girls had decided that they would not leave Richmond. How could three young women move an invalid mother in a hurry, and besides, where could they go that would be safe? No, they would just remain in the house on Franklin Street and hope for the best. So this Sunday afternoon, they sat at the windows of the brick house and watched as sudden panic gripped the populace. All of Richmond, rich and poor, highborn and lowly, seemed to be scrambling to leave the city. Wagons and carriages piled high with furniture and barrels jostled the endless stream of heavily laden pedestrians, all intent on getting away, somewhere, anywhere, to escape the dreaded Yankees. Through the open casements the family listened to the sounds of flight, the tramping of feet, the creak of wagon wheels, the cries of children, and the whinnies of frightened horses, as "grim terror spread in wild contagion."[100]

By midafternoon, looting began. A motley horde of deserters, camp followers, and released prisoners rampaged through the streets, attacking empty houses and shops, smashing windows and breaking open commissary supplies. Down near the waterfront the mob discovered that departing soldiers had poured the government's liquor supplies into the streets, and with whoops of glee they scooped up the filthy, undiluted whiskey with hands, cups, and buckets. Then, reeling, they staggered to their feet to pillage some more, aware that the city lay helpless before them, since police and all able-bodied men had gone to join Lee's battered forces near Amelia Court House. Like many other families where only women and servants remained, the Lees bolted their doors, secured their shutters, and listened on into the night to the frightening sounds of breaking glass, boxes being dragged over cobblestones, and hoarse shouts and obscenities. Gradually, near midnight, the orgy subsided as the crowd, worn out by greed, exertion, and alcohol, drifted away to sleep off their drunkenness.

But few persons could sleep long that night. Suddenly the darkness and calm were shattered by a violent explosion that rattled windows. Peering through the shutters at the rear of their home, the Lee girls saw flames and billowing smoke, which drifted back toward them with the distinctive odor of burning tobacco. The tobacco warehouses by the James River were on fire, either set deliberately by fleeing soldiers or accidentally fired by straggling looters. As they watched, the fire spread quickly along the waterfront toward the east, fanned by a brisk breeze.

An hour later another gigantic explosion rocked the city. Rushing again to their window, the girls could see new flames behind the warehouse fires, and then a sudden cascade of sparks and small explosions spewing into the night air in all directions. The navy's ships, tied up at river docks, had caught fire, and ammunition stored below decks was exploding and spiraling upward like a thousand firecrackers. By the light of this new conflagration, the girls realized that the main part of the fire had moved rapidly to the east, the whole sky ablaze with flame, smoke, and flying rafters. The sight was so awesome and mesmerizing that it must have been difficult for them to tear themselves away to go downstairs to calm the servants and bring their mother up to date on the progress of the fire.

Just before dawn the girls were flung from their couches by an earsplitting shock, like the sound of "a hundred cannon at one time."[101] The city's powder magazine had blown up, and the noise all but drowned out the crackle and roar of the fire which already had consumed most of the city's business district, as well as the ironworks and other shops by the river.

Dawn came, and the sun rose like a "dull, ghastly . . . disk" in the smoky atmosphere to cast its murky light upon a city that only yesterday had been rain-fresh and hopeful.[102] Now Richmond was "one vast, livid flame [which] roared and screamed before the wind."[103] Fiery rafters and tar paper from warehouse roofs curled upward, then blew in all directions to fall and set fires blocks away in a crazy, hopscotch pattern.

About noon the wind shifted, and the fire turned toward the west, creeping nearer and nearer toward Capitol Square, President Davis' home, St. Paul's Church, and the house on Franklin Street where Mrs. Lee sat quietly, her knitting in her lap. Friends rushed to warn of danger and offered to evacuate the family. Mrs. Lee was polite, but adamant. She was not moving. Her stubborn calm and defiant dignity were echoed by a neighbor who sat upon her packed trunk in front of her home at the corner of Franklin and Eighth streets, "attired in her handsomest dress, her best bonnet, veil, and gloves," watching the approaching fire through her lorgnette.[104] Though they might lose possessions and freedom, Mrs. Lee and Mrs. Stanard were determined to face fire and Yankees with whatever dignity remained to them.

Suddenly the steeple of the church on the north side of Franklin Street directly across from the Lee home caught fire. Friends formed a bucket brigade to dampen down the roof at 707, while Mary Custis perched herself on the top step, a container of water beside her, prepared to put out any errant sparks. But miraculously, the flames suddenly lost their momentum and the wind died down. Still smoldering around Capitol Square, the fire moved no farther west than the burning church, and the lower side of Franklin Street was saved. The sun went down, bloodred, "with a lurid, angry glare," and a bright moon rose over the broken city, where now only the murmur of the river and the sound of Federal soldiers' marching feet broke the stillness.[105]

Tuesday morning, when the girls unbolted their door and opened the shutters, they saw just how close the devastation had come. From a few doors away and on to the east for block after block there remained only blackened walls and fallen timbers where nine hundred homes and business establishments had stood two days before. Just as heartrending was the sight of the old, familiar Union flag above the Capitol building, limp and listless in the heavy, smoke-filled atmosphere. (The city had formally been surrendered to Federal authorities at dawn on Monday morning.) In their hearts, the Lees must have echoed the feelings of another young woman, who cried as she saw the "Southern Cross dragged down. . . . Was it to this end . . . that the wives and children of many a dear and gallant friend were husbandless and fatherless . . . that our homes were in ruins, our State devastated?"[106] Though they still professed to believe in the future of the Confederacy, the Lees must have realized that morning that the war was almost over.

Sunday and Monday had been so tumultuous that the rest of the week passed like a dream. Well-disciplined Federal troops took over the city, put out the few remaining fires, re-established order, posted guards at many homes, and issued ration cards to people whose Confederate money no longer had any value. General Godfrey Weitzel, the Union commanding officer, offered to move Mrs. Lee in an ambulance to a place of greater safety and comfort, and when she refused, he posted a guard at the door to make sure that she and the girls were not disturbed. The first sentry assigned to their home was black, but upon Mrs. Lee's request he was replaced by a series of white guards, who paced up and down before the brick structure and ate their meals on the front steps. Sometime during the latter part of the week, the girls ventured out of the house to apply for ration cards and procure a few groceries. If they were out on the afternoon of April 4, they might have seen Abraham Lincoln riding slowly through the blackened streets in an open carriage, his eyes sad and haunted. Behind him came a rabble of cheering, singing freed slaves, who welcomed the president with shouts of joy.

One week after the city had been abandoned, the booming of a cannon announced to its citizens that Lee's army had surrendered. With an outward show of optimism, Mrs. Lee refused to accept defeat. "General Lee is not the Confederacy," she was quoted as saying. "There is life in the old land yet."[107] But within a day or two, Custis was home, corroborating the news of the surrender and giving details of the unequal numbers of Union and Confederate troops and the starving condition of Lee's men. Custis had been captured briefly, and he heard while a prisoner that his mother had died. Requesting a parole to return to the city quickly, he was overjoyed to find that Mrs. Lee and his sisters had survived the terrible days of the past week.

Quietly he, his mother, and the girls waited for the general's return. On Saturday, April 15, a small group of horsemen rode without fanfare into Richmond—General Lee, Rooney, and five of Lee's former staff officers. They had hoped to get into the city unnoticed, but the imposing figure of Robert E. Lee astride Traveller was too familiar not to be recognized. By the time the party had arrived in front of 707 Franklin Street, a crowd had gathered, cheering the general, trying to catch hold of his hand or touch his old gray coat. As the girls peered through their shuttered windows, their father dismounted, doffed his hat to the group, and turned to walk up the front steps. Two years earlier, he had written Mildred and Agnes of his hope that with an early end to the war the family could be reunited. The war was over, but not as they would have wished. Stirred by emotions of pride, relief, and despair, the girls welcomed General Lee into the house and closed the door behind him.

6

Saints, Yearlings, and Leaders of the Herd

1865–1873

IN THE FIRST WEEKS AFTER APPOMATTOX the Lees found themselves, in spite of their relatively secure financial position, facing questions similar to those troubling most Southerners. Where should they settle? What would they do? And even more troubling, how could they overcome the bitterness and loss of hope that accompanied defeat?

General Lee had specific suggestions for his soldier sons, the same advice he urged upon all his fellow officers—to put aside anger, apply for pardon, take the oath of allegiance, and then go back home to rebuild their lives. "Our returned soldiers . . . must all set to work," he wrote his aide-de-camp, Colonel Walter Taylor, "and if they cannot do what they prefer, do what they can. Virginia wants all their aid, all their support, and the presence of all her sons to sustain and recuperate her."[1] Lee himself made application for pardon on June 13, 1865, though he did not sign the oath until four months later.*

But he had no immediate counsel for the women of the Confederacy, assuming that they would follow the lead and advice of their menfolk.

---

*Robert E. Lee's signed oath, sent to Washington, D. C. early in October 1865, was misplaced and lost for many years. His application for the reinstatement of his civil rights was not acted upon until 1975, when Congress, by a special resolution, returned his citizenship—105 years after he had requested it (Charles Bracelon Flood, *Lee: The Last Years* [Boston: Houghton Mifflin Company, 1981], 276).

He seriously underestimated, however, both the fierce resentment that noncombatants felt toward Yankees and the independence and responsibility thrust upon Southern women by the exigencies of war. Suddenly plantation mistresses had acquired new managerial skills, and feminine refugees of necessity had taken jobs never before filled by women. To return to the passive, unobtrusive roles of prewar years now seemed unthinkable. "It is impossible to believe that women will . . . move in the same narrow ruts as before," wrote one observant North Carolina lady soon after the surrender. "They cannot if they would."[2]

Though Mildred, Agnes, and Mary Custis had not managed estates or worked as clerks in the War Office, they had for the first time lived and traveled independently. More dramatically, they had nursed the sick, been subjected to house arrest by the enemy, and endured frightening days of fire and occupation without the support of father or brothers. Their own sense of hopelessness about the future was intensified by Lee's inability to understand their lingering bitterness and their new self-reliance.

As children, the Lee girls had been quite sure what their adult lives would be like. Courted by plantation neighbors or distant relatives as their mother and grandmothers had been, they would marry with their father's consent and move away to new households where their talents and energies would be directed toward the benefit of husbands and children. Their schooling and the homilies in their girlhood books trained them to become wives and mothers "perform[ing] faithfully all those little household cares and duties on which the comfort and virtue of" their families depended, as the heroine of a favorite story expressed it.* If, by chance, one of them should not marry young, she would be expected to stay at Arlington under her father's supervision, assisting with housekeeping and teaching younger relatives, with the possibility of a late marriage to a widower in search of a surrogate mother and housekeeper for his orphaned brood.

Even after the family abandoned Arlington, the girls' confidence in their future remained, exemplified by Annie's quiet assurance about the war-related skills she would "have to tell my children" someday.[3] But as fighting continued for month after weary month, as casualties mounted and friends like Hettie Cary were widowed within weeks of their

---

*Elizabeth Stuart Phelps, *The Angel Over the Right Shoulder* (Philadelphia: W. P. Draper, 1852), 29.

weddings, the girls laid aside their personal ambitions to concentrate on victory and the vindication of the Confederacy. Now, after bitter defeat and what appeared to be the meaningless deaths of a quarter of a million young Southern men, there seemed to be absolutely nothing to look forward to. Like their friend Mrs. Judith McGuire, they felt they had "no country, no government, no future," and their anger toward Yankees, kindled by the occupation of Arlington and deepened by the destruction of the White House, the capture of Rooney, and the hanging of Orton Williams, hardened into bitter animosity during the early months of Federal occupation.[4]

Agnes and Mildred, however, had little time to ponder their despair or hatred, for they were too busy finding food and bed linen for the people now staying in the Franklin Street house—General Lee; Rooney; Custis; their aunt, Mrs. Smith Lee; and her sons, John, Fitz, and Dan. At night Mildred became her father's companion on long, silent walks about the ruined city, while Agnes assisted Mrs. Lee in preparing for bed.

Though her sisters engaged in unobtrusive feminine roles, Mary Custis chose an assertive and more visible task. With Rooney, Custis, and her cousins, she sought to protect General Lee from the hundreds of visitors who crowded around the house hoping for interviews. While her father remained upstairs reading, writing letters, or strolling about the tiny back balconies, Daughter and the boys spoke to the never-ending stream of inquirers, which included Confederate comrades seeking a final farewell, Union officers trying to reestablish friendship from old army days, Southern women hoping for information about missing relatives, newspaper reporters, photographers, and casual tourists from the North eager for a glimpse of the fallen hero. Sometimes Lee, hearing the name of a guest or recognizing a voice, would come downstairs, but much of the time Mary Custis, Rooney, and Fitz were able to acknowledge the visitors' interests and send them away, for they all realized that each interview added to the general's emotional and physical exhaustion.

The family's concerns were compounded by the continued absence of Rob, who had not been heard from for several weeks after the surrender. Now twenty-one, Rob had been on his way to Lynchburg with his troops when news of Appomattox reached him. Unwilling to surrender at once, he had traveled by back roads till he met Jefferson Davis' tiny retinue near Greensboro, North Carolina. There his uncle, Smith Lee, persuaded him to return to Virginia and apply for pardon. He arrived unannounced in Richmond about the middle of May, to the great relief of his sisters and mother.

He came to the Franklin Street home too late, however, to see Rooney, who had already become restless and ill at ease in the crowded household. Having lost far more during the war than his brothers, Rooney was the first to take his father's advice, returning to his Pamunkey plantation to build a shanty and begin farming on his burned-over fields. Lee offered Rob tuition for a final year at the University of Virginia, but the young man demurred, believing that his father needed "any means he might have in caring for my mother and sisters."[5] So Rob joined Rooney in cultivating the White House farm, with plans to work his own estate at Romancoke the following spring.

Through letters and personal conversations, offers of all sorts poured in upon General Lee, promising fine houses, outright monetary gifts, and chances for positions of power or prestige. They were tempting inducements for, like Custis, Lee no longer had a professional career upon which to build, and Arlington, which both of them had managed, was now a Federal cemetery. But neither man was interested in opportunities in which he would serve as a mere figurehead. Instead Custis sought to find a teaching job somewhere, and Lee began looking for property to farm. Eager to get Mrs. Lee away from another scorching Richmond summer and still restricted in his personal freedom by the crowds, he considered purchasing a tract of land along the Pamunkey, a hope that was dashed by his sons' pessimistic reports of the "utter desolation" of their neighborhood.[6]

Late in the spring a letter arrived from Mrs. Elizabeth Cocke of Cumberland County that seemed to provide the perfect offer. With consummate tact, Mrs. Cocke suggested that the Lees use an unoccupied four-room cottage on her property, where there would be an ample supply of fresh vegetables, but few visitors. Best of all, the cottage, called Derwent, would be easy for Mrs. Lee to reach by canalboat, as it was near the James River, fifty miles west of Richmond. Here was a chance to get away from the heat and confusion of the city for a few months to a place where the general could find rest and quiet without undue obligation to his benefactress. After a respite at Derwent, he and Custis could settle upon some livelihood remunerative enough to provide for Mrs. Lee and the girls.

Though there is no indication that they were consulted about the move, Mildred and Agnes were probably happy to leave Richmond, with its somber reminders of defeat and fire and its oppressive atmosphere under military occupation. Group gatherings had been forbidden and besides, there was no enthusiasm for social functions. "We suffered terribly . . . for want of something in which we might occupy ourselves," one of their friends wrote about that summer. "The sultry days were begun and rounded by hours of listless endurance, followed by troubled sleep."[7] If Derwent proved to be half as pleasant as Bremo had been the summer before, they would find their stay congenial and restful.

Mary Custis was less sure about the new venture. Now almost thirty, she had achieved greater independence during the war than her sisters, living away from the family more than she had been with them, and for almost a year she had been completely cut off from parental counsel, correspondence, and support. So it is not surprising that, though she left Richmond with her parents and sisters, she never settled at Derwent, traveling instead to Staunton for a prolonged visit with relatives.

Despite their differing views of the new destination, all three young women found it hard to say good-bye to neighbors they had grown close to during periods of sorrow, privation, and terror. Mildred's friend Louise Haxall and others came to bring farewell gifts and to ask General Lee for mementos, locks of his hair and buttons from his Confederate coat. More acquaintances waited down at the packet landing on the afternoon of June 30 for final farewells. When their personal belongings had been loaded onto the flat-bottomed shallow boat and Mrs. Lee had been carried aboard, the family turned to wave to the small knot of friends on shore.

As tow horses pulled the cumbersome vessel in the direction of the setting sun, the Lees moved away from the burned bridges and twisted wreckage of the city toward more restful scenes round each bend of the James, where greening fields and plowed gardens attested to the healing touch of summer's abundance. Darkness fell, and the women tried to sleep in the tiny, stifling cabin, while General Lee preferred to stretch out on deck, wrapped in his field coat, as he had slept so many hundreds of nights in recent years. All of them must have lain awake for a long time, listening to the unaccustomed silence and wondering what lay ahead for them in the weeks and months to come.

At sunrise the vessel arrived at Pemberton Wharf, near the Cocke plantation of Oakland. Here they were met by Mrs. Cocke's eldest son, Edmund, and by Custis, who had ridden out on Traveller several days before. The two young men escorted the family in a carriage on the brief ride through Cartersville and on to the Cocke home, set far back from the road with fifty enormous oak trees on the front lawn. Though Oakland had been raided several times by Federal troops, the three-thousand-acre estate had survived with little damage, and the Lees were treated to an old-fashioned plantation breakfast of batter bread, hot rolls, loaf bread, beaten biscuits, sausage, ham, and broiled tomatoes.[8] Mrs. Cocke, a widow in her fifties, was a gracious and charming hostess, but Mildred and Agnes no doubt enjoyed even more becoming acquainted with her sons, Edmund, Preston, and Tom, all of whom were young Confederate veterans.

The girls soon found, however, that Derwent was far less appealing than Oakland. Set in deep woods several miles from the plantation house, their cottage was not only isolated but also cramped, with only four small rooms for living, eating and sleeping.* "A retired little place with a straight up house," Mrs. Lee called it, whose "outbuildings are dilapidated & the garden . . . a mass of weeds."[9] Having spent years growing used to noisy city streets, they all found the silence "profound," so still they could almost "number the acorns falling from the splendid oaks that overshadowed the cottage."[10] Fortunately, kind neighbors supplied them bountifully with fresh produce and ice.

With characteristic optimism, Lee called the house "comfortable but small."[11] Years later Mildred recalled how cheerful her father was during those months at Derwent and how hard he worked to keep up the family's spirits. His enthusiasm and his "interest in a *home* life, however humble, after those five years in a tent" made life endurable for them all, in spite of "petty trials of wretched service, cooking, market-ing—an ugly meanly built little house with ordinary surroundings [and] provincial society."[12]

The family had been at Derwent only a short time when Agnes became very ill with a severe case of typhoid fever. Mildred nursed her day and night until at last the debilitating temperature was checked, and Lee could put away his fear that a second daughter might be taken from him, far away from doctors and medications. "Mildred is my only reliance & support," he wrote to Rooney. "She is very active & attentive & but for her I do not know what Agnes would do."[13] The increased compatibility between Precious Life and her father, stimulated by noc-

---

*Although Oakland was in Cumberland County, Derwent, part of the same estate, was over the county line in Powhatan County.

Derwent

turnal walks in Richmond the past spring and now augmented by their joint care of Agnes and Mrs. Lee, was to continue and become a precious element in the lives of both daughter and father.

As Agnes slowly recovered and required less constant care, Mildred found that Derwent had little to offer in the way of diversion. The most exciting event each day was a walk to the spring with Custis and her father. She saw the Cocke boys from time to time and she made the acquaintance of Lucy Blain, a young girl several years her junior who was spending the summer on a nearby estate, but Mildred could not often get away from her patient for long periods of time. Heretofore, when she needed companionship, she had acquired kittens or the unsatisfactory squirrel, Custis Morgan. At Derwent she began collecting chickens, the first she had kept since leaving Arlington, naming them after friends and relatives. "My chickens are a great comfort," she told Lucy.[14]

But even these feathered pets and a wide assortment of books were not enough to dissipate Mildred's pervasive sense of futility. "Oh! Lucy," she wrote to her younger friend, "enjoy yourself while you can. When you get *my age* [nineteen], when your heart & hopes have been withered as mine have been; when where your heart once *was, there* remains only a *heap* of *ashes, then*, & *not till then*, will you believe that life is all 'vanity and vexation of spirit.'"[15]

Fortunately, cheerful letters arrived from Rooney and Rob, who had completed their makeshift shelter and were preparing to harvest a bumper crop of field corn. Custis, too, had good news—the possibility of a teaching position at the Virginia Military Institute in Lexington, provided the school could raise enough funds to reopen. Daughter, the family learned, had moved from the Peytons' in Staunton to Liberty, where she was visiting the Burwell family. From there she expected to go on to the Eastern Shore of Maryland to be with Goldsborough cousins.

By now the summer was nearly over, and still Robert E. Lee had made no decision about his future plans. He had accepted Mrs. Cocke's generosity for the summer months only, and besides, the small cottage at Derwent would scarcely be suitable for winter use. Late in August, however, an unexpected guest brought a message that was to change the lives of them all.

The day had begun like all the rest, a quiet breakfast and Mildred's assisting her mother and Agnes to get dressed, when suddenly the family noticed a stranger riding up toward the door. Dismounting from his horse, the gentleman introduced himself as Judge John Brockenbrough of Lexington. He was tall and angular, the girls noticed, shabbily dressed in an ill-fitting suit. As he and General Lee talked alone, Mildred and Agnes must have wondered what business could have been so important that a judge must travel three days and nights on horseback to discuss it with their father. Only later did they learn details of the surprising message that the Lexingtonian had brought and of the part that their sister had played in the sequence of events leading up to his visit.

While Mary Custis had been in Staunton, she had attended a party where another guest had been Colonel Bolivar Christian, a lawyer from Lexington. In her usual outspoken way, she had commented in Colonel Christian's presence that "the people of the South are offering my father everything but work; and work is the only thing he will accept at their hands."[16] Daughter probably thought no more about her remark, but its implications stuck in Colonel Christian's mind. As a trustee of Lexington's struggling, war-damaged Washington College, he was about to attend a board meeting for the purpose of choosing a new college president. During the course of that meeting a few days later, Colonel Christian, with some hesitation, mentioned Mary Custis Lee's remark. Not really believing that General Lee would accept, the board unanimously elected him president and dispatched their rector, Judge Brockenbrough, to carry the invitation to Derwent. Though he had to borrow money and a suit of respectable clothes for the trip, the judge was eloquent enough to take away with him General Lee's promise to consider the unexpected offer.

None of the family had ever seen Lexington, but the college itself was not unfamiliar to Robert E. Lee. His father, "Light Horse Harry" Lee, had been instrumental in persuading George Washington to make a handsome gift of canal stock to Liberty Hall, which in gratitude had changed its name to Washington Academy. Lee's half brother Henry had attended the school in 1806–07, and his brother-in-law, Louis Marshall, was the son of a former president of the college who had served from 1830 to 1834.[17]

The school very nearly closed during the war, though its trustees valiantly advertised for students month after month in the Richmond papers. Its enrollment dropped to only a handful of boys too young for military service, and most of its classes were preparatory in nature. General Hunter's raid had spared the college buildings, though Federal troops had set fire to neighboring V.M.I., but the library had been looted and scientific equipment destroyed. By the end of the war, many of the town's leading citizens, including the few Washington College faculty members, were living precariously close to starvation.

For several days General Lee pondered his decision. His pay as president would not be large, only fifteen hundred dollars a year plus a portion of each student's tuition, as well as the promise of a house and garden plot. These perquisites, supplemented by railroad bonds and other securities that had survived the war, should, he thought, be enough to support Mrs. Lee and the girls simply but adequately. More important, the offer would give him a chance to set a concrete example for the South by earning his own living and, at the same time, assisting to rebuild the region. On the other hand, he realized that the move would mean carrying the family farther away from familiar friends and scenes of the past.

Two Lexington acquaintances wrote, urging him to take the position—former Governor John Letcher, whom he had known in Richmond in the early days of the war, and his artillery chief, General William Pendleton, who had returned to his old duties as rector of the town's Episcopal Church. Their cordial letters not only gave Lee added encouragement, but also assured him that there were at least two families with whom Mrs. Lee and the girls would be congenial. Late in August, he made his decision and wrote the board of trustees a letter of acceptance. Then, five months to the day from his return to Richmond in defeat, Robert E. Lee rode Traveller toward the west, bound for a new life and a new career in Lexington.

Mrs. Lee showed little enthusiasm for his departure. "The papers will have told you," she wrote to Miss Emily Mason, "that the Gen'l has decided to accept the position at Lexington. I do not think that he is very fond of teaching, but he is willing to do anything that will give him honorable support."[18] In a week she and the girls received a letter recounting Lee's first impressions. His journey had been hot, he told them, but the scenery along the way was beautiful. Lexington nights were much cooler, and he was needing both a blanket and a "coverlid." He assured them that the college buildings were "beautifully located," but unfortunately, the home to which he had soon hoped to bring them was still occupied by its wartime resident, a local doctor who was having trouble finding other accommodations.[19]

In subsequent notes Lee continued to speak of the loveliness of the mountains, but he acknowledged to Agnes that Lexington "is a beautiful spot by nature—man has done but little for it."[20] When he finally viewed the inside of the president's house, he found it in wretched repair. Still, he felt sure that before long it could be made attractive and livable, with the new tables, chairs, and beds he had recently ordered from Baltimore, a complete set of bedroom furniture provided by their benefactress, Mrs. Cocke, and the old carpets and draperies from Arlington, which had remained at Tudor Place throughout most of the war. In addition to giving details about the house, Lee wrote chattily of the pretty girls he saw walking around town and the increase in the numbers of students, both at Washington College and at the Virginia Military Institute, which reopened its doors on October 16. Custis, appointed professor of civil engineering at V.M.I., moved into an undamaged classroom at the institute and ate his meals with his father at the hotel.

Lee's letters did little to convey the excitement that his coming to Lexington had generated in the little community. Before the end of 1865 more than one hundred students had enrolled at the college and the number of faculty had doubled. The town even made national news on October 6, when a reporter from the *New York Herald* (the same man who had covered the surrender at Appomattox) arrived to write a story on General Lee's inauguration as president of Washington College. Though the trustees had hoped for a gala occasion, Lee insisted upon only a simple oath-taking and the signing of a pledge to uphold the best for the school.

Meantime, the ladies of Lexington were busy preparing the empty house for the arrival of the Lee family. As each room was painted and varnished, they cleaned woodwork and windows, laid the carpets sent by Aunt Brit Kennon (folded under at the corners because these rooms were much smaller than those at Arlington) and hung the old Arlington curtains.

Back at Derwent, Rob was now keeping his mother and sisters company till they could move to Lexington. After a summer of unac-customedly hard manual labor and a rewarding harvest, Rob had come down with a persistent case of malaria. In spite of cooler weather at Derwent and later at Lexington, his chills lasted for months, inspiring Lee to change his nickname from "Robertus" or "Bertus" to "Robertus Sickus."[21]

When the days turned cold in early November and still the president's house was not ready, Mrs. Lee, the girls, and Rob moved from Derwent to Bremo and the weather-tight house of Dr. and Mrs. Cocke some twenty-five miles farther upstream on the James. About this time Agnes received an invitation from her Richmond friend, Sally Warwick, to take part in Sally's wedding and prenuptial festivities. Unlike Mary Custis, who simply moved from place to place on her own whim, Agnes felt constrained to ask her father's permission to go. "My precious little Agnes," he replied, "it is very hard for you to apply to me to advise you to go away from me. . . . But in order to help you make up your mind, if it will promote your pleasure & Sally's happiness, I will say, go." Later in the letter, he added, "I hope Life is not going to desert us too."[22]

With his lukewarm consent Agnes hastened to Richmond, leaving only Mrs. Lee, Mildred, and Rob to make the journey to Lexington by packet boat. Departing from Bremo on Thursday, November 30, they traveled for forty-eight hours aboard the private conveyance of the president of the James River and Kanawha Canal Company, a boat that offered ample sleeping accommodations and a dining room, complete with a cook to prepare their meals. The journey up the James River to

Balcony Falls and then twenty miles along the North River in Rockbridge County was much more comfortable than their trip five months earlier, but the farther west they moved, the more unfamiliar the topography became. The narrowing river gorges, turbulent rapids, moss-covered stone locks designed to lift the boat over rough water, and frowning crags must have seemed mysterious and forbidding to the passengers, used to the sunny open shores of the Potomac.

The morning of December 2 was crisp and cool as Mildred and Rob stood on deck for their first glimpse of Lexington. To the left a high cliff rose abruptly from the water's edge, covered with undergrowth and cedars. To the right lay the wharves and warehouses of Lexington's canal terminal, where packets were tied up to the shore with great iron rings. Here General Lee and Custis were waiting to transport them across the river on a small ferry, assist them into a waiting carriage, and escort them up the winding dirt road, past the still-damaged barracks of the Virginia Military Institute, and toward the three colonnaded brick buildings of Washington College.

The *Lexington Gazette*, noting their arrival, reported that "General Lee's family took possession of the Presidential Residence on College Hill," but to Mildred's eyes, their new home a few hundred yards from the college hardly looked presidential.[23] The house was of brick, two-storied in the center, with matching one-story wings, and a front porch with large pillars—almost a dollhouse-sized model of Arlington's architecture. Inside, the front parlor was empty save for an enormous grand piano of carved rosewood, inlaid with pearl, a gift from a piano manufacturer in Baltimore. Behind it in the dining room, Lee's campstools and mess kit substituted for the new furniture, which had not yet arrived, and for the still-buried family silver.* But on the makeshift table the wife of the college's mathematics professor had placed a hot breakfast, and in spite of their weariness and the strangeness of their new surroundings, Rob wrote that "we were all very grateful and happy— glad to get home—the only one we had had for four long years."[24]

---

*Before Rob returned to eastern Virginia, he and a retired sergeant from V.M.I. dug up the silver and the family papers from the spot where Sergeant Hampsey had buried them for safekeeping prior to Hunter's raid. The silver was tarnished, but with polishing it was usable; most of the irreplaceable Washington and Custis letters had rotted or mildewed and had to be burned. According to Mrs. Lee, "Our Washington [letters and papers] were destroyed by the damp during the long time they were underground. I almost wept as I had to commit to the flames papers that had been cherished for nearly a century; those that remained were all defaced and stained" (William Couper, *History of the Shenandoah Valley* [New York: Lewis Historical Publishing Co., 1952], 2:969–71; Mrs. REL to Miss Gertrude Deutsch, 31 January 1873, VHS).

As soon as they had unpacked, Mildred and Rob took a quick look at the town, which stood high above the river with mountains ringing it as far as the eye could see, "shading away in their tints from deep emerald to dreamy blue as they become more and more remote."[25] Simple frame and stone buildings on the narrow streets provided housing and shops for fewer than twenty-five-hundred residents. Lexington was the county seat, as well as the site for two colleges, and the weekly newspaper gave as much space to agricultural concerns and records of local court cases as it did to notices of student debates.

Since the community was so isolated, with the canal route its only direct link with other sections of Virginia, citizens tended to be provincial and straitlaced.* Visitors often commented on the "general tone of soberness and propriety" in the town, which had been founded by Scotch-Irish immigrants, an atmosphere "remarkable when one remembers that . . . seven or eight-hundred boys are there at college."[26] One new student found the townspeople "severe to the point of simplicity; intense in their religious fervor . . . loving and possessing education, yet often narrow-minded."[27] It seemed to him that even the hedges were trimmed with Presbyterian severity. Not surprisingly, Mildred sometimes referred to Lexingtonians as "the Saints."[28]

A few months earlier, Lucy Blain, who had relatives in Lexington, had assured Mildred that she would find her new home "a delightful place." But in February Mildred confessed that she disagreed "in toto. I am often dreadfully lonely, know no one well in the whole town—& have got to such a state that I am delighted whenever the door bell rings. . . . Lucy, do you know what starvation of the *heart & mind is*? I suffer & am dumb!"[29] Though Lee was very busy, the rest of the family led such a quiet life that it could hardly have appealed to a twenty-year-old woman. "Custis is promenading the floor," her father wrote to Agnes, still in Richmond, "Rob reading the papers & Mildred patching her dress. Your Mama is up to her eyes in news, & I am crabbed as usual."[30]

---

*The nearest train was the Chesapeake and Ohio, which stopped in Goshen. From there passengers took a twenty-three-mile, eight-hour stagecoach ride over "the worst and rockyest [sic] roads I ever saw" (David Fleet to his family, 2 September 1871, in *Green Mount After the War, The Correspondence of Maria Louisa Wacker Fleet and Her Family*, ed. Betsy Fleet [Charlottesville, Va.: University Press of Virginia, 1978], 62). Mail and freight arrived by packet boat three times a week or by the daily stagecoach from Staunton, which traveled along the old Plank Road, passing through Lexington on its way to Fincastle and the West. No wonder Robert E. Lee is reported to have said that it made "but little difference" which route people used in coming to Lexington, "for whichever . . . you select, you will wish you had taken the other" (Robert E. Lee, Jr., *My Father, General Lee* [New York: Doubleday & Co., 1904, 1924, 1960], 346).

Slowly, as she became acquainted with neighbors, Mildred changed her mind about the community. One of the family's earliest callers was Margaret Junkin Preston, a gifted poet, daughter of Washington College's former president, sister-in-law and close friend of Stonewall Jackson. Able to combine heavy domestic responsibilities with a lively life of the mind, Mrs. Preston helped Mildred to realize that life in a small town, the dull routine of housework, and the management of unskilled servants need not stultify her intellectual interests. One of Life's first close friends was Elizabeth Preston, Margaret Preston's stepdaughter and a girl about Mildred's own age.

And there were other young women in the community whom she came to know well: two of the Pendleton girls who had been at the Virginia Female Institute with Annie and Agnes; Lizzie Letcher, who had spent the early years of the war in Richmond; and a half-dozen faculty daughters in their early twenties. Indeed, there seemed to be so many young single women that Mildred exclaimed to Lucy Blain, "The number of old maids here quite appalls me. My fate was decided from the first moment I put my foot on shore."[31]

One of the most difficult aspects of Mildred's new life was adjusting to poorly trained servants. Like many Southern women of her generation, she was no doubt glad to be relieved of the chore of managing slaves, but she would have preferred more able household assistants. Before her arrival, her father had hired a man-of-all-work who proved to be "tolerable" but "not very energetic."[32] The cook was even less well prepared, and Mildred had had no experience in teaching basic culinary skills. At Arlington one generation of slaves had trained the next. She knew how to make fancy desserts, but rendering lard, making potato yeast, and pickling peaches were beyond her abilities. "What the cook can't do, remains undone," she admitted.[33] Lee "encouraged us in all our homely duties—in our efforts in dressmaking—housekeeping—would admire the calico dresses we made, with our unskilful [sic] hands—the tomatoe [sic] catsup that would explode!"[34]

Mildred's housekeeping woes were similar to those of many women all over the South, as "high-born ladies" were "demoted from supervisors in the home to manual laborers." Twenty years after Appomattox, in a survey to determine "how the war had most significantly changed" the lives of Confederate women, "all said that doing their own work or adjusting to hired Negro domestics was their major postwar problem."[35]

Nevertheless, in spite of Mildred's inexperience and the cook's uncertain talents, the pantry and larder were well filled. As a New Year's present, twenty-four Confederate veterans from the county gave the family nine hams, two "shoulders," one turkey, one "middling" [salt pork], thirty pounds of buckwheat flour, one barrel of white flour, twenty-two bushels of corn, half a bushel of dried peaches, two bushels of corn meal, one jug of molasses, and crocks of apple and quince butter.[36]

Precious Life was alone with her parents and Custis that first Christmas, as Agnes stayed on in eastern Virginia, Mary Custis remained in Maryland, and Rob, finally well, left for the White House. The winter was long and cold, and in March there were heavy snows. The dismal weather depressed Mrs. Lee, who was used to an earlier spring season at Arlington and Richmond. When warm days finally arrived, Lee set out rose bushes in the front yard and planted a vegetable garden, but Mrs. Lee remained unhappy, for "the sweet spring . . . & all the early flowers in bloom" made her acutely homesick for her old home and "my roses at Arlington."[37] Still hoping to recover the estate, she confided to Mrs. Jefferson Davis that "I feel as a stranger & exile always looking forward to some change in my condition."[38]

Agnes traveled to Lexington from Norfolk in May, bringing Rooney with her for a short visit. Mildred was grateful to have an assistant with the cooking, and Rooney cheered Mrs. Lee. "Fitzhugh has become quite stout," she wrote, "but in spite of all his afflictions . . . has still a gay light heart."[39] Mary Custis stayed in Maryland, moving from the Shore to Baltimore. "We rarely hear from Mary," Mrs. Lee complained. "She is a bad correspondent."[40]

Daughter was probably too busy to write, for she was an active participant in one of the first great charity endeavors of the postwar period. In 1866 a group of Baltimore women, aware of acute suffering below the Mason-Dixon line, organized the sale of donated articles from prominent ladies all over the South, proceeds from which would be sent to Confederate widows and orphans. Heretofore, well-bred women had never permitted their names to be used publicly, for "a woman's name should appear in print but twice—when she marries, and when she dies."[41] Now, suddenly, Mrs. Jefferson Davis, Miss Mary Lee, Mrs. Andrew Johnson, and others permitted their names to be advertised as the donors of portraits, books, and handwork, which sold at huge prices. Mary Custis contributed "a beautifully embroidered cushion, valued at thirty dollars," according to a newspaper article, and Margaret Junkin Preston's long wartime poem *Beechenbrook*, bound in hardcover, was the runaway bestseller of the fair.[42] The Southern Relief Fair drew enormous crowds, not only from Baltimore but also from Washington and Richmond, garnering in one month more than $108,000, which was divided among refugees and veterans' survivors in Maryland, Virginia, and other Southern states. Aristocratic women, including Mary Custis Lee, did not yet feel free to "work publicly," but within the "women's sphere" of church and philanthropic work they demonstrated their ability in the Baltimore Fair of 1866.[43]

Daughter finally came to Lexington in time to greet her parents and sisters just back from a quiet summer at Rockbridge Baths, a family-style spa about eleven miles from Lexington. The new college term opened on September 16, with nearly four hundred students in attendance. Though Mildred had complained of the number of old maids in the community, the ratio of men to eligible young women heavily favored the ladies. Elizabeth Preston commented that "you must have had a crooked back or a squint eye *not* to have had 'suitors' in a town of ... [so many] young men and only thirty girls."[44] For the next five years, the Lee daughters enjoyed a constant round of social life, from the beginning of each college term in the fall through elaborate commencement exercises. Modern readers may consider their activities dull, but there is no question that the young people loved them all and had ample opportunities to court and be courted.

Visiting after supper—or "running," as it was sometimes called—was the principal social function.[45] Each evening young men would go from house to house, chatting with parents, daughters, and each other for an hour or so, then proceed to another home for more rounds of conversation. The Lee girls entertained in the front parlor, while their parents sat in the dining room beyond, with the door between closed discreetly. As the clock struck ten, Lee walked into the parlor to close the front shutters. If this hint were not taken, he said in a firm voice, "Good night, young gentlemen." Occasionally, even this remark was not acted upon readily enough, in which case Lee replaced his daughter in her tête-à-tête. Not having come for sentimental conversation with General Lee, the embarrassed swain made a hasty departure.[46]

In addition to chatting in the parlor, the girls and their friends took long walks, rode horseback, went ice-skating and sleigh riding in cold months, listened to debates and special lectures, and took part in informal dances and formal "hops." Once they attended the performance of a traveling circus when it came to town, though "before the war, a circus had not been considered a very high class entertainment." Agnes' escort was surprised and relieved to see General Lee in the audience. Having the college president there, he felt, "lent dignity even to a circus."[47]

Mary Custis was more fond of walking than her sisters, often taking long, solitary walks along the narrow dirt roads leading toward House Mountain, a rocky mass that dominated the landscape west of town. During one such excursion she met a country man whose horse and wagon had become "mired in a mud hole."[48] Unable to extricate the animal, the mountaineer was striking the horse mercilessly. Always a horse lover, Mary Custis ordered him to stop beating the creature, and she showed him how to maneuver horse and wagon free. Before he could get away, she insisted that he give her his name and directions as to how to reach his cabin on House Mountain. When she returned home, she wrote a note to a member of the student YMCA, explaining the incident and suggesting that some of the young men find the wagoneer, named John Moodispaugh,* and persuade him to attend the student-run Sunday School class held weekly in a tiny chapel not far from where the man lived. Evidently the encounter with Mary Custis had a profound effect upon Moodispaugh, for he stopped drinking, attended chapel regularly, and ultimately became a model citizen.

The winter of 1866–67 was even colder than the preceding one, and the North River froze solid. Before the Lees arrived, ice-skating by ladies was frowned upon as being the recreation of "Yankee women," but no one could question the Southern credentials of Agnes and Mary Custis, who spent long hours on the river. Another cold-weather excursion that same year was a sleigh ride that Mary Custis and Agnes took with two young bachelor faculty members from V.M.I. "In the evening we astonished the natives," Captain Marshall McDonald wrote, "by a genuine old fashioned sleighing party. . . . We drove out about 6 miles into the country and got back about 8 o'clock P.M. We all enjoyed it very much." But strict Lexingtonians disapproved because the two couples had been without a chaperone![49]

---

*The spelling is Mary Custis Lee's, in her words, "so *pronounced*, about the *othography* [sic] I am doubtful." Current spelling in the Lexington telephone directory gives the name three ways: *Muterspaugh, Muterspaw*, and *Mutispaugh*.

In the fall of 1866, the young women of the community organized a coeducational Reading Club, which met weekly on Wednesday nights. "They . . . read a little and talk a great deal," one observer commented.[50] Lee characterized the organization as "a great institution for the discussion of apples & chestnuts, but [it] is quite innocent of the pleasures of literature."[51] Both Agnes and Mary Custis were charter members, and the group met at least once at the Lee home. Agnes wrote to Mildred, who was visiting in Richmond, that the event had been a "real 'success'. . . . We had cake, apples, nuts, & 'iced punch' [which] seemed very palatable."[52] She did not mention books or topics for discussion.* An even more entertaining meeting was held at V.M.I., where the bachelor officers hosted a supper in the cadet laboratory and used the "Engineering Academy" for dancing.[53] "The dancing was kept up until 3 o'clock," one of the hosts, Captain McDonald, reported, "& then I could only get them to leave by having the reel played & sending the music away."[54]

Dozens of young men—students, faculty, and townspeople—became friends of the Lee girls during the years of their father's presidency. There were the "yearlings," as Lee called them, teenagers like shy, fifteen-year-old John Blackmar from Columbus, Georgia, who was made to feel welcome in the Lee home, and there were sophisticated veterans such as brilliant Milton Humphreys, who often knew more than his professors did. There were single teachers—by Lee's characterization "leaders of the herd"—and at least two widowers, Dr. H. T. Barton and Captain John Mercer Brooke, with children nearly as old as Mildred.[55] Dr. Barton, the V.M.I. Post physician and the father of three red-haired orphans, was such a persistent swain of Mildred's that Lee called him "the last rose of summer,"[56] and Captain Brooke, an able naval officer during the war and now professor of astronomy at V.M.I., was a special friend of Agnes'. Forty years of age, with a heavy gray beard and bald head, Brooke seemed too old for Agnes, who was ten years his junior, but friends of the captain hoped she would accept his suit. "If

---

*Though the girls who organized the Reading Club in Lexington were probably not in correspondence with other like-minded groups, similar reading societies were springing up in the 1860s and 1870s all over the country. A respected columnist for young ladies, writing in the *North Carolina Presbyterian*, endorsed the phenomenon as a means for young women to "make themselves fit companions for acute and thoughtful men" (Mrs. Cornelia Phillips Spencer, "Young Ladies' Column," *North Carolina Presbyterian*, 21 September 1870). Though individual groups were usually short-lived, this impetus toward continuing education evolved by the turn of the century into more formalized chautauqua programs, women's clubs, and other literary and cultural vehicles for self-improvement.

Brooke has been so fortunate as to win Agnes Lee," Catesby Jones wrote in 1867, "he is indeed to be congratulated. She was one of my favourites."[57]

As different as the callers were, they were alike in their enormous admiration for General Lee and their uneasiness at meeting him and his family for the first time on a social basis. But quickly made comfortable by the Lee ladies, they returned again and again because they found the daughters attractive and entertaining company. Most agreed that Agnes was the prettiest of the three, Mary Custis the least feminine, and Mildred the most vivacious and appealing. One young law student from Kentucky, Lucius Desha, stated categorically that Mildred "has more good sense than all of them."[58] He also described her as "splendid and lively."[59] An undergraduate, Samuel H. Chester from Mount Holly, Arkansas, was convinced that Mildred was "her father's favorite. She was not beautiful," he recalled many years later, "but had a bright, interesting face . . . a pleasing personality . . . fine literary taste" and a comfortable sense of humor.[60]

On Sundays, when there was a ban on "running," everyone went to church, often more than once. After evensong one night, Mildred walked home with Frank Preston, Elizabeth's brother who had lost an arm during the war and was now teaching Greek and Latin at the college. It was such a pretty evening that he talked her into sitting on the steps for a little while. "Minutes slipped away," Preston remembered later, and "the lingering was lengthening into an un-Sabbatical visit, when the front door opened and the figure of the General stood quietly in the light." The pair jumped to their feet, and Frank Preston disappeared into the shadows, hoping not to have been detected. But he was close enough to hear Mildred say, in a flustered tone, "Ah—Father, is it you? Was there anyone here while I was gone?"

"No, my daughter," Lee replied gravely. "Gentlemen do not visit at my house on Sunday night."[61]

Instead of socializing on Sunday, the Lees, like most of their neighbors, spent their leisure time reading. The girls read novels by Thackeray, Dickens, and Goldsmith, as well as collections of Victorian poetry. Sometimes Lee read aloud from his new copy of the *Iliad,* whose translator, a young English poet named Philip Worsley, had dedicated the volume to him. Only Mrs. Lee scanned contemporary newspapers, keeping the rest of the family up to date with her version of political events and the evils of newly passed Reconstruction acts. "I am the only person in the house except the girls occasionally who reads the papers," she wrote to a friend. "The Genl. & Custis will not look at them, better perhaps for their tempers & peace of mind."[62]

In 1867 General and Mrs. Lee, Mildred, and Agnes joined Grace Episcopal Church near the campus, and the whole family, including Mary Custis, became active in church affairs. Lee served on the vestry, Mrs. Lee directed the church's sewing group from her sitting room, and both Agnes and Mary Custis taught Sunday School when they were in town. In addition, Daughter collected books for the depleted church library, organized benefit bazaars for the building fund, and every Christmas made sure that a cedar tree, elaborately decorated with handmade ornaments, stood in the chancel to be lit at a special Christmas Eve service.

Lee was a gregarious man, and there is no question that he enjoyed observing the social ritual played out by his daughters and their gentleman visitors. But it is equally clear that he was not eager to lose his girls in marriage, for whenever they were away, even on short visits, he missed "their love, care, and attention."[63] He was not, however, opposed in principle to women marrying, even members of his own family, and he told Markie Williams that "you must not say you will never marry. It may be proper as well as becoming in you to marry some of these days."[64] Perhaps what he really hoped for was that his daughters would not marry during his lifetime.

Mrs. Lee was far more concerned that the girls did not appear to be interested in marriage. "My children," she fretted, "seem not to be disposed for matrimony."[65] In another letter, she worried that "the girls. . . seem to be in the position of 'poor Betty Martin' who, you know the song said, could never 'find a husband to suit her mind.' I am not in the least anxious to part with them; yet think it quite time, if they intend to change their condition."[66]

She had reason to feel that Mary Custis' matrimonial prospects dimmed with each year of their stay in Lexington, for after the postwar veterans had graduated, she was much older than most of the students. Agnes was consistently friendly and kind, but to many young men she seemed aloof and reserved. Harry Wickham, frequently in the Lee house during his years at Washington College, was convinced that she was still grieving over the lost Orton Williams. Only Mildred, twenty when she arrived on the campus, had several serious romantic attachments. Samuel Chester, who saw her almost daily from 1869 to 1873, wrote that she "was much sought after by men whose alleged love, she knew, was 'mingled with respect.'" Yet "somehow the right man from her standpoint never came along."[67] Mildred told a friend years later that at least one suitor "had declared his ardent love for her,"[68] but she did not divulge whether she herself had turned the young man down, or whether Lee had refused his suit, as Elizabeth Preston's father had done when she was twenty. The most compelling explanation for Mildred's not marrying is that she was unable to find a young man who could match her father. "To me," she wrote, "he seems a Hero—& all other men small in comparison."[69]

Though their home on the campus had only four bedrooms, the Lees usually kept as boarders a number of young relatives who were attending college. Partly because of the crowded conditions, the girls frequently indulged themselves in long visits away from home,* making sure that at least one of them was always home to keep house and care for Mrs. Lee. Mary Custis traveled the most and the farthest, even venturing north to New York City for a winter with her old friend Helen Peters. Agnes spent time away for her health, and in her longest absence Mildred went with her father to Rooney's wedding to a Petersburg belle, Tabb Bolling. At the festivities Lee was much amused by Mildred's enthusiasm for pretty clothes and stylish hairdos. He wrote his wife that she was "perfectly happy, as she had on last evg. [evening] a dress about 2 yds longer than Norvell's."[70] He described her as "all life, in white & curls."[71]

When two of the girls were away at the same time, there were extra beds for visiting friends and relatives, including Markie Williams, who came several times a year bringing two small orphaned nieces with her. At the end of each academic session, the house overflowed with guests invited to enjoy Washington College's week-long commencement festivities, followed immediately by V.M.I.'s official ceremonies, hops, and parades. Lee wrote to Rob in June of 1869 that "Mildred is full of housekeeping and dresses, and the house is full of young ladies— Misses Jones, Albert, Burwell, Fairfax, and Wickham; others in expectation."[72] The following spring there were so many visitors that Lee relinquished his own room to sleep in the library. Mildred never seemed to have enough of graduation excitement, though her father drily suggested once that she "ought to be . . . satisfied with commencements for this year, having participated in three"—two in Lexington and one at the University of Virginia.[73]

---

*A settlement of the Smith Island property, one item of their grandfather's estate, had brought to each of the three surviving granddaughters more than $3,000 apiece, providing them with travel money without having to request it from their father.

Her various enthusiasms delighted Lee, who called her his "light-bearer" and said that "the house is never dark when she is in it!"[74] Yet he constantly teased her about her handwriting, her weight, her pets, and her habit of offering unsolicited advice. She was a far better correspondent than Mary Custis, but sometimes her handwriting was hard to read. "We held a family council over it [your letter]," Lee commented on one occasion. "It was passed from eager hand to hand & attracted wondering eyes & mysterious looks. . . . Your mother's commentary . . . was that you had succeeded in writing a wretched hand."[75]

For years Mildred had been concerned about being overweight, and once while she was away visiting, she spoke of the rich meals that her hosts provided. "I am delighted at your increased bodily dimensions," her father replied. "One hundred & twenty eight avoirdupois is approximating a proper standard."[76]

Always fond of cats, Mildred now had a whole houseful, including Sidney Baxter (named for a former Virginia attorney general), whom Lee described as the "fashionable colour of moonlight on the water"; Tom the Nipper, a fine mouser who had been "reared in the stable" with Traveller, from whom he had learned "the most refined manners"; and frequent broods of new kittens, whose arrival, Lee wrote, made Life so happy that "the world wags cheerily with her."[77]

During their early months in Lexington, Lee had made fun of Mildred's culinary ineptitude. Now, as she grew accustomed to managing the household and as her self-confidence increased, he teased her about her willingness to offer gratuitous advice to neighbors and relatives. Life "expends her energies in regulating her brother," he wrote to Rob.[78] Later he claimed that she "rules . . . my nephews with an iron rod, and scatters her advice broadcast among the young men of the college. . . . The young mothers of Lexington ought to be extremely grateful to her for her suggestions . . . as to the proper mode of rearing their children."[79] She knew better than to tell her father what to do!

Whenever she was at home, Mildred and her father took long daily rides in the country, Lee erect and dignified on Traveller, Life trotting along behind on Lucy Long, a mare which had been stolen by the Yankees and later returned to the family. "Nothing seemed to rest him like these rides," Mildred recalled, "he would laugh & tease me & let Traveller out to his fullest speed—leaving me far behind on slow little Lucy—then wait for me at the top of the next hill—his eyes sparkling with fun. If I was silent—he would often say 'Life tell me something—tell me about those schoolmates whom [sic] Rob says have experienced every calamity but matrimony!'"[80]

During the summer of 1869 Lee and Mildred took a three-day horse-back trip of thirty-five miles to the Peaks of Otter, a cluster of mountains rising three thousand feet above Liberty, which Mrs. Lee, Agnes, and Mary Custis had visited during the war. Leaving Lexington at daybreak, the pair arrived in time for an early supper at a small hotel perched on the "saddle" between the two main peaks. Next morning they ascended the summit, riding within half a mile of the top, tethering their horses there, and then clambering the rest of the way on foot. The view from the top was magnificent in both directions, to the east a great patchwork of farms and woods, broken by undulating streams, and to the west ridge after ridge of mountains stretching toward the horizon. They "sat for a long time on a big rock," Mildred recounted, "looking at the glorious panorama beneath—the Virginia he loved. He seemed to feel it with all his heart & was very silent."[81]

The descent was quicker, though they were caught in a rainstorm and had to take shelter in a mountain cabin, muddying the floor of the irate housewife. The poor woman was overcome with mortification and embarrassment to learn the identity of her bedraggled visitors. When they reached Liberty and the home of the Burwells, their clothes were still wet, but Mildred was equal to the occasion. She had managed to pack in her small saddlebag not only a fresh dress but also her carefully telescoped hoopskirt. At the dinner hour she swept into the dining room, dry and "glorified in crinoline," much to her father's amusement.[82] They spent the next evening with Captain Buford, who took a special fancy to Mildred, pronouncing her "a real chunk of a gal."[83] Soon after the visit, he sent her a cow as a gift, on condition that she learn to milk it and send him a sample of the butter she had churned.

After living in the "Presidential Residence" for three and a half years, the Lees moved in the spring of 1869 into a new, much larger home nearby, with a spacious downstairs bedroom for Mrs. Lee and a veran-dah around three sides of the house where she could sit in the sunshine and fresh air. Some biographers of Lee have suggested that he modified the house design to incorporate several features from his boyhood home at Stratford, such as four matching chimneys and deep-set win-dows with built-in shutters. But whatever Lee's influence on the architec-tural plans, Mrs. Lee certainly tried to make their new home reminiscent of Arlington. The buff tints of her bedroom and front hall, the "nite green" of the dining room and library, and the rose tone of the parlor were similar to the colors on the first floor of her old home and complemented the rugs and velvet curtains that had originally been chosen to go with the settees and chairs at West Point and Arlington.[84] In the new house there was enough wall space for the Custis portraits and other paintings stored for so long at Ravensworth.*

Though the family lived simply when they were in Lexington, they treated themselves during the summer to vacations at resort spas, six of which were within a forty-mile radius of Lexington. White Sulphur Springs, which had reopened two years after the surrender at Appomattox, quickly renewed its old reputation as a stylish summer watering place. The Lees were there in 1867 and 1869, staying in the "Harrison Cottage," a comfortable, white frame building with a wide porch. Mrs. Lee remained in her room or on the verandah except for daily baths in the mineral waters, but Lee, Custis, and the girls enjoyed walks about the handsome grounds, eating in the spacious dining room, and taking part in balls, concerts, and other evening entertainment. "The girls are always busy at something, but never ready," their father complained. He himself preferred "more quiet."[85]

Memories of the war were still fresh in the minds of Southern guests at White Sulphur Springs, and former Confederates often ostracized the increasing number of Yankee patrons, a situation that distressed Lee and stimulated him to give his first recorded advice to young Southern women concerning reconciliation. Noting a group of Northern guests sitting alone at the side of the ballroom one evening, Lee asked Mildred's friend, Christiana Bond, to help him greet the new arrivals. "I want you to take a message to your young friends" back home, he told her. "Tell them from me that it is unworthy of them as women, and especially as Christian women, to cherish feelings of resentment against the North. Tell them that it grieves me inexpressibly to know that such a state of things exists, and that I implore them to do their part to heal our

---

*At least one of the famous paintings from Arlington had been stolen during the war, the beautiful portrait of Robert E. Lee's mother. During one of her trips abroad years later, Mildred recognized the painting on the wall of an Italian villa. Its embarrassed owner, who had bought the picture not knowing its true identity, hastily returned it to Lexington. Other portraits, notably the West paintings of Colonel and Mrs. Lee made in 1838, were damaged when they were being transported by canalboat to Lexington in 1871. The boat sank, but the portraits were rescued with little damage; they were subsequently sent to Baltimore for restoration (Francis A. MacNutt, "A Lee Miscellany," *Virginia Magazine of History and Biography* 33, no. 1 [January 1925]: 371. See also Mrs. REL to W. W. Glenn, 1 August 1871; Mrs. REL to George A. Kinnear, 16 August 1873, 17 September 1873, and n.d., W&L).

country's wounds."[86] Miss Bond never forgot his words, but Lee's own daughters did not always live up to his injunctions.

During other summers, the family visited Hot Springs, Healing Springs, Rockbridge Alum Springs, and the small hotel at Rockbridge Baths that Lee had visited soon after his arrival in Lexington. In 1868 they were at the Warm Springs Hotel, where Mildred contracted typhoid fever. Lee never left her bedside until, at the end of a month, she was pronounced out of danger. Her recuperation was exceedingly slow, and she did not regain her old vitality and energy till late fall. Grateful for her complete recovery, her father gave her that year every Christmas gift she asked for.

When the college was in session, General Lee worked long hours in his office in the basement of the school's chapel, changing and modernizing the curriculum, counseling students, and handling a voluminous correspondence. Several times between 1865 and 1869 he was ill, his symptoms usually beginning with a chill and congestion, followed by lingering weariness and a sense of weakness. In October of 1869, he again caught a heavy cold, but this time his problems were compounded by severe chest pains and discomfort in his right arm. A student, seeing the president on campus that fall, was "painfully struck with the change in his appearance."[87]

The faculty, also aware of his increasingly poor health, urged him to relinquish his duties temporarily and take a trip south, where, they hoped, warmer weather and plenty of sunshine would revitalize him. Reluctantly, he agreed, and an itinerary was worked out for him and Agnes, also in poor health, to travel by packet boat to Richmond, then down by train through the Carolinas to Florida.

More than any other place, Lee wanted to visit Annie's grave near Warrenton, North Carolina. In 1866 some ladies from the area had erected a monument to Annie's memory in the small Jones Springs cemetery, but he had been unable to attend the ceremonies since his parole did not allow him at that time to leave Virginia. Now he and Agnes drove alone in a buggy to the small graveyard, where Agnes placed white hyacinths and gray moss at the foot of the simple granite obelisk. Together they read the inscriptions—Annie's name and the names of her parents, the dates of her birth and death, and two lines from a favorite hymn.

Perfect and true are all His ways
Whom heaven adores and earth obeys.[88]

"My visit to dear Annie's grave was mournful yet soothing to my feelings," Lee wrote to his wife, "& I was glad to have the opportunity of thanking the kind friends for their care of her while living and their attention to her since her death."[89] Agnes told her mother that the monument looked just as it had been described to them, adding quietly that "it was a great satisfaction to be there."[90]

The remainder of their journey was less restful. Word spread from town to town that General Lee was passing through, and at every train stop there were bands, serenades, and crowds of persons eager to see or speak to him—"wounded soldiers, servants . . . working-men . . . [and] the sweetest little children," Agnes wrote her mother. She enjoyed seeing jasmine and magnolia in bloom, and in Augusta, Georgia, she went roller-skating for the first time in her life. But, like her father, she was worn out by the adulation and the confusion, though she felt that "Papa has borne the journey and the crowds far better than I thought he would."[91] Lee wrote his wife that he hoped he was stronger, but he still complained of "the pain in my chest whenever I walk."[92]

In May he and Agnes were back in Virginia, joining Mrs. Lee at Rooney's home at the White House. (She and Markie Williams had traveled by packet boat to Richmond and from there by railroad.) Mrs. Lee felt that her husband looked "fatter but I do not like his complexion and [he] seems still stiff," and that Agnes appeared "thin, . . . partly owing," she decided, to the girl's new hairdo, an "*immense chignon* which seemed to weigh down and absorb everything."[93]

For more than a year, the *Lexington Gazette* had advertised the ease with which travelers could reach St. Louis by railroad. Soon after Agnes and her father returned to Lexington, Mary Custis decided to journey overland to the city where her parents, Custis, and Rooney had lived in 1838. After six weeks in St. Louis, she joined a group traveling by riverboat up the Mississippi to southern Minnesota. It proved to be an unpleasant excursion, for she was bothered by swarms of mosquitoes, exceedingly high temperatures, and numerous sick children on board. Almost every night she had to leave her steamy stateroom to sleep out on the open deck. A month's stay in Wisconsin and Minnesota was more enjoyable, with boating, picnicking, riding rafts, sightseeing, and even trout fishing. (Though her letter describing her adventures did not mention with whom she stayed, it is possible that she visited her first cousin, Louis Marshall, and his wife, Florence, in Minnesota. After the war, they had gone to the Northwest, where Marshall ran a dairy and engaged in ranching.)[94]

Mary Custis was in Detroit when the new term at Washington College began, her father again in the president's office. His voice was strong as he spoke to the assembled student body in the chapel on September 15, and for the next two weeks he spent part of each day in his office, working on routine matters. During the morning of September 28 he talked to students, wrote a letter, and placed his signature on a photograph for a college sophomore. Then, about one-thirty, he walked slowly up the hill to the new president's house for his midday meal, "as usual, a plate of grapes & then his ordinary dinner," followed by a nap in his favorite armchair by the dining room window, which faced the distant mountains.[95]

He could not rest long, however, because at four he was to attend a vestry meeting. Before leaving the house, he sat in his armchair, listening to Mildred play Mendelssohn's "Songs Without Words" on the piano. When she switched to the dreary "Funeral March," he smiled and commented, "Life, that is a doleful piece you are playing." He did not really want to attend the meeting, he told her, for he hated to "listen to all that pow-wow." Kissing her as he always did before leaving home, he stepped off the porch into steady rain.[96]

The afternoon slipped by, as several students came to call on Mildred. Entertaining them in the parlor, she scarcely noticed when her father returned, till suddenly Custis summoned her to the dining room. "Papa . . . was seated in his place at the head of the table," she wrote, "his head bowed down & looking very strange & speaking incoherently."[97]

For two weeks General Lee lay in his low bed, brought downstairs to the dining alcove, while the doctors worked to rally him. As heavy rains poured down incessantly, the distraught girls tried to tend to his unspoken needs. Mildred nursed her father during the day, Agnes at night, rubbing his hands as they used to do by the fireside at Arlington. Outside, tiny streams turned into raging torrents, forcing the North River over its banks, destroying houses and barns, carrying away the new covered bridge, and cutting Lexington off from mail or telegraph communication.

Days went by, with little change in Lee's condition. He spoke occasionally but most of the time lay quiet, his dark lustrous eyes following the girls about the room or resting upon Mrs. Lee, sitting helpless in her wheelchair by his side. The weather finally cleared one morning, long enough for Mildred to notice sunshine and bright berries in the hedge. That evening Agnes was too busy trying to persuade her father to take his medicine to notice a rare, spectacular display of the aurora borealis lighting up the night sky. But Lexingtonians with their Scotch-Irish heritage shuddered, for they remembered an old Highland superstition, set down in a well-known book of Scottish verse.

All night long the northern streamers
Shot across the trembling sky:
Fearful lights that never beckon
Save when kings or heroes die.[98]

He was so much worse on October 11 that the doctors suggested the family remain with him all night. After an attempt at sleep before midnight, Mildred, Agnes, Custis, and Mrs. Lee knelt beside his bed while Dr. Pendleton read the prayers for the dead. All was still except for the sound of Lee breathing "hard & painfully."[99]

Wednesday, October 12, "a lovely October day . . . found us still watching," Mildred wrote many years later. Around nine o'clock her father "seemed to be struggling—I rushed out for the Doctor." Dr. Madison hurried into the room, took one look, "& without saying a word walked quietly away."[100] At nine-thirty it was all over. Robert Edward Lee was dead at the age of sixty-three.*

For the first time, Mrs. Lee gave way. She put her arms around Mildred and said "do be kind to me now!" Later Mildred wrote, "Oh how my heart aches at the memory of those words—& the need for them——"[101]

The bells in the college chapel and town churches tolled on and on while Agnes dressed her father's body in the black broadcloth suit he

---

*Neither Mrs. Lee nor Mildred recorded any final words by Lee; rather they indicated that he was unconscious on October 12. Colonel William Preston Johnson placed Lee's words, "Tell Hill he must come up!" and "Strike the tent!" near the end of his account of Lee's death, thereby suggesting that these words came within a few hours of the general's death. As this book concentrates on the daughters' story, it seemed best to adhere to Mildred's account (See J. William Jones, *Personal Reminiscences, Anecdotes, and Letters of Gen. Robert E. Lee* [New York: D. Appleton & Co., 1874], 451; *Father*, 440).

The exact time of death was recorded by Fitzhugh Lee, Lee's nephew, in *General Lee* (New York: University Society, 1894), 412.

had purchased for Rooney's wedding. She did not dress him in his Confederate uniform because it "would have been 'treason' perhaps!"[102] Rooney and Rob arrived a few hours later, summoned by telegram as soon as communication was possible. Mary Custis did not reach Lexington until after the funeral.

On the day of the public service, the girls left their mother alone in her room reading old letters to walk with Rooney and Rob down the hill to the chapel, which was draped with black ribbons. October 15 was a warm day, almost Indian summer, but Mildred remembered little except "the crowds, music,—the solemn words [which] made me feel like fainting." She tried hard not to cry as she gazed through her heavy veil at the flower-covered coffin in front of her. Outside, the overflow congregation on the grassy slopes sang her father's favorite hymn, "How Firm a Foundation, Ye Saints of the Lord."[103]

In some ways Mrs. Lee accepted her husband's death more easily than did the girls. Custis took over the presidency of the college, which was renamed Washington and Lee University, and the family stayed in the house which had been built for them but which belonged, at their insistence, to the school. Totally housebound now, Mrs. Lee spent much of her time raising money for the renovation of Grace Episcopal Church by tinting small copies of Custis and Lee portraits that were sold all over the South. For Agnes, Lee's death recalled all the vivid details of Annie's last hours almost exactly eight years before. And Mildred found she could not bear to ride horseback, even avoiding visits to Traveller and Lucy Long in their stalls.* Both girls were haunted by their father's last days, the silence of his sickroom, and his dark, beseeching eyes.

Before Lee's final illness, Rob had announced his engagement to Charlotte Haxall of Richmond, a close friend of Mildred's. Both Agnes and Mildred attended the wedding in October of 1871, a year after their father's death. Their absence left Mary Custis in Lexington to keep house and care for her mother and brother. After her adventures in the West, Daughter found Lexington dreary. "I go no where," she wrote a friend, "see as few people as possible, take long walks & rides in the country & teach my Sunday School."[104]

---

*Nine months after his master's death, Traveller developed lockjaw after stepping on a rusty nail and died. Lucy Long lived on for another twenty years, finally put to death at the age of thirty-three because "she had ceased to enjoy life" (*Father*, 251).

During Advent, she began recruiting students and V.M.I. cadets to sing in the annual carol service and to fix the elaborate Christmas tree. A freshman cadet—or "rat," as a new student at V.M.I. is designated—wrote to his family that Miss Mary Lee, "one of the pillows [*sic*] of the church," had requested his help in the choir, "as she heard I had a very sweet tenor voice."[105] With as little tact as spelling ability or modesty, Cadet Fleet described Miss Mary as being "right old and ugly, but . . . one of the most pleasant ladies I ever saw." He not only sang for the service, but assisted in placing white candles on the tall cedar tree, decorating it "prettier than it ever had been fixed."[106]

After New Year's, when the river ice grew thick, Mary Custis turned to ice-skating, acknowledging that she was quite "proficient. . . . It is the only amusement in which I have partaken for a long time." Already she was eager for another trip, "if Agnes can be forced home by that time."[107] This excursion was to be to Europe, a venture that Mrs. Lee encouraged "if she can find a suitable escort & we can raise the means."[108] However, she admitted that in some ways it "was not so convenient for her to go."[109]

With Agnes back home again and both money and chaperonage arranged, Daughter sailed from New York in June of 1873, visiting England, Scotland, France, Belgium, and Italy. During the winter she wrote that Rome was fragrant and beautiful with "oleanders & violets & roses in bloom."[110] She was still there when she received news of the death of Rob's young bride, the "Beautiful Lottie," who had succumbed to tuberculosis less than a year after her wedding.[111]

From time to time since Appomattox, Mrs. Lee had attempted to retrieve her possessions from Arlington and regain title to her father's property. In 1869 President Andrew Johnson had given permission for the Washington memorabilia to be returned to her, but Congress intervened and forbade their removal from the Patent Office. Again in 1872 Mrs. Lee formally petitioned Congress, this time for compensation for the Arlington estate, and her suit was supported by many Northerners as well as Confederate sympathizers. But as the case dragged on with little prospect of early solution, the invalid decided that she needed to see her old home once more before her death. "The longing I have to revisit it is almost more than I can endure," she had acknowledged three years earlier.[112]

Traveling that distance was not easy for her. Accompanied by Rob, she probably traveled by carriage to Staunton, and from there by train to Alexandria for a short visit with Aunt Maria Fitzhugh, now aged and infirm but nonetheless cordial. From Ravensworth, Mrs. Lee drove in a carriage along the old pike to the familiar Arlington wharf and up the winding road to the mansion house itself. The handsome trees were gone, the house stood empty and ghostlike, and Federal graves had been placed in rows up to the portico itself. "I rode out to my dear old home," Mrs. Lee wrote to a friend, but it was "so changed it seemed but as a dream of the past. I could not have realized that it was Arlington but for the few old oaks they had spared & the trees planted on the lawn by the Genl & myself which are raising their tall branches to the Heaven which seems to smile on the desecration around them."[113]

After her mother's return, Mildred was unusually busy trying to get the house ready for winter and prepare for several college-age cousins coming to live with them. Agnes was sick again, as she had been so many times in recent years, this time with a debilitating intestinal disorder. But Mildred was unaware of just how fragile her sister had become till she moved Agnes from their shared bedroom at the back of the house to Mary Custis' empty room with its eastern exposure and greater ventilation. Always delicate, Agnes now had to lean heavily on Mildred's arm as she tried to walk from one bed to the other. Even the "delicious sunshine" of "those golden Oct. days" and the roses that Mildred placed on the dresser could not bring light to Agnes' "tired eyes" or strength to the listless "white hands." By October 12—the third anniversary of the "day my Father died"—it was apparent even to Mildred that her sister was terminally ill. Agnes tried to be grateful for "all this kindness & nursing," but her suffering was too intense for many words. "In the afternoon my poor suffering mother was brought up in her chair—& sat close to her bedside holding her hand—the tears streaming down her face." Agnes lay much of the time in a stupor, rousing occasionally to murmur that "I never cared to live long, I am weary of life" and to request that Markie be given her Bible. "You know *Orton* gave it to me," she said. Night came on, and the firelight flickered in the silent room, so like the scene in the dining room three years before, except that tonight the stars were shining brightly outside the window. In the darkness Agnes asked for Custis. When he came and took her hand, she whispered, "You must not forget me when I am gone." He stroked her hand, saying, "Aggie none of us will do that."[114]

Then the breaths came slower and slower, until "one gasp—& all was over for ever! Day was just about dawning in the East, when her pure, her heroic spirit took its flight—ah whither, who can tell! I rushed down stairs to tell Mama. . . . when I told her Agnes was dead, [she] cried 'my poor child, that I should have outlived her. Oh that I could have seen her again!'" Mildred then "laid two roses on Agnes' dead heart, gathered from the bush Papa planted."[115] Eleanor Agnes Lee was only thirty-two.*

The death of her favorite child was more than Mrs. Lee's frail constitution could endure. Her mind began to wander and she thought herself back at Arlington, with all her "little children again." Occasionally, sitting in an old red morocco chair with Love, her "much petted cat," in her lap, she would smile "in her sweet old way," but she wept whenever Agnes' name was mentioned. Watching her mother, Mildred could not help feeling that "the God she had so faithfully served had deserted her in that time of peril and I resented her cruel tortures." The physical and mental deterioration lasted only a fortnight. "The end was drawing near—the life of unselfish Love—of daily sacrifice—of high poetic tastes, & simple faith in Christ, of total self abnegation, was closing forever."[116] By the time Rooney and Rob had returned from eastern Virginia, their mother was already unconscious. She died in the night on November 5, at the age of sixty-six. The cause of death was listed as "rheumatism."[117]

Together, the three brothers and Mildred buried her between General Lee and Agnes, whose grave was still covered with flowers placed there only three weeks before. "Ah, how sacred the Chapel had become," Mildred later reminisced. Custis and Mildred spent that winter alone in the "emptied silent house, where every room echoed with dead voices!"[118]

---

*Two days after Agnes' death, David Fleet, still at V.M.I., wrote to his mother that "Miss Agnes Lee . . . died two . . . days ago with cholera morbus." The term, used frequently in the late nineteenth century, is defined in a medical dictionary as "any acute severe gastroenteritis" (David Fleet to his mother, 17 October 1873, quoted in *Green Mount After the War*, 116. Blakiston's *Gould Medical Dictionary* [New York: McGraw-Hill Book Co., 1931], 301).

7

"The Pathways of Life Alone"

1873–1918

OF THE FOUR SISTERS, only Mildred and Mary Custis were left now, the youngest and the eldest, nearly ten years apart in age and utterly different in temperament and interests. Mildred had inherited from her father his warm, sensitive, family-oriented nature, with a strong sense of duty, while Mary Custis, assertive and unafraid, exhibited his qualities of leadership, persuasiveness, and zest for new adventures. With few family ties to hold them together, the two women grew further and further apart as their lives moved in remarkably divergent paths.

Mildred was only twenty-seven when she buried her mother, but by the end of that first long, dreary winter alone, she had begun to look years older, her lined face and graying hair visible signs of exhaustion and tension. A decade later, when a classmate from St. Mary's saw her at White Sulphur Springs, she hardly recognized in the "large, fleshy woman, . . . [whose] hair was snow white" the blithe Mildred Lee she had known in boarding school.[1]

In contrast, Mary Custis grew more striking as she aged, her dark curls and erect carriage making her a handsome and arresting figure. During the summer when Mildred and Mrs. Parker met at the "Old White," Mary Custis was in Mexico City, where the American consul,

David Strother, described her in his diary. "She is dark," he noted, "about 50 years of age, of good figure . . . great vivacity, & good sense." A former correspondent for *Harper's Magazine* and a Union officer during the war, Strother was surprised to find himself liking Mary Custis more each day of her visit, in spite of what he termed "the bias of her southern education & position."[2]

In 1873 Mary Custis had already embarked on a routine of travel and new experiences. But Mrs. Lee's death forced Mildred to adjust her life greatly. As long as she could remember, she had tried to "take care of Mama," and after the war she had assumed new responsibilities, nursing Agnes and providing emotional support for her father in his readjustment to civilian life. With all three gone, life seemed unbearably empty. "The winter has glided by," she wrote early in 1874, "teaching me to bear the stillness and coldness of my present life."[3] As she answered letters of condolence, sorted through her mother's belongings, and discarded mementos from Agnes' happier days, she was understandably bitter that Mary Custis, in Rome, was too far away to share her painful tasks. "Mary you know is still abroad," she told her cousin Harry Lee, "and Custis and I have to bear our sorrow alone—and together—in a home once so happy, but now so desolate."[4]

Instinctively, she reached out to friends for comfort and support. Washington and Lee's professor of history and English literature offered her volumes of verse and religious treatises. Margaret Junkin Preston wrote a touching poem, "Agnes Has Gone," whose words, Mildred wrote gratefully, expressed "just what my weary heart was silently moaning, all those glorious, decaying, autumn days."[5] Her most congenial companion that winter, however, was neither scholar nor literary figure, but a housewife about her own age, Mary McDonald, the wife of V.M.I.'s chemistry professor. An unpretentious and friendly young woman, Mrs. McDonald frequently sent tasty treats from her kitchen to the Lees' lonely table and often invited Mildred to have tea with her and her husband, Marshall, along with their lively three-year-old daughter, Rose.* It was the first time in her life that Mildred had been close friends with a young couple, and she warmed to their kindliness and the spontaneous affection of their winsome child.

---

*Colonel and Mrs. Marshall McDonald spelled their name *McDonald*, as his record in the V.M.I. alumni files indicates. Their daughter, Rose, the author of a valuable biography of Mrs. Lee, spelled her name *MacDonald*.

Her fondness for the McDonalds and her loneliness at home stimulated a sudden longing for marriage and family. There was little happiness, she said, "for those who tread the pathways of life *alone*," and her future as a single woman now seemed unutterably bleak. "Time flies & life is soon over," she wrote to a former suitor on the occasion of his marriage, "& in the quiet grave we are soon forgotten."[6] Perhaps she had been shortsighted when she measured every young man against her enormously attractive father. "Most women when they lose such a Father," she admitted, "replace it [*sic*] by husband & children. I have had nothing———"[7]

If Mildred Lee had lived a decade or two later, she might have filled the vacuum by taking up a career or engaging in charitable activities. But in the years just after the Civil War, few high-born Southern women worked outside the home unless forced to do so by economic necessity. For Mildred to have taught school or served as a "companion" to an elderly heiress would have implied that her father had been unable to provide adequately for her support. She did take part in a variety of church endeavors, supplying treasured recipes for money-making parish cookbooks and working for church bazaars and dinners. But she had been so thoroughly trained to believe that women's service must be channeled primarily through the home that any outside projects seemed extraneous to the all-important tasks of the homemaker. She now understood with frightening clarity that the loss of Arlington had taken from her not only a physical abode, but a portion of her identity and purpose as well. "Be thankful you have your own little home," she told a friend sadly. "Anything can be endured if you have that."[8]

Respectability decreed that an unmarried woman live with relatives, devoting all her energies toward promoting their happiness, whether or not this brought any personal satisfaction. "The single woman embroiders the clothes of other people's children," a correspondent for a women's column wrote bitterly in 1870. "She climbs other people's stairs, or sits by her solitary fire contriving how to benefit other people's families."[9]

Mildred was fortunate in having three brothers with whom she might choose to live, all three fond of her and all probably willing to welcome her into their households. She had always found Rooney the most congenial, but he and his wife now had more than enough to occupy them, with a growing family, a recent move from the White House plantation to Ravensworth (which Rooney had inherited in 1874 from Fitzhugh relatives), and the serious illness of their youngest child. It seemed far more logical for Mildred to stay in Lexington with Custis or move to Romancoke to be with Rob, who did not remarry till 1894.

She was eager to be of use to Custis, whom she regarded with the combined respect and affection of a much younger sister. "Few sisters are blessed with such a guide and protector as I have in Custis," she wrote.[10] But the two were very different. He was painfully shy, reticent, and neat to the point of fastidiousness, while she was effervescent and outgoing. The quiet, orderly household he sought contrasted sharply with the relaxed, hospitable home she would have preferred. And Custis was having problems of his own. After years of remission, rheumatoid arthritis, the disease that had crippled his mother, suddenly returned to plague him.* At the same time, he came to the realization that Washington and Lee's board of trustees had chosen him as president more for his name than for his initiative. Physically sick and emotionally frustrated, trapped as "the beneficiary of an undesired nepotism," he simply withdrew into himself.[11] He did not even seem to need his sister as housekeeper since his valet, William Price—"my chamber maid, who is a man," Custis used to call him—ran the household, organized the kitchen, and supervised the boarding students still living in the president's house.[12] The only time Mildred sensed that Custis was truly grateful for her presence was at graduation, when she served as a kind of hostess for the many guests at the college.

She was far happier with Rob "in his solitary home,"[13] keeping herself busy gardening, housecleaning, "arranging, destroying, casting out, repairing all day."[14] "There is not a hole or corner of the house," she wrote a friend, "that has not been swept & garnished."[15] In spite of a constant battle with slovenly, poorly trained servants, she found time to read books, ride horseback, and enjoy "the society of one man, whom I happen to love!"[16]

For more than fifteen years Mildred alternated between Romancoke and Lexington, usually spending the autumn and winter months on the Pamunkey with Rob and returning to Custis' home late each spring in time for commencement. Though she now felt no enthusiasm for the hectic pace of the graduation period, indeed wishing she could "cross the ocean to avoid" its confusion, she felt duty-bound to "help Custis by

---

*Custis' first symptoms of arthritis came in 1859, when he was stationed in San Francisco in the army, but the stiffening and disability seem to have lessened in the years between 1860 and 1874.

being there," as she presided over the annual president's reception, attended commencement balls attired in white muslins and silks, and planned meals and made beds for the influx of guests arriving to see sons and friends graduate.[17] "Miss Mildred has a houseful of company," a young visitor wrote one summer, adding perceptively that a crowded house was "a thing she cannot endure."[18]

The young guest had sharper eyes than most of Mildred's friends, who seldom sensed her continuing malaise and inner unhappiness. Reared to be entertaining and outwardly cheerful, she showed appropriate enthusiasm for Lexington news and always seemed interested in activities at the college, such as the literary society debates and the annual boat races at graduation between two rowing teams, the "Harry Lees" and the "Albert Sidney Johnstons." When she was on the campus, students continued to find her a warm and sympathetic friend and showed their appreciation by christening one of the school's racing shells "The Mildred Lee." Years later John M. Glenn, an undergraduate from the class of 1879, remembered that she had been "one of the brightest, most stimulating, & wittiest women I ever met."[19]

To many Southern women struggling against the grinding poverty of the Reconstruction period, Mildred's life must have appeared easy and glamorous, as she lived comfortably with Rob and Custis, traveled to summer resorts in hot weather, and took a number of trips abroad. From far-off places she wrote back charming letters about her adventures, describing Queen Victoria's Jubilee processions where "royal coaches in scarlet livery" whisked "kings & queens of every nation, clime, & colour" past her admiring eyes,[20] cataloging the icebergs, spouting whales, and eider ducks she viewed on a voyage to the North Sea, and recounting her arduous ascent up the great pyramid of Egypt, "with the assistance of 4 Arabs, who clutched & pinched me in every part of my body."[21]

Only occasionally in letters from abroad did she hint at the pervasive loneliness she could not escape even in the midst of crowds or in the excitement of new experiences. From the chateau country of Brittany she wrote of her longing to be in Lexington, in "that quiet valley . . . where my loved ones lie sleeping!"[22] On a Mediterranean journey she acknowledged that she felt "the need of someone to take care of me, sadly. Oh, celibacy, where are the charms!"[23] One spring day in Venice, as she sat on the hotel balcony with gondolas gliding silently along the canals below, she felt frighteningly alone until she opened letters from home that made her "happy to know there are kind true hearts . . . who are thinking of me sometimes, & who care whether I live or die!"[24]

When Mrs. Preston asked permission to write the story of her life, Mildred was understandably flattered, but at first she demurred with typical Victorian modesty, suggesting that she had not "done anything that the world should wish to know my face or story!" The request touched a hidden chord of bitterness, however, and she went on to indicate that "the true history of my life—and I suppose of any woman's—would read stranger, sadder, more inexplicable than any romance that ever was written."[25] She was no doubt referring in part to her personal disappointment at not having married, but her mention of collective unhappiness surely reflected the frustration that she, and other Southern women of her generation, felt at the passivity imposed on them by society. Their helplessness was eloquently described a few years later by Virginia-born Ellen Glasgow as she wrote of the dilemma facing girls who had been born prior to the Civil War.

> Every girl . . . was destined for a heritage of love or of barrenness—yet she was forbidden to exert herself either to invite the one or to avoid the other. . . . Was that a woman's life after all? Never to be able to go out and fight for what one wanted![26]

An undercurrent of uneasiness for the entire family was the continued uncertainty regarding Arlington. Custis had begun in 1874 a series of attempts to reclaim the estate, but the case moved slowly and was finally referred to the Supreme Court. In 1882 that body ruled that the national government had acted illegally in seizing Arlington and must either return the property or pay appropriate indemnity. Since Custis had no desire to live in a Federal cemetery and since forty thousand graves could hardly be relocated, he accepted the offer by Congress of $150,000 in return for formally relinquishing the family's claim to the mansion and its eleven-hundred-acre estate. Once the sum had been paid to him as residuary legatee, he divided a portion of the total between his two remaining sisters as completion of their grandfather's legacy.

The women accepted the irrevocable loss of Arlington and the accompanying financial settlement in characteristically different ways. For Mildred no monetary worth could be placed upon the "Kingdom of my childhood," and she remembered nostalgically her mother's rose garden, her own favorite hiding place under an old seringa bush, and her grandparents' graves, "inseparably associated with the old life at Arlington."[27] But neither legal decision nor payment of fees could remove from her the values that Arlington symbolized and by which she continued to live her life—gracious hospitality, carefully nurtured family ties, and the traditional social conservatism of an antebellum household.

Though she had vigorously supported Custis in his suit, Mary Custis had little sentimental attachment to the house and estate, and she had no qualms about using her share of the money. Whether or not she ever acknowledged the fact, even to herself, it was undeniably true that with the loss of Arlington she acquired more personal liberty than she could ever have had in her prewar role of hostess and occasional domestic manager of the plantation.

Travel, constant change, and novel experiences came to be as important to Mary Custis as a home environment was to Mildred. Between 1870 and the outbreak of the First World War, she lived abroad most of the time, visiting more than twenty-six different countries. Often she made her headquarters near colonies of American expatriates in London, Rome, or Paris, taking short excursions and then returning to her central location. But she did spend an entire year in Australia, traveling about with free passes on the New South Wales and Victoria railroad lines, and she took at least one round-the-world cruise with stops in India, Ceylon, Java, Hong Kong, and Japan. More unusual than the number of countries she visited was the ingenious way she managed to experience out-of-the-ordinary adventures, occasionally initiating escapades that could have been disastrous.

She dined with the Dutch governor of Java, sat through formal dinners with the American legation in Tokyo and Rome, attended a meeting of the International Medical Congress in London by pretending to be "the 'wife' of a doctor," and received an invitation for a special audience at the Vatican with His Holiness, Pope Leo XIII. She bought silks in Japan, played roulette in Monaco, traveled overland in Russia without a guide, took the cure at Baden-Baden, and spent an extraordinary Christmas vacation "at a native court" as the guest of an Indian maharaja, a week she described as "a piece out of the Arabian Nights!" In rural England she sustained a nearly calamitous fall through the ceiling of an old cathedral, and in Constantinople she bribed her way into the Moslem mosque of Santa Sophia where any woman—especially a female infidel—would be killed if apprehended. Only the inability to change schedules kept her from making "an impression never to be erased" by paddling to the upper reaches of the Congo River where no white woman had ever ventured, in the company of the Reverend William Taylor, Methodist Bishop of Africa.*28

In 1878 she was the unwitting cause of a potential international incident when she accidentally set fire to her mosquito netting in a Naples hotel. Two young American tourists, Samuel Melton and Washington Clark, gallantly responded to her cries for help, beating out the flames and rescuing as many of her belongings as they could—"purse, jewelry, slippers, burning shawls, and all sorts of woman's doings." When the Italian hotel keeper asked for exorbitant reparations, the youthful travelers grew angry. Hot words were followed by fisticuffs, and a real brawl might have resulted if the American consul had not arrived to arbitrate the dispute. After their nocturnal adventure, Melton and Clark were too weary to tour Pompeii, but Mary Custis departed in good spirits, charred luggage and all, bound for Marseilles. "Luck go with her," Samuel Melton wrote to his wife. "I wish I'd never seen her."29

Similar sentiments had been expressed in February of that same year by a group of Americans living in Egypt, after Mary Custis had arrived for an extended visit in Cairo. The Americans, most of them former Confederate and Union officers working for the Egyptian army, were glad to arrange trips to the pyramids and escort the visitor to the native quarter to see dancing dervishes. They were distinctly annoyed, however, when she refused to attend a dinner party given by the senior American official, Colonel Charles P. Stone, in honor of former President and Mrs. Ulysses S. Grant. "I wouldn't sit down at the same table with General Grant to save his life," Mary Custis was quoted as announcing. Her outspoken comment prompted one American to remark wryly that she was not only "middle-aged [and] uninhibited," but also had a "mind of her own" and was "as unrestrained in her speech as she was unconventional in her conduct."30 Young Fanny Stone was less charitable. Irri-

---

*Bishop Taylor was a native of Rockbridge County, Virginia, who soon after his ordination preached in San Francisco during the Gold Rush, then served as an itinerant evangelist in England, Australia, India, and South America. In his travels he may well have met Mary Custis (See Charles W. Turner, "'California' Taylor of Rockbridge: 'Bishop of the World,'" in *Rockbridge Historical Society Proceedings* 9:97–108, 1975–79).

tated that the visitor had refused to attend her father's party, Fanny described Mary Custis as "a horribly ugly old maid, and very *queer*."[31]

Her subsequent visits to Egypt were far pleasanter after she had made the acquaintance of Horatio Herbert Kitchener, England's flamboyant, mustachioed military hero who was later knighted in honor of his conquest of the Sudan. On one occasion in Constantinople, Mary Custis was excluded from an excursion party bound for Egypt. She immediately notified Kitchener of her predicament. Members of the party were astonished to learn that Kitchener promptly sent a private ship to carry Mary Custis to Egypt. One member exclaimed, "What in the world is she—merely the daughter of a defeated General—that General Kitchener should take such notice of her?" "That is the reason," another replied. "She *is* the daughter of that defeated General."[32]

On her occasional visits back to the United States, Mary Custis was eagerly interviewed by Northern newspaper reporters, whose descriptions of General Lee's daughter ranged from effusive to unflattering to critical. One story, for example, characterized her as a "brilliant, original, and cultivated" woman, whose "handsome and intellectual personality . . . makes whomever she visits warm friends as well as ardent admirers." This journalist was struck by her jewelry and exotic necklaces of "uncut stones of great value" and curious items fashioned from family keepsakes, like the "silver and Rhine-stone [*sic*] buckles" once worn by Geroge Washington which now decorated her shoes. Another reporter, however, spoke of her as "large and masculine-looking," with a "proud, calm face" and "a reputation for extreme hautiness [*sic*]." Whatever their personal bias, these Northerners all acknowledged that "Miss Lee has become one of the ever-increasing colony of Americans who find in Continental Europe a freedom from social responsibility that oppresses them at home."[33]

Southerners tended to be baffled by her, admiring her courage and adventuresome spirit but uncomfortable at the contrast between the daughter and her illustrious father, whose unsullied image grew larger and less realistic with every passing year. They were particularly disturbed by her arrest in Alexandria, Virginia, in 1902 for allegedly breaking newly enacted Jim Crow laws. Boarding a streetcar in company with her black maid, Mary Custis had sat down with the servant in the back section of the car reserved for "colored" patrons. When she refused to move, she was arrested by the embarrassed conductor, forced to post a bond of five dollars, and summoned to police court before the city's mayor. She simply ignored the arraignment and forfeited her bond.[34]

But in spite of her action, she was no reformer and like her parents regarded blacks as inherently inferior. Rather, her response appears to have been a purely personal reaction to an irritating regulation that interfered with her traditional travel arrangements.

Southern conservatives also feared that, because of her independent ways and uninhibited attitudes, she was an advocate of women's votes. But she was not interested in women's suffrage, stating emphatically that "a woman, if she is reasonably attractive, can get everything she wants from men without a vote."[35]

Living abroad so much and growing apart from the rest of the family, Mary Custis seldom felt the need to come to Lexington. When she was in the community, she did not stay with Custis but instead paid long visits to old friends, who found the disruption of their households wearing. Their children were even more uncomfortable, endlessly pressed into running errands for the demanding guest in return for what seemed like worthless trinkets from all over the world.[36]

The two sisters seldom crossed paths, and indeed they were not often in the United States simultaneously. In 1884, however, they were invited together to attend the unveiling of a statue of their father in New Orleans, and six years later they rode in the same carriage through the streets of Richmond for the dedication of that city's Lee Memorial. In 1891 they met again, this time at Ravensworth for a sadder purpose, to be with Rooney in his last illness.

After his move to Ravensworth, Rooney had entered politics, first as a state senator and later as an immensely popular United States congressman from Virginia's Eighth District. He was taken ill not long after his reelection and suffered intensely during the summer and early fall of 1891. Yet he managed to creep outdoors into the old familiar garden, to sit under the shade of the catalpa trees, and to reminisce about days gone by with his sisters. In October his condition worsened, and on the fifteenth of the month, "the same day Agnes died—nineteen years ago," Mildred recalled, William Henry Fitzhugh Lee died at the age of fifty-four.[37] The family buried him at Ravensworth, beside his grandmother Lee, several Fitzhugh ancestors, and the two daughters and tiny son from his second marriage who had died in infancy.*

---

*In 1922 his body was moved to the family crypt in Lee Chapel, Lexington.

While her brothers and Mary Custis prepared to return to Lexington, Mildred retired to the library, "with the firelight, & warmth, & flowers, & light," to write out an account of the death of her "warm & loving-hearted brother." It seemed uncanny, almost malevolent, that Rooney should have died on the anniversary of Agnes' death, the same day in October on which, twenty-one years earlier, her father had been buried. As she stared out the window, she saw "the same golden sunshine [and] changing foliage" she had viewed those other sad autumn days, while within herself she experienced "the same tears & pain at parting. . . . Dear, dear Fitzhugh—Goodnight."[38]

The four surviving siblings were in Lexington together for Christmas that year, with both women at the president's house and Rob now residing in the area as the executive of a Rockbridge County mining company. Mary Custis made plans to travel to Bermuda, but Mildred, distraught and troubled, found the holiday season difficult and was not yet able, she wrote, "to take up my old life & thoughts."[39] Rob's move from Romancoke to Lexington had broken the fragile pattern of her yearly routine, and she missed the relaxed atmosphere and quiet companionship she had enjoyed with him on his farm.

When Rob left Lexington in 1893, he did not return at once to Romancoke but moved instead to Washington to enter the real estate business. A year later he married a young cousin, Juliet Carter, from a river plantation not far from Romancoke. Returning to the farm after their marriage, the couple made a special effort to make Mildred feel welcome, and once more she found herself happier at Rob's home than anywhere else. "I was very well & very happy at Romauncoke," she told a friend. "I was so much interested there in gardening & improving, & lived out of doors chiefly. . . . It is always a comfort to be with Rob, who is so good to me."[40]

After the birth of two nieces, Mary Custis and Anne Carter Lee, she found the attraction of Romancoke even greater. "My two precious nieces occupied my entire time & heart," she confessed. "One must have *something* to love in this world. They are the most fascinating, sweetest little beings, I ever saw."[41]

She had little opportunity during 1897, however, to visit with Rob and his wife but instead spent weary months with Custis, who was finally leaving the presidency of the college after twenty-six years. Late in December of 1896, sick and despondent, he had submitted his sixth letter of resignation to the board of trustees, indicating that he felt "utterly useless" as the president and foresaw "little probability of ever

being useful to the University."[42] Heretofore, the board had persuaded
him to reconsider, but this time it accepted what he had wanted for so
long, voting him the title of "president emeritus" and offering him
continued use of the president's house.

Though it would have been simpler to have remained in Lexington,
Custis was determined that "the original plan should be carried out"
and the house made available for the new president, William L. Wilson,
who had served as postmaster general under Grover Cleveland. "It
would be different if we were in want," Mildred wrote to a member of
the board, "but as it is, it would be impossible to accept so much." More
telling was the argument, "as Custis always says, 'Our Father refused this
house & we should be guided by him.'"[43]

When Dr. Wilson arrived in Lexington for a visit early in March, he
found Mildred far more helpful and informative than Custis, whom he
saw only in his "darkened bed-room." The new president noted in his
diary that Mildred seemed "bright" and unusually knowledgeable
about college affairs, and he expressed "a pang in anticipating the
occupancy of a house, endeared to her by so many sacred memories of
parents, and now darkened by the ill health and despondency of her
brother."[44]

During the next four months Mildred sorted and packed furniture,
books, and other accumulations of thirty years' residence in one house.
She sent the most valuable heirlooms and documents to Ravensworth,
gave large pieces of furniture to Lexington friends, and put much of the
rest into boxes in the attic above Traveller's old stall. One of her hardest
tasks was going through the large number of souvenirs from all over the
world that Mary Custis, presently in Rome, had accumulated and stored
in the house.

Most trying of all was parting with intimate family items. Custis had
sometimes teased her about her reluctance to give away household
reminders that had belonged to their parents and grandparents. "It's as
hard to get blood out of a beet," he used to say, "as to get anything out of
Mildred."[45] Now, however, she had no choice. She and Custis managed
to distribute "nearly everything . . . in the way of mementos or relics."[46]
Often Mildred included poignant notes in her parcels. "I have just
mailed you a little box containing some souvenirs of my dear Father &
Mother," she wrote Mary Cocke of Bremo. "I know how much you loved
them—& want you to have these little tokens"—a smoking cap, gold
braid from an overcoat, and a Bible of General Lee's, along with a paper
cutter "constantly used by my Mother until her death." Her letter was

brief, she explained, because "we are just about to break up our home—I am too tired & weary & sad to write about it."[47]

Finally, on July 29, 1897, Mildred left the house to which she had moved thirty years before, and Custis departed four days later to take up residence at Ravensworth at the invitation of Rooney's widow, Tabb. Once away from the campus, he gradually improved in health,* living on at Ravensworth for another fifteen years, puttering about the gardens, working on small architectural designs at his engineer's bench, and enjoying "a quiet, more or less secluded life."[48]

Months of packing and decision making had left Mildred exhausted, physically and emotionally. To regain her strength, she took a trip to Europe, but new scenes did little to cheer her. "I am very weak nervous & low spirited," she wrote to her friend Mrs. Hay. "I never in all the trials & sorrows of my life have suffered more than in the last 3 months—not so much physically—but in the feeling of loneliness, & helplessness . . . feeling so far away & so *alone*." She longed for the happier days of the past "with Custis & all the kind good friends at home" in Lexington.[49]

Mary Custis came from England to France to be with her, but there was now little congeniality between the two sisters. "You know she is not sympathetic with weakness or nervousness," Mildred confided to Mrs. Hay, "& is always absorbed in self first & foremost. . . . I try to steel myself against her sharp words . . . but now, weak & wretched as I am, it is doubly hard to bear."[50]

Slowly over the next few years Mildred regained her emotional equilibrium and much of her old enthusiasm, spending winter and spring months at Romancoke as before, then traveling to the mountains in hot weather. In 1905 she went to New Orleans for Mardi Gras and visited the widow of her old friend, William Preston Johnston. Easter was late that year and the weather was already balmy for the Shrove Tuesday parades on March 7. There were so many people to see, including

---

*Though Ollinger Crenshaw, in the university's official history, *General Lee's College*, does not mention the possibility that at least some of Custis Lee's problems might have come from heavy drinking, there are suggestions in contemporary letters that alcohol aggravated his attacks of melancholia. The only outright confirmation the author can find to substantiate this rumor comes from an interview that Greenlee Letcher had, many years later, with William Patton, a clerk in "Larrick Gents Clothing Store" in Lexington, in which Patton testified that Custis "drank and would get on sprees, but that no one ever saw him as he kept close in the house if such was the case" (Greenlee Letcher's interview with William Patton, 10 April 1940, TS, W&L).

Washington and Lee alumni and Confederate veterans, that she lingered on for several weeks after the holiday. All who saw her remarked on how unusually well and cheerful she seemed.

On the evening of Sunday, March 26, a group of old soldiers came to call. When she showed them to the door to say good-bye, she announced that she was "seriously thinking of buying a house here and settling down and spending the remainder of my days" in New Orleans.[51] She had always been a favorite among veterans' groups, and these men who had fought under General Lee were excited to think that she might live among them for a quarter century or more.

The following morning, when she failed to appear for breakfast, her hostess knocked at her closed door. There was no response. Entering her bedroom, Mrs. Johnston was horrified to find Mildred sprawled on the floor unconscious with what appeared to be a massive stroke. In spite of the attempts of doctors to revive her, Mildred Lee died at nine o'clock in the morning on March 27, 1905, at the age of fifty-nine.

The suddenness of her death shocked the entire South. Flags flew at half-mast, and at the Soldiers' Home in New Orleans the Confederate Stars and Bars were draped in black crepe. A group of veterans and Washington and Lee alumni accompanied the coffin on the long train ride east to Atlanta and from there north to Lynchburg. All along the route people who had known her, or her father, brought floral tributes or simply stood silent as the train moved slowly through Spartanburg, Charlotte, and Danville. At dusk on March 30, the special funeral cars from Lynchburg pulled into the Lexington depot to be met by faculty members and students from both Washington and Lee and V.M.I., as well as official delegations of veterans and the United Daughters of the Confederacy.

In the R. E. Lee Memorial Episcopal Church, only a few doors from the president's house, the rector led family members and an overflow congregation in the simple burial service, which included the singing of the hymn used at her father's funeral, "How Firm a Foundation." Then eight student pallbearers carried "the body . . . across the University campus, on the most lovely of spring days," to the crypt where her parents and Agnes already lay.[52]

The eulogies, editorials, and tributes to Mildred Childe Lee were numerous and affectionate. The college faculty remembered "the esteem in which this University was ever held by Miss Mildred";[53] Confederate veterans commented on "her frank, ingenuous manner, and that utter lack of assumption which marks the high-bred woman";[54]

and the Mary Custis Lee Chapter of the United Daughters of the Confederacy claimed "a precious memory of her radiant girlhood in her father's home here in Lexington."[55] But the comment she perhaps would have appreciated most came from a group of college students, the Harry Lee Boat Club, who wrote:

> In the death of Miss Mildred Lee our club has lost a true, loyal and warm supporter whose place cannot be filled.... We hereby express our deep sense of appreciation for the past and our sorrow for the loss of her whom we have so lo[ng] honored.[56]

Among the signers of that resolution was Lucius Junius Desha, the son of the Kentucky law student who in 1871 had called his friend Mildred Lee "splendid and lively." The warm, spontaneous appreciation of father and son, representing thirty-five years of collegiate friendship, was an exceptional tribute accorded to few women.

———

Mary Custis was in Nice when she learned of Mildred's death. To return for the funeral was impossible, so for the third time she was absent at the final rites of a sister. Except for occasional visits in the United States, she lived abroad for the next decade in southern France, Germany, Italy, and Egypt until the outbreak of the First World War. Caught in Germany when hostilities began, she managed to work her way through Holland to London, where she was interviewed by the British correspondent for the *New York World*. She had learned enough about modern battle and trench warfare to be sickened. "I am a soldier's daughter, and descended from a long line of soldiers," she declared. "But what I have seen of this war, and what I can foresee of the misery which must follow, have made me nearly a peace advocate at any price. My father often used to say that war is a terrible alternative, and should be the very last . . . I often wonder, with many misgivings, if, in this case, war was the last alternative." Remembering the "dark days of one of the world's great civil wars," she concluded, "my sympathy is with suffering wherever it exists, with the brave men who are fighting and suffering in the trenches and with the brave women who in practically all homes in Europe are waiting and suffering."[57]

Coming back to the United States in 1914, she established residency in Washington, staying much of the time at the Shoreham Hotel. The city had changed enormously since her childhood. Now streetcars clanged along paved boulevards where pigs once wallowed, and row houses filled the meadows between Pennsylvania Avenue and Georgetown. When she was not visiting in Richmond or Savannah, she attended luncheons and teas in the District, dined with her fellow Virginians, President and Mrs. Woodrow Wilson, and tried not to permit her gaze to wander across the Potomac toward the dilapidated, empty mansion where she and her sisters had been born. She was the only sibling left now; Custis had died in 1913 and Rob a year later.

In the fall of 1917, at the age of eighty-two, she returned to Lexington, boarding only a few doors from the Washington and Lee campus. Crippled with arthritis, wearing shabby, ill-fitting black dresses, and carrying an old-fashioned, lace-edged parasol, she hardly resembled the handsome young woman whom Jeb Stuart had admired or the strong-willed adventurer who had sailed up the Nile. But in spite of her infirmities, she had lost neither her keen mind nor her fierce independence. She revised her will without legal assistance, answered in her own handwriting a student appeal for funds, and wrote out a detailed description of the Custis and Lee portraits she was giving to Washington and Lee.

She had been told by relatives that her share of the family pictures was "12 3/8, whatever that may mean!" she wrote to Dr. Henry Louis Smith, who had become president of the university in 1913, and she was scornful of the current cataloging of the portraits—"so many stupid mistakes." Since she had been "brought up with them at 'Arlington' & received my knowledge of them first hand from my grandfather himself," she decided to make "a new & more correct list," including "who the artists were, when taken, etc. etc." At the same time, she presented to the college her father's camp chest and her own cabinet of "curios . . . simply souvenirs of my travels," since she had no central place to keep them, "no home of my own."[58]

To the students she sent a short handwritten note along with a donation, suggesting that they probably wanted a piano not only for their "gymnastic exercises," but more importantly for their "strenuous efforts at . . . Hops and Balls!" She hoped they would always remember the two men for whom the college had been named and "live up to such examples."[59]

In the autumn months of 1918, not long before the end of the First World War, she moved to the Homestead Hotel at Hot Springs, Virginia. The building was not the same one where she had taken her mother during the early days of the Civil War. That old structure had burned and was now replaced by a handsome brick edifice with every luxury. Although the weather was cold, she was well cared for and as comfortable as possible with her debilitating arthritis. A few days after the Armistice, she was suddenly taken ill. In spite of the ministrations of the hotel's physician, she died on November 22 at the age of eighty-three.

Even in death she refused to be bound by convention. Influenced perhaps by foreign cultures and by increasing interest in England for alternative ways of burial, she had made precise arrangements for her own cremation, her ashes to be brought to Lexington in a "marble or alabaster urn" inscribed with her name, date of death, and the statement that she was "the last surviving child of General Robert E. Lee." Her decision, she noted in her will, grew from her "life long horrow [sic] of being boxed up in a *coffin*."[60]

No one in Lexington or Rockbridge County had ever been cremated.* So, understandably, people were disconcerted and uncomfortable with her decision, for they had anticipated paying her the same kind of tribute they had paid to Mildred in 1905. Instead of escorting her coffin from the train station, placing flowers on her bier, attending a service at the Episcopal church, and following student pallbearers across the campus, Lexington's citizens could only attend a short service of committal at the crypt.

Alone among the four sisters to leave a will, Mary Custis divided her estate of $156,000 among churches, favorite charities, historic and educational institutions, nieces, nephews, and cousins. One relative was willed a larger sum than others because he had a "large family." She donated $10,000 to refurbish the R. E. Lee Episcopal Church, "built in memory of my father," with the provision that no "other alteration in the building other than a chancel be adopted." She also bequeathed $10,000 to Christ Church of Alexandria, "the church of my parents and grandparents and of my own childhood . . . associated with many of my

---

*Theories concerning cremation had been widely discussed in England and, to a lesser degree, in the United States since the 1880s. But the practice spread slowly. In America fewer than one percent of those who died in 1918 were cremated, and in the eastern United States in 1918, there were only two crematoriums, one of them in Washington, D. C.

happiest days." To Washington and Lee went a similar sum to fireproof the building in which the Lee and Custis portraits were to be displayed. Smaller amounts were given to the "needy Confederate Women's Home" in Richmond and to a fund to keep her father's monument in Richmond "in repair." Stipends went to the Society for the Preservation of Virginia Antiquities, to the Confederate Museum, to the Virginia Historical Society, and to the Virginia Division of the United Daughters of the Confederacy, "not in putting up tablets, etc., but in the good charitable work . . . of which there is always much need in our State."[61] In spite of having revised the document by herself when she was over eighty, Mary Custis Lee had put together a sensible, balanced will that clearly revealed her innate practicality, her pride in her heritage, and a belated sense of family loyalty.

Standing before the crypt at Lee Chapel, one is impressed by the simplicity and reticence of the inscriptions. There, carved in the stone, are the names and dates of death of Robert E. Lee's three daughters who are buried in Lexington: Eleanor Agnes Lee—Died October 15, 1873; Mildred Childe Lee—Died March 27, 1905; Mary Custis Lee—Died November 22, 1918. Because her father requested that she not be moved, Annie's body is still in the quiet, rural cemetery in North Carolina where Agnes and her mother laid her. The inscription over her grave is more revealing, giving her name, the names of her parents, and the place and date of both her birth and death.

Born at Arlington, died and buried miles from home—these two details epitomize the story of the Lee girls. Beginning life in luxury, with a rich heritage and strong family ties, they were forced to adjust to privation, to the dissolution of family and social unity, and to a sense of rootlessness which all four felt when driven from their home. The Lee girls would scarcely recognize their beloved Arlington today, with endless crosses on its green slopes, walkways slicing through the old orchard and the gardens, and thousands of cars speeding along the Potomac's edge where they once ice-skated and rode their Mexican pony. Only the great house with its immense portico appears unchanged, serene and aloof on the hilltop, a silent reminder of their early years and the bitter war that irrevocably changed their lives.

A Family Tree

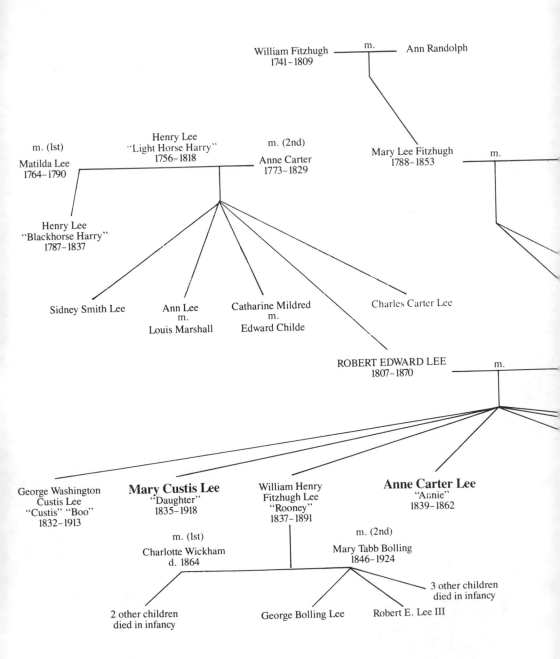

William Fitzhugh
1741–1809 ——— m. ——— Ann Randolph

Henry Lee
"Light Horse Harry"
1756–1818

m. (2nd)
Anne Carter
1773–1829

m. (1st)
Matilda Lee
1764–1790

Mary Lee Fitzhugh
1788–1853 ——— m.

Henry Lee
"Blackhorse Harry"
1787–1837

Sidney Smith Lee

Ann Lee
m.
Louis Marshall

Catharine Mildred
m.
Edward Childe

Charles Carter Lee

ROBERT EDWARD LEE
1807–1870 ——— m.

George Washington
Custis Lee
"Custis" "Boo"
1832–1913

Mary Custis Lee
"Daughter"
1835–1918

William Henry
Fitzhugh Lee
"Rooney"
1837–1891

Anne Carter Lee
"Annie"
1839–1862

m. (1st)
Charlotte Wickham
d. 1864

m. (2nd)
Mary Tabb Bolling
1846–1924

2 other children
died in infancy

George Bolling Lee

Robert E. Lee III

3 other children
died in infancy

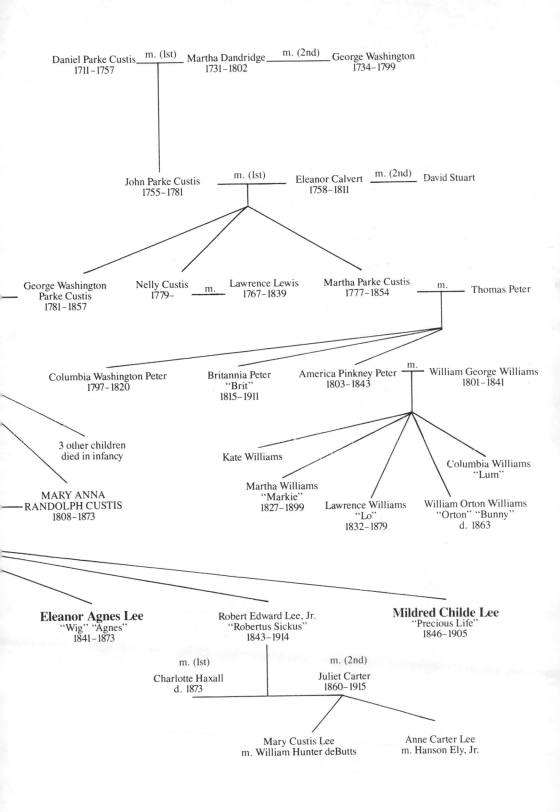

Schools, spas, and estates well known to the Lee girls.

(These are approximate locations.)

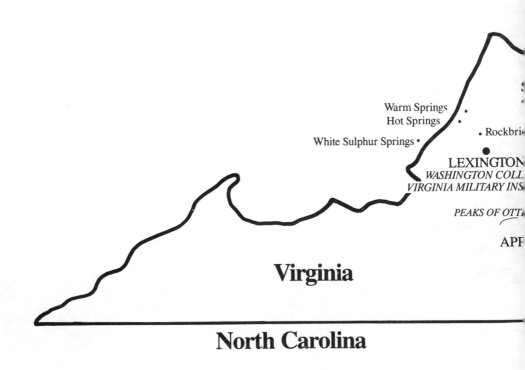

Warm Springs

Hot Springs

White Sulphur Springs •

• Rockbri

LEXINGTON
WASHINGTON COLL
VIRGINIA MILITARY INS

PEAKS OF OTT

APF

Virginia

North Carolina

District of Columbia

Audley ■

Tudor Place ■

ARLINGTON ■

● WASHINGTON

Kinloch ■

Ravensworth ■

■ ALEXANDRIA

Mount Vernon ■

Richland

Maryland

Cedar Grove ■

STAUNTON ●

Chatham

Clydale

Stratford ■

TUART HALL

Rappahannock River

Chantilly ■

ge Baths

Pamunkey River

Hickory Hill ■

Romancoke ■

Potomac River

RICHMOND ●

Bremo

EGE ●

Shirley ■

White House ■

TITUTE

Oakland ■ ■ ■ Belmead

James River

Derwent

R ●

MATTOX

● WARRENTON
Jones Springs

● RALEIGH
ST. MARY'S COLLEGE

Notes

Dates of Agnes' journal entries have been transcribed exactly as they appear in the journal. Dates of letters have been standardized. Dates separated by slashes indicate that the letter was begun on the first day and concluded on the second day.

ABBREVIATIONS

Persons

ACL	Anne Carter Lee (Annie)
EAL	Eleanor Agnes Lee (Agnes)
GWCL	George Washington Custis Lee (Custis)
HB	Helen Bratt
Markie	Martha Custis Williams
MCL	Mary Custis Lee (Daughter)
MilCL	Mildred Childe Lee (Life, Precious Life)
Mrs. Custis	Mrs. George Washington Custis
Mrs. REL	Mrs. Robert E. Lee (Mary Anna Randolph Custis Lee)
REL	Robert Edward Lee
REL, Jr.	Robert Edward Lee, Jr. (Rob)
WHFL	William Henry Fitzhugh Lee (Rooney)
Mrs. WHFL	Mrs. William Henry Fitzhugh Lee (Mary Tabb Bolling Lee)

MANUSCRIPT COLLECTIONS

ARLINGTON   Collections of Arlington House, The Robert E. Lee Memorial, administered by the National Park Service, Arlington, Va.

DUKE   Manuscript Department, Duke University Library, Durham, N.C. Robert Edward Lee Papers except where otherwise noted.

L-J   Lee-Jackson Memorial Foundation, Charlottesville, Va.

UNC   Southern Historical Collection, Library of the University of North Carolina, Chapel Hill, N.C.

USC   South Caroliniana Library, University of South Carolina, Columbia, S.C.

VHS   Virginia Historical Society, Richmond, Va. Lee Family Papers except where otherwise noted.

W&L   Special Collections, the University Library, Washington and Lee University, Lexington, Va.

OTHER

Father   Robert E. Lee, Jr. *My Father, General Lee*. New York: Doubleday & Co., 1904, 1924, 1960.

Freeman   Douglas Southall Freeman, excerpted from *R. E. Lee*, volumes 1 and 4. Copyright 1934, 1935 Charles Scribner's Sons; copyright renewed ©1962, 1963 Inez Gooden Freeman. Reprinted with the permission of Charles Scribner's Sons.

Journal   Journal of Eleanor Agnes Lee, 1852–1858, VHS. At the end of the Journal are entries by Mildred Childe Lee.

Letterbook   A book kept by Robert E. Lee from 3 December 1838 to 4 February 1860 containing copies of his correspondence, some in his handwriting and some in another's. VHS.

MacDonald   Rose Mortimer Ellzey MacDonald. *Mrs. Robert E. Lee*. Boston: Ginn & Co., 1939.

O.R. *Official Records of the Union and Confederate Armies.* Gettysburg: National Historical Society, 1972.

Sanborn Margaret Sanborn. *Robert E. Lee.* 2 vols. Philadelphia: J. B. Lippincott Co., 1966–67.

Scrapbook 1732–1892, Scrapbook 1816–1892, Scrapbook 1912–1914 Mary Custis Lee's scrapbooks, Lee Papers, VHS.

Chapter 1. Bright Flowers of Arlington, 1834–1848

1. M. E. A. Lewis to C. M. Conrad, 5 March 1835, TS, Lewis Family Papers, Mount Vernon Ladies' Association, Mount Vernon, Va.

2. Mrs. [Frances] Trollope, *Domestic Manners of the Americans* (London: Whittaker, Treacher, & Co., 1832), 187.

3. Godfrey T. Vigne, *Six Months in America* (London: Whittaker, Treacher, & Co., 1833), 55.

4. Mrs. REL to Mrs. Custis, Sunday [1831], VHS.

5. REL to Mrs. REL, 21 August 1835, by permission of The Huntington Library, San Marino, Calif., HM 20561.

6. REL to Andrew Talcott, 25 November 1835, Talcott MSS, VHS.

7. REL to Andrew Talcott, n.d. [1835 or 1836], Talcott MSS, VHS.

8. REL to Andrew Talcott, 5 May 1836, Talcott MSS, VHS. See also REL to Andrew Talcott, 23 May 1836, 22 June 1836, Talcott MSS, VHS.

9. REL to Andrew Talcott, 5 May 1836, Talcott MSS, VHS.

10. Mrs. REL to Mrs. Andrew Talcott, 21 November [1835], Talcott MSS, VHS.

11. Freeman, 1:137.

12. REL to Mrs. REL, 10 September 1837, VHS.

13. Sanborn, 1:108.

14. REL to Mrs. REL, 16 October 1837, VHS.

15. REL to Mrs. REL, 10 September 1837, VHS.

16. Mrs. REL to Mrs. Custis, Friday [March 1838], VHS.

17. MacDonald, 75.

18. REL to Mrs. Andrew Talcott, 29 May 1838, Talcott MSS, VHS.

19. MCL to Dr. Henry Louis Smith, 15 December 1917, W&L.

20. REL to Mrs. Custis, 20 March 1839, VHS.

21. MilCL to Mrs. Emily Hay, 29 November [n.d.], W&L.

22. MacDonald, 75–76.

23. REL to Andrew Talcott, 18 May 1839, Talcott MSS, VHS.

24. J. William Jones, *Personal Reminiscences, Anecdotes, and Letters of Gen. Robert E. Lee* (New York: D. Appleton & Co., 1876), 369.

25. REL to Mrs. Custis, 26 July 1839, VHS.

26. Sanborn, 1:129.

27. U.S. Quartermaster Corps, *Arlington and Its Associations* (Fort Humphreys, Va., 1932), 25.

28. REL to Mrs. Custis, 7 November 1839, VHS.

29. REL to Mrs. REL, 4 August 1840, VHS.

30. REL to Jack Mackay, 18 March 1841, TS, Colonial Dames Collection, Georgia Historical Society.

31. Ibid.

32. Mrs. REL to Mrs. Custis, 27 October 1844, VHS.

33. REL to Henry Kayser, 16 November 1844, *Missouri Historical Society* 3 (1936): 361. Original at the Robert E. Lee Collection, Missouri Historical Society, St. Louis, Mo.

34. REL to GWCL, 1 June 1844, VHS.

35. Mrs. REL to Mrs. Custis, 10 Wednesday [n.d.], VHS.

36. Mrs. REL to Mrs. Custis, 29th [1844], VHS.

37. MacDonald, 95.

38. Mrs. REL to Mrs. Custis, 10 Wednesday [n.d.], VHS.

39. Will of Robert E. Lee, Will Book 19, p. 361, Rockbridge County Court Records, Lexington, Va.; probated 7 November 1873.

40. Mrs. REL to Mrs. Custis, 29th [1844], VHS.

41. WHFL to GWCL, dictated to REL, with a postscript by REL, 18 December 1845, VHS.

42. Mrs. REL to Mrs. Custis, 25 December [1845], VHS.

43. REL to GWCL, postscript to letter from WHFL to GWCL, 18 December [1845], VHS.

44. Mrs. REL to Mrs. Custis, 25 December [1845], VHS.

45. REL to Mrs. Custis, 14 February, 24 March 1846, VHS.

46. REL to Mrs. REL, 14 January 1846, VHS.

47. Sanborn, 1:165.

48. REL to GWCL and WHFL, 24 December 1846, VHS.

49. Journal, Sept. 2nd [1855], VHS.

50. REL to EAL, 12 February 1848, VHS.

51. REL to ACL, 29 February 1848, W&L.

52. *Father*, 4.

53. Mrs. REL to Cora Caroline Peters, 16 February [1849], W&L.

54. *Father*, 9.

55. Mrs. Burton [Constance Cary] Harrison, *Recollections Grave and Gay* (London: Smith, Elder & Co., 1912), 33.

56. Marietta Minnigerode Andrews, *Memoirs of a Poor Relation* (New York: E. P. Dutton & Co., 1930), 91.

57. *Father*, 4.

Chapter 2. Marble Steps and Iron Railings, 1848–1855

1. Mrs. REL to Mrs. Custis, 25 December [1845], VHS.

2. Mrs. REL to Cora Caroline Peters, 16 February [1849], W&L.

3. *Father*, 5.

4. Henry Taylor Wickham, "Address, Delivered Before the Joint Session of the General Assembly of Virginia," Virginia State Document No. 10 (Richmond: 1940), 5.

5. Mrs. REL to Cora Caroline Peters, 26 October [1848], W&L.

6. Mrs. REL to Cora Caroline Peters, 16 February [1849], W&L.

7. REL to Mrs. REL, 23 June 1849, VHS. .

8. Joseph Packard, *Recollections of a Long Life*, ed. Thomas J. Packard (Washington: Byron S. Adams, Publisher, 1902), 158.

9. Folder, "Girls' Seminary, 1856–57, Principal: M. Louise Hiser," Maryland Historical Society, Baltimore, Md.

10. *Literary Budget* 1, no. 5 (September 1852). Newspaper edited by the "Young Ladies of Misses Kilbourn & Healy's Academy," Maryland Historical Society, Baltimore, Md.

11. J. William Jones, *Life and Letters of Robert Edward Lee: Soldier and Man* (New York: Neale Publishing Co., 1906), 73.

12. REL to Charles Carter Lee, 10 May 1855, Letters of Robert E. Lee (#990), Manuscripts Department, University of Virginia Library, Charlottesville, Va.

13. Henry E. Shepherd, *Life of Robert Edward Lee* (New York: Neale Publishing Co., 1906), 44–45.

14. *Father*, 11.

15. Mrs. REL to Mrs. Custis, enclosed in letter from REL to Mrs. Custis, 26 March 1851, VHS.

16. Mrs. REL to Cora Caroline Peters, 7 May 1849, W&L.

17. Mrs. REL to Cora Caroline Peters, [1848], W&L.

18. Mrs. REL to Cora Caroline Peters, 26 [July 1850], W&L.

19. Mrs. REL to Cora Caroline Peters, 16 February 1849, W&L.

20. Mrs. Custis to Cora Caroline Peters, 20 February 1851, W&L.

21. REL to Jerome Bonaparte, Jr., 19 September 1850, Jerome Napoleon Bonaparte Papers, MS. 144, Manuscripts Division, Maryland Historical Society Library, Baltimore, Md.

22. MacDonald, 106.

23. Mrs. Custis to Cora Caroline Peters, 3 December [n.d.]. W&L.

24. Ibid.

25. REL to Mrs. Custis, 17 March 1852, VHS.

26. REL to GWCL, 13 April 1851, VHS.

27. Freeman, 1:311.

28. MacDonald, 107.

29. Jones, *Life and Letters*, 76–77.

30. MilCL, account at end of Journal, 20 July 1890, VHS.

31. Ibid.

32. Constance Cary Harrison, "Washington at Mount Vernon After the Revolution," *Century Magazine* 37 (April 1889): 841.

33. Journal, 20th [October 1853], VHS.

34. Reginald Pelham Bolton, "Bolton Priory at Pelham Manor," *Westchester Historian* 6, no. 3 (1930): 54–58.

35. Marielle [MCL] to Mrs. REL, 20 May [1853], VHS.

36. Journal, Christmas Eve December 24th 1852, VHS.

37. Journal, March 2nd [1853], VHS.

38. Journal, 20th [April 1853], VHS.

39. Mrs. Custis to Cora Caroline Peters, 20 February 1851, W&L.

40. REL to ACL, 25 February 1853, VHS.

41. Code of Virginia, Ch. 3, §15, 17 (1819), 424–25. Cumulative Supplement to Revised Code of Virginia (1833), Ch. 186, 244–45.

42. Journal, 23rd [February 1853], VHS.

43. REL to Markie, 23 June 1853, by permission of The Huntington Library, San Marino, Calif., HM 8818.

44. Mrs. E. P. Lewis to C. M. Conrad, 14 August 1847, TS, Lewis Family Papers, Mount Vernon Ladies' Association, Mount Vernon, Va.

45. Journal, May 4th [1853], VHS.

46. Mrs. William Fitzhugh to Mrs. Abby Nelson, April 1853, *Virginia Magazine of History and Biography* 35 (January 1927): 23.

47. Journal, July 13th [1853], VHS.

48. Journal, 20th [July 1853], VHS.

49. Journal, August 6th [1853], VHS.

50. Journal, 20th [July 1853], VHS.

51. Journal, Friday 26th [August 1853], VHS.

52. Ibid.

53. Journal, 8th Tuesday [1853], VHS.

54. Journal, Oct. 18th [1853], VHS.

55. Journal, Feb. 9th [1854], VHS.

56. Burke Davis, ed., *Jeb Stuart, The Last Cavalier* (New York: Rinehart & Co., 1957), 23.

57. Journal, Jan. 22nd 1854, VHS.

58. REL to Markie, 2 January 1854, by permission of The Huntington Library, San Marino, Calif., HM 8821.

59. REL to Markie, 16 September 1853, by permission of The Huntington Library, San Marino, Calif., HM 8820.

60. Journal, Feb. 9th [1854], VHS.

61. Journal, 28th May [1854], VHS.

62. Journal, June 18th [1854], VHS.

63. REL to Markie, 26 May 1854, by permission of The Huntington Library, San Marino, Calif., HM 8825.

64. Journal, Feb. 9th [1854], VHS.

65. Journal, June 18th [1854], VHS.

66. Journal, 18th [July 1854], VHS.

67. Journal, Sunday eve. Dec. 31st [1854], VHS.

68. Ibid.

69. Journal, March 11th [1855], VHS.

70. ACL to HB, 29th [1855], W&L.

71. Journal, 13th [March 1855], VHS.

72. ACL to HB, 7 November [1854], W&L.

73. Journal, March 11th [1855], VHS.

74. EAL to HB, enclosed in letter of ACL to HB, 18 January [1855], W&L.

75. Journal, March 11th [1855], VHS.

76. ACL to HB, 22 February 1855, W&L.

77. "To Helen," ACL to HB, [February 1855], W&L.

78. Journal, March 11th [1855], VHS.

79. Ibid.

80. ACL to HB, 29th [spring 1855], W&L.

81. Journal, 17th [April 1855], VHS.

82. ACL to HB, 3 May 1855, W&L.

83. Journal, 17th [April 1855], VHS.

84. Journal, 13th [March 1855], VHS.

85. ACL to HB, 13 July [1855], W&L.

86. ACL to HB, 3 May 1855, W&L.

87. Journal, July [1855], VHS.

88. MilCL, account at end of Journal, 20 July 1890, VHS.
89. Journal, 20th [April 1855], VHS.

Chapter 3. Schools, Spas, and Secession, 1855–1860

1. REL to Mrs. REL, 1 July 1855, VHS.
2. ACL to HB, 13 July [1855], W&L.
3. Ibid.
4. Journal, July 8th [1855], VHS.
5. Journal, Sept. 2nd [1855], VHS.
6. Journal, 11th [June 1855], VHS.
7. Ibid.
8. ACL to HB, 13 July [1855], W&L.
9. REL to Mrs. REL, 3 September 1855, VHS.
10. Journal, March 16th 1856, VHS.
11. ACL to HB, [November 1855], TS (original presumed lost), W&L.
12. Ibid.
13. Catalog of Virginia Female Institute (1857): 3, Stuart Hall, Staunton, Va.
14. Journal, March 16th 1856, VHS. See also catalog of Virginia Female Institute (1856): 2, 17, Stuart Hall, Staunton, Va.
15. Catalog of Virginia Female Institute (1856): 2, 17, Stuart Hall, Staunton, Va.
16. Ibid, 6–7.
17. Ibid.
18. Journal, March 17th [1856], VHS.
19. EAL to HB, 1 February 1856, TS (original presumed lost), W&L.
20. ACL to HB, 12 April [1856], W&L.
21. Journal, March 27th [1856], VHS.
22. REL to Mrs. REL, 1 July 1855, VHS.
23. REL to MilCL, 1 April 1861, VHS.
24. ACL to HB, 25 January [1856], W&L.
25. Journal, Sunday morn 23rd [March 1856], VHS.
26. ACL to HB, 25 January [1856], W&L.
27. *Staunton Spectator*, 23 April 1856.
28. Journal, March 16th [1856], VHS.
29. Journal, Sunday morn 23rd [1856], VHS.
30. Journal, [Sunday] night [April 1856], VHS.
31. *Staunton Spectator*, 16 April 1856.

32. Journal, Sunday [April 1856], VHS.
33. ACL to HB, 12 April [1856], W&L.
34. Journal, 26th [May 1856], VHS.
35. REL to MilCL, 28 April 1856, VHS.
36. Blanche Berard, "Arlington and Mount Vernon, 1856," *Virginia Magazine of History and Biography* 57 (1949): 161, 162, 164.
37. EAL to REL, 24 May 1856, VHS.
38. EAL to HB, 25 August 1856, W&L.
39. Journal, August 30th [1856], VHS.
40. REL to Mrs. REL, 1 September 1856, VHS.
41. ACL to HB, n.d. [November 1855], TS (original presumed lost), W&L.
42. ACL to HB, 12 April [1856], W&L.
43. ACL to HB, 25 January [1856], 4 August [1856], 28 November 1856, 7 March 1857.
44. EAL to HB, 25 August 1856, W&L.
45. ACL to HB, 4 August [1856], W&L.
46. EAL to HB, 25 August 1856, W&L.
47. REL to Mrs. REL, 18 August 1856, VHS.
48. EAL to HB, 25 August 1856, W&L.
49. Harrison, "Washington at Mount Vernon," 842.
50. ACL to HB, 28 November 1856, W&L.
51. Journal, Oct. 20th [1856], VHS.
52. EAL to REL, 19/21 October 1856, VHS.
53. ACL to HB, 28 November 1856, W&L.
54. REL to Mrs. REL, 27 December 1856, VHS.
55. REL to Mrs. REL, 7 March 1857, VHS.
56. REL to MilCL, 22 March 1857, VHS.
57. REL to MilCL, 9 January 1857, VHS.
58. REL to MilCL, 22 March 1857, VHS.
59. EAL to REL, 9 April 1857, VHS.
60. EAL to Mrs. REL, 2 April [1856 or 1857], VHS.
61. Mrs. REL, quoting ACL, to REL, 17 March [1857], VHS.
62. Mrs. REL to EAL, 14th [spring 1857], VHS.
63. REL to Mrs. REL, 18 May 1857, VHS.
64. Mrs. REL to REL, 22 May/4 June [1857], VHS.
65. REL to Mrs. REL, 12 August 1857, VHS.
66. REL to General Winfield Scott, 11 August 1857, Letterbook, VHS.
67. Mrs. REL to REL, 22 May/4 June [1857], VHS.
68. Journal, Jan. 3rd 1858, VHS.

69. ACL to HB, 3 July 1857, W&L.

70. REL to Mrs. REL, 15 June 1857, VHS.

71. Mrs. REL to REL, 22 May/4 June [1857], VHS.

72. Porte Crayon [David Strother], *Virginia Illustrated* (New York: Harper & Brothers, Publishers, 1857), 270.

73. ACL to HB, 3 July 1857, W&L.

74. ACL to REL, 30 July 1857, VHS.

75. ACL to HB, 30 August 1857, W&L.

76. Journal, 13th [October 1857], VHS.

77. REL to Mrs. REL, 22 August 1857, VHS.

78. REL to Charlotte Wickham, 10 October 1857, Letterbook, VHS.

79. Markie to EAL, 29 December [1863], VHS.

80. REL to ACL, 8 August 1857, VHS.

81. *Daily National Intelligencer*, 14 October 1857.

82. Journal, 13th [October 1857], VHS.

83. Journal, Oct. 11th 1857, VHS.

84. Mrs. REL to Mrs. Hackley, 19 February 1857, Talcott MSS, VHS.

85. Will of George Washington Parke Custis, Will Book 7, pp. 267–69, Alexandria County Court Records, Alexandria, Va.; probated 7 December 1857. Copy on file in Research Document Collection, Arlington.

86. Freeman, 1:381, quoting inventory of the estate of George Washington Parke Custis.

87. Journal, 3 January 1858, VHS.

88. Journal, Dec. 13th [1857], VHS.

89. REL to Markie, 5 December 1857, by permission of The Huntington Library, San Marino, Calif., HM 8830.

90. ACL to HB, 10 February 1858, W&L.

91. REL to GWCL, 17 January 1858, Duke.

92. REL to GWCL, 15 February 1858, Duke.

93. Sanborn, 1:276.

94. Mrs. REL to Benson Lossing, 25 November 1857, Arlington.

95. ACL to HB, n.d. [summer 1858], W&L.

96. Ibid.

97. Sanborn, 1:278.

98. Gail Hamilton [Mary Abigail Dodge], *Gail Hamilton's Life in Letters*, ed. H. Augusta Dodge (Boston: Lee & Shepard, 1901), 1:172.

99. ACL to HB, 12 December 1858, TS (original presumed lost), W&L.

100. ACL to HB, 30 December 1858, TS (original presumed lost), W&L.

101. ACL to HB, 15 February 1859, W&L.

102. GWCL to EAL, 18 May 1859, Duke.

103. ACL to HB, 29 September [1858], W&L.

104. MilCL, account at end of Journal, 20 July 1890, VHS.

105. REL to GWCL, 30 May 1859, Duke.

106. Mrs. REL to [Benson Lossing], 20 July 1859, W&L.

107. Ibid.

108. Jones, *Life and Letters*, 102.

109. Mrs. REL to [Benson Lossing], 20 July 1859, W&L.

110. REL to Hon. J. B. Floyd, Secretary of War, 1 February 1860, Letter-book, VHS.

111. REL to ACL, 25 March 1860, VHS.

112. Ibid.

113. REL to WHFL, 2 April 1860, George Bolling Lee Papers, VHS.

114. REL to ACL, 16 June 1860, VHS.

115. REL to EAL, 8 June 1860, VHS.

116. REL to Mrs. REL, 1 July 1860, VHS.

117. Mrs. REL to ACL, Saturday [August 1860], VHS.

118. Mrs. REL to ACL, 10/13 [August 1860], VHS.

119. REL to Markie, 22 January 1861, by permission of The Huntington Library, San Marino, Calif., HM 8831.

120. Mrs. REL to ACL, 10/13 [August 1860], VHS.

121. REL to Mrs. REL, 18 June 1860, VHS.

122. 1858 Brochure about Mr. and Mrs. Charles L. Powell's Female Seminary, p. 3, Handley Library, Winchester, Va.

123. Mrs. REL to ACL, Saturday [August 1860], VHS.

124. 1858 Brochure about Mr. and Mrs. Charles L. Powell's Female Seminary, p. 10, Handley Library, Winchester, Va.

125. Mrs. REL to ACL, Saturday [August 1860], VHS.

126. Mrs. REL to MilCL, 8 September [1860], VHS.

127. Invitation to Miss Agnes Lee, dated 12 October 1860, Arlington.

128. Mrs. REL to ACL, 21 October [1860], VHS.

129. REL to GWCL, 5 December 1860, Duke.

130. 1858 Brochure about Mr. and Mrs. Charles L. Powell's Female Seminary, pp. 3, 5, 10, Handley Library, Winchester, Va.

131. REL to MilCL, 22 October 1860, VHS.

132. Mrs. REL to MilCL, 4 December [1860], VHS.

133. REL to Mrs. REL, 23 January 1861, VHS.

134. Mrs. REL to MilCL, 17 January 1861, VHS.

135. Mrs. REL to Helen [Peters], 1 February 1861, W&L.

136. Charles Francis Adams, *An Autobiography* (Boston: Houghton Mifflin Co., 1916), 91.

137. Mrs. REL to Helen [Peters], 1 February 1861, W&L.

138. Mrs. REL to MilCL, 25 [1861], VHS.

139. Mrs. REL to MilCL, 19 [February 1861], VHS.

140. Mrs. REL to Helen [Peters], 1 February 1861, W&L.

141. REL to Markie, 22 January 1861, by permission of The Huntington Library, San Marino, Calif., HM 8831.

142. REL to MilCL, 1 April 1861, VHS.

143. REL to MilCL, 15 March 1861, VHS.

144. Mrs. REL to "my dear child" [MilCL], 10 April [1861], VHS.

145. Elizabeth Lindsay Lomax, *Leaves From an Old Washington Diary 1854–1863*, ed. Lindsay Lomax Wood (New York: E. P. Dutton & Co., 1943), 148.

146. *Father*, 27.

147. EAL to MilCL, 19 April [1861], VHS.

148. Ibid.

149. Jones, *Life and Letters*, 132.

150. *Father*, 26–27.

151. Miss S. L. Lee, "War Time in Alexandria," *South Atlantic Quarterly* 4, no. 3 (July 1905): 235, Duke University Press.

152. *Alexandria Gazette*, 20 April 1861.

153. Lee, "War Time in Alexandria," 235.

154. Alexander J. Wedderburn, *Historic Alexandria, Va., Past and Present* (Washington, D.C.: Sudwarth Printing Co., 1907), n.p.

155. John Esten Cooke, *A Life of Gen. Robert E. Lee* (New York: D. Appleton & Co., 1871), 32.

Chapter 4. The Broken Circle, 1861–1862

1. George Washington Cullum, *Biographical Register of the Officers and Graduates of the United States Military Academy* (New York: Houghton Mifflin & Co., 1891), 2:375–76.

2. Mrs. REL to REL, 9 May 1861, VHS.

3. Ibid.

4. ACL to EAL, 2 May [1861], Duke.

5. Mrs. REL to [MilCL], 11 May [1861], VHS.

6. REL to Mrs. REL, 26 April 1861, VHS.

7. REL to Mrs. REL, 30 April 1861, VHS.

8. EAL to ACL, 6 May [1861], VHS.

9. EAL to ACL, 10 May [1861], VHS.

10. Markie to EAL, 8 May 1861, VHS.

11. EAL to ACL, 6 May [1861], VHS.

12. Mrs. REL to EAL, 30 June [1861], VHS.

13. Mrs. REL to General Charles W. Sandford, 30 May 1861, Enoch Aquila Chase Papers, 1861–1928, VHS.

14. Ibid.

15. Mrs. REL to REL, 9 May 1861, VHS.

16. *Father*, 34.

17. REL to Mrs. REL, 2 July 1861, VHS.

18. REL to Mrs. REL, 8 July 1861, VHS.

19. Ibid.

20. REL to MilCL, 29 June 1861, VHS.

21. Mrs. REL to MilCL, 11/12 June 1861, VHS.

22. Markie to Mrs. REL, 13 July 1861, VHS.

23. Mrs. REL to Mrs. Francis Asbury Dickins, 18 June [1861], Dickins Papers, the Manuscript Collection, Arlington.

24. Sallie Ann Brock Putnam, *Richmond During the War: Four Years of Personal Observation by a Richmond Lady* (New York: G.W. Carleton & Co., 1867), 64.

25. Margaret Elizabeth Clewell, "A Volunteer Nurse," 76–77, Gertrude Jenkins Papers, Duke.

26. REL to Mrs. REL, 27 July 1861, VHS.

27. Freeman, 1:543.

28. REL to Mrs. REL, 4 August 1861, VHS.

29. REL to Mrs. REL, 9 September 1861, VHS.

30. EAL to MilCL, 20 August [1861], VHS.

31. Sanborn, 2:29.

32. Mrs. REL to ACL and EAL, 12 September [1861], VHS.

33. Ibid.

34. REL to MilCL, 15 November 1861, VHS.

35. *Father*, 55–56.

36. *Letters of General J. E. B. Stuart to His Wife, 1861*, ed. Bingham Duncan (Atlanta: Emory University, 1943), 25.

37. REL to Mrs. REL, 25 December 1861, VHS.

38. REL, Jr. to ACL, 1 December 1861, VHS.

39. Putnam, *Richmond During the War*, 87.

40. EAL to MilCL, 10 November [1861], VHS.

41. EAL to Orton Williams, 1 December 1861, VHS.

42. Emily V. Mason, *Popular Life of General Robert Edward Lee* (Baltimore: John Murphy & Co., 1877), 90–91.

43. Jones, *Personal Reminiscences*, 388.

44. Ibid.

45. REL to ACL, 2 March 1862, VHS.

46. Constance Cary Harrison, "A Virginia Girl in the First Year of the War," *The Century Illustrated Monthly Magazine* 30 (August 1885): 610.

47. REL to Mrs. REL, 4 April 1862, VHS.

48. Frontispiece to Scrapbook 1816–1892, VHS.

49. Fitzhugh Lee to MCL, 20 March 1862, Scrapbook 1816–1892, 164, VHS.

50. REL to Charlotte Wickham Lee, 22 June 1862, George Bolling Lee Papers, VHS.

51. J. E. B. Stuart to MCL, 19 March 1862, Scrapbook 1816–1892, 79, VHS.

52. Mrs. Virginia Clay-Clopton, *A Belle of the Fifties: Memoirs of Mrs. Clay of Alabama* (New York: Doubleday, Page & Co., 1904), 171.

53. REL to Mrs. REL, 4 April 1862, VHS.

54. REL to Mrs. REL, 22 April 1862, VHS.

55. Cooke, *A Life*, 61.

56. Dr. George Lyman, "Some Aspects of the Medical Service in the Army of the United States During the War of the Rebellion," *Papers of Military Historical Society of Massachusetts* 8 (1913): 193–94.

57. REL to EAL, 29 May 1862, VHS.

58. Putnam, *Richmond During the War*, 129–31.

59. ACL to Mrs. REL, 18 June [1862], VHS.

60. REL to Charlotte Wickham Lee, 22 June 1862, George Bolling Lee Papers, VHS.

61. Putnam, *Richmond During the War*, 154.

62. Markie to Mrs. REL, 25 July 1862, VHS.

63. REL to Mrs. REL, 28 July 1862, VHS.

64. GWCL to ACL and EAL, 18 August 1862, Duke.

65. Mrs. REL to ACL, 21 September [1862], VHS.

66. ACL to Mrs. REL, 10 August 1862, VHS.

67. Lizzie Wilson Montgomery, *The Saint Mary's of Olden Days* (Raleigh, N.C.: Bynum Printing Co., 1932), 15.

68. Annie Moore Parker, "Personal Recollections of St. Mary's," *The St. Mary's Muse* 11, no. 4 (December 1906): 23.

69. Ibid.

70. Comment from an alumna whose grandmother attended St. Mary's with Mildred Lee, passed on to the author by Martha Stoops, historian at St. Mary's.

71. EAL to MilCL, 13 October 1862, VHS.

72. EAL to MilCL, 23 November 1862, VHS.

73. EAL to MilCL, 13 October 1862, VHS.

74. Mrs. REL to MCL, 18/19 October [1862], VHS.

75. Ibid.

76. EAL to MCL, 7 November 1862, VHS.

77. EAL to MilCL, 20 October [1862], VHS.

78. Mrs. REL to unnamed recipient [MCL], Saturday night [October 1862], VHS.

79. Mrs. REL to MCL, 23 October 1862, VHS.

80. Walter H. Taylor, *Four Years with General Lee* (New York: D. Appleton & Co., 1877), 76.

81. *Father*, 79–80.

82. REL, Jr. to Mrs. REL, 30 October 1862, VHS.

83. EAL to MilCL, 20 October [1862], VHS.

84. Markie to EAL, 18 November 1862, VHS.

85. *Father*, 85–86.

86. EAL to MilCL, November 1862, VHS.

87. REL to Mrs. REL, 18 November 1862, VHS.

88. Mrs. REL to MilCL, postscript to letter above.

89. REL to EAL, 26 December 1862, VHS.

90. Davis, *Jeb Stuart*, 251.

91. John Esten Cooke, *Wearing of the Gray* (Baltimore: J. S. Morrow, 1867), 327.

92. C. A. Williams, "Light on a War Mystery," *Confederate Veteran* 29 (July 1921): 263.

93. William G. Beymer, *On Hazardous Service: Scouts & Spies of the North & South* (New York: Harper & Brothers, 1912), 59.

94. Wickham, 7.

95. Ibid.

96. MilCL, account at end of Journal, 5 February 1884, VHS.

Chapter 5. The Streets of Richmond, 1863–1865

1. William Miller Owen, *In Camp and Battle with the Washington Artillery of New Orleans: A Narrative of Events During the Late Civil War*

from Bull Run to Appomattox and Spanish Fort (Boston: Ticknor & Co., 1885), 295.

2. Harrison, *Recollections*, 153.

3. *Daily Richmond Examiner*, 28 August 1863.

4. "To Miss Agnes" from "K.G.S.," Richmond, 17 May 1863, Album of EAL 1854–1870, VHS.

5. Marietta Minnigerode Andrews, *Scraps of Paper* (New York: E. P. Dutton & Co., 1929), 71.

6. REL to EAL, 6 February 1863, VHS.

7. REL to EAL, 20 February 1863, VHS.

8. REL to Mrs. REL, 29 January 1863, VHS.

9. *The Wartime Papers of R. E. Lee*, ed. Clifford Dowdey and Louis H. Manarin (Boston: Little, Brown & Co., 1961), 428.

10. REL to EAL, 11 April 1863, VHS.

11. REL to Mrs. REL, 23 May 1863, VHS.

12. REL to EAL, 11 April 1863, VHS.

13. REL, Jr. to "my dear Sister" [Charlotte Wickham Lee], 18 January 1863, VHS.

14. Problems of families in King George County have been gleaned from Nannie Brown Doherty's "Some Recollections of the Civil War," unpublished TS on deposit in Central Rappahannock Regional Library, Fredericksburg, Va.

15. Emory M. Thomas, *The Confederate State of Richmond* (Austin: University of Texas Press, 1971), 124.

16. REL to EAL, 25 May 1863, VHS.

17. REL to Mrs. REL, 12 April 1863, VHS.

18. REL to Mrs. REL, 27 March 1863, VHS.

19. REL to Mrs. REL, 31 May 1863, VHS.

20. Martha Stoops, *The Heritage: The Education of Women at St. Mary's College, Raleigh, North Carolina, 1842–1982* (Raleigh: Saint Mary's College, 1984), 161.

21. REL to Mrs. REL, 12 April 1863, VHS.

22. Stoops, *The Heritage*, 160.

23. *Daily Richmond Examiner*, 13 June 1863.

24. REL to Mrs. REL, 14 June 1863, VHS.

25. O.R., ser. 1, vol. 23, pt. 2, p. 397.

26. Ibid., 398.

27. O.R., ser. 1, vol. 23, pt. 2, pp. 415–16.

28. Beymer, *On Hazardous Service*, 55.

29. *Daily Richmond Examiner*, 3 July 1863.

30. O.R., ser. 2, 5:763.

31. *Daily Richmond Examiner*, 3 July 1863.

32. *Chattanooga Rebel*, 17 June 1863.

33. Beymer, *On Hazardous Service*, 58.

34. *Detroit Free Press*, 10 June 1863; clipping pasted in Scrapbook 1816–1892, 158, VHS.

35. Wickham, 10.

36. REL to Mrs. REL, 11 June 1863, VHS.

37. *Wartime Papers*, ed. Dowdey and Manarin, 561.

38. REL to Charlotte Wickham Lee, 26 July 1863, George Bolling Lee Papers, VHS.

39. Mrs. Thom. C. Cruikshank, "A Few Recollections, 1863–64," *The St. Mary's Muse* 10, no. 9 (April 1906): 13.

40. Circular letter from Dr. Aldert Smedes, 11 July 1863, pasted in Scrapbook 1816–1892, 126, VHS.

41. REL to MilCL, 27 July 1863, VHS.

42. Ibid.

43. Judith Brockenbrough McGuire, *Diary of a Southern Refugee* (Richmond: J. W. Randolph & English, 1889), 233.

44. Mrs. REL to E. G. W. Butler, March 1860, TS (original presumed lost), Duke.

45. REL to Mrs. REL, 9 August 1863, VHS.

46. REL to Mrs. REL, 4 September 1863, VHS.

47. REL to Mrs. REL, 9 August 1863, VHS.

48. Mrs. REL to "my dear child" [MilCL], 16/19 [August 1863], VHS.

49. REL to MilCL, 10 September 1863, VHS.

50. Ibid.

51. Lizzie Wilson Montgomery, *The Saint Mary's of Olden Days*, 20.

52. REL to MilCL, 10 September 1863, VHS.

53. REL to Mrs. REL, 28 October 1863, VHS.

54. MacDonald, 171.

55. Mrs. REL to "my dear child" [MilCL], 16/19 [August 1863], VHS.

56. REL to Mrs. REL, 27 December 1863, VHS.

57. Mrs. Binnie Mason to "Cousin Mary" [Mrs. REL], 7 January 1864, VHS.

58. Markie to EAL, 29 December [1863], VHS.

59. Mary Boykin Chesnut, *A Diary from Dixie*, ed. Ben Ames Williams (Boston: Houghton Mifflin Co., 1949), 385.

60. REL to Mrs. REL, 6 February 1864, VHS.

61. REL to Mrs. REL, 24 January 1864, VHS.

62. REL to Mrs. REL, 24 March 1864, VHS.

63. REL to Mrs. REL, 30 March 1864, VHS.

64. Mrs. REL to Mrs. Francis Asbury Dickins, n.d. [1864], Dickins Papers, the Manuscript Collection, Arlington.

65. REL to Mrs. REL, 24 March 1864, VHS.

66. REL to Mrs. REL, 23 April 1864, VHS.

67. REL to Mrs. REL, 7 July 1864, VHS.

68. REL to MilCL, 28 June 1864, VHS.

69. REL to MilCL, 5 July 1864, VHS.

70. REL to Mrs. REL, 10 July 1864, VHS.

71. Phoebe Yates Pember, *A Southern Woman's Story: Life in Confederate Richmond* (New York: G. W. Carleton & Co., 1879), 129.

72. REL to Mrs. REL, 29 May 1864, VHS.

73. Edward A. Pollard, *Life of Jefferson Davis with a Secret History of the Southern Confederacy* (Philadelphia: National Publishing Co., 1869), 487; Francis Butler Simkins and James Welch Patton, *The Women of the Confederacy* (Richmond: Garrett & Massie, 1936), 182.

74. Emma Mordecai, June 17th [1864], Emma Mordecai Diary, UNC.

75. Putnam, *Richmond During the War*, 303.

76. MacDonald, 179.

77. Mrs. REL to Mrs. Francis Asbury Dickins, 11 August [1864], Dickins Papers, the Manuscript Collection, Arlington.

78. REL to Mrs. REL, 23 April 1864, VHS.

79. REL to MilCL, 5 July 1864, VHS.

80. Mrs. REL to Mrs. Francis Asbury Dickins, 11 August [1864], Dickins Papers, the Manuscript Collection, Arlington.

81. REL to Mrs. REL, 31 July 1864, VHS.

82. REL to Mrs. REL, 7 August 1864, VHS.

83. REL to Mrs. REL, 5 September 1864, VHS.

84. REL to EAL, 20 November 1864, VHS.

85. REL to MilCL, 6 November 1864, George Bolling Lee Papers, VHS.

86. W. W. Blackford, *War Years with Jeb Stuart* (New York: Charles Scribner's Sons, 1945), 261.

87. Putnam, *Richmond During the War*, 350.

88. L. Minor Blackford, *Mine Eyes Have Seen the Glory: The Story of a Virginia Lady, Mary Berkeley Minor Blackford, 1802–1896* (Cambridge: Harvard University Press, 1954), 239.

89. A. A. and Mary Hoehling, *The Day Richmond Died* (New York: A. S. Barnes & Co., 1981), 78.

90. Sally Nelson Robins, "Mrs. Lee During the War—Something About 'The Mess' and Its Occupants," in *Gen. Robert Edward Lee: Soldier, Citizen, and Christian Patriot*, ed. R. A. Brock (Richmond: Royal Publishing Co., 1897), 330–34.

91. REL to EAL, enclosed in letter to Mrs. REL, 28 March 1865, VHS.

92. Blackford, *War Years*, 261.

93. REL to EAL, 31 March 1865, VHS.

94. Mrs. REL to Colonel Francis Smith, 30 March [1865], S. Smith Papers, VHS.

95. McHenry Howard, *Recollections of a Maryland Confederate Soldier* (Baltimore: Williams & Wilkins Co., 1914), 361.

96. REL to EAL, enclosed in letter to Mrs. REL, 28 March 1865, VHS.

97. T. C. DeLeon, *Belles, Beaux, and Brains of the 60's* (New York: G. W. Dillingham Co., 1909), 399. The account suggests that it was Mary Custis Lee who was rescued, but memory must have played tricks on Jimmy Clark, for it was Agnes Lee who was in Petersburg that night.

98. Katharine M. Jones, *Ladies of Richmond* (Indianapolis: Bobbs-Merrill Co., 1962), 293.

99. Hoehling, *The Day Richmond Died*, 105.

100. Katharine Jones, *Ladies*, 273.

101. Putnam, *Richmond During the War*, 365.

102. Pollard, *Life of Jefferson Davis*, 497.

103. T. C. DeLeon, *Four Years in Rebel Capitals: An Inside View of Life in the Southern Confederacy, from Birth to Death* (Mobile: Gossip Printing Co., 1890), 361.

104. Robert Beverley Munford, Jr., *Richmond Homes and Memories* (Richmond: Garrett & Massie, 1936), 178.

105. Putnam, *Richmond During the War*, 368.

106. Nellie Grey, *A Virginia Girl in the Civil War 1861–1865: Being a Record of the Actual Experiences of the Wife of a Confederate Officer*, ed. Myrta Lockett Avery (New York: D. Appleton & Co., 1903), 363–64.

107. Matthew Page Andrews, *Women of the South* (Baltimore: Norman Remington, 1920), 412.

Chapter 6. Saints, Yearlings, and Leaders of the Herd, 1865–1873

1. *Father*, 162.

2. Mrs. Cornelia Phillips Spencer, "The Young Ladies' Column," *North Carolina Presbyterian*, 2 February 1870.

3. Robins, "Mrs. Lee During the War," in *Gen. Robert Edward Lee*, 326.

4. Katharine Jones, *Ladies*, 289.

5. *Father*, 161.

6. MacDonald, 198.

7. Katharine Jones, *Ladies*, 308, 310.

8. Elizabeth Randolph Preston Allan, *A March Past* (Richmond: Dietz Press, 1938), 55–56.

9. Mrs. REL to Cora Caroline Peters, 18 July 1865, W&L.

10. MacDonald, 200.

11. REL to REL, Jr., 10 July [1865], VHS.

12. MilCL's account at end of Journal, 21 August 1888, VHS.

13. REL to WHFL, 29 July 1865, George Bolling Lee Papers, VHS.

14. MilCL to Lucy Blain, 14 August 1865, W&L.

15. Ibid.

16. Franklin L. Riley, *General Robert E. Lee After Appomattox* (New York: Macmillan Co., 1930), 75–76.

17. Francis Pendleton Gaines, *Lee: The Background of a Great Decision* (Lexington, Va.: 1934), n.p.

18. MacDonald, 204.

19. REL to Mrs. REL, 19 September 1865, VHS.

20. REL to EAL, 26 October 1865, VHS.

21. MilCL's account at end of Journal, 21 August 1888, VHS.

22. REL to EAL, 16 November 1865, VHS.

23. *Lexington Gazette*, 6 December 1865.

24. *Father*, 203.

25. John S. Wise, *The End of an Era* (Boston: Houghton Mifflin & Co., 1899), 234.

26. Orra Langhorne, *Southern Sketches from Virginia, 1881–1901*, ed. Charles E. Wynes (Charlottesville: University Press of Virginia, 1964), 50.

27. Wise, *The End of an Era*, 239.

28. MilCL to Mrs. Emily Hay, 1 March [n.d.], W&L.

29. MilCL to Lucy Blain, 7 February 1866, W&L.

30. REL to EAL, 5 December 1865, VHS.

31. MilCL to Lucy Blain, 7 February 1866, W&L.

32. Robins, "Mrs. Lee During the War," in *Gen. Robert Edward Lee*, 348.

33. MilCL to Lucy Blain, 7 February 1866, W&L.

34. MilCL's account at end of Journal, 21 August 1888, VHS.

35. Mary Elizabeth Massey, *Bonnet Brigades* (New York: Alfred A. Knopf, 1966), 280, 281.

36. J. C. Davis to REL, 20 January 1866, VHS.

37. Mrs. REL to Cora Caroline Peters, 4 May 1866, W&L.

38. Mrs. REL to Mrs. Jefferson Davis, 6 February 1867, The Museum of the Confederacy.

39. Mrs. REL to Cora Caroline Peters, 4 May 1866, W&L.

40. Robins, "Mrs. Lee During the War," in *Gen. Robert Edward Lee*, 347.

41. Myrta Lockett Avary, *Dixie After the War* (New York: Doubleday, Page & Co., 1906), 23, footnote.

42. *Lexington Gazette*, 18 April 1866.

43. Marjorie Stratford Mendenhall, "Southern Women of a 'Lost Generation,'" *South Atlantic Quarterly* 33 (1934): 346–47, Duke University Press.

44. Allan, *March Past*, 240.

45. Ibid., 252.

46. *Father*, 245. See also Riley, *General Robert E. Lee*, 91–92.

47. W. W. Scott, "Some Personal Memories of General Robert E. Lee," *William and Mary Quarterly* 2d ser., 6 (October 1926): 286.

48. Samuel H. Chester, "At College Under General Lee," MS, W&L, ca. 1920, 1.

49. Marshall McDonald to Mary E. McCormick, 22 January 1866 [1867], Marshall McDonald Papers, Duke.

50. Marshall McDonald to Mary E. McCormick, 18 November [1866], Marshall McDonald Papers, Duke.

51. REL to MilCL, 21 [December 1866], VHS.

52. EAL to MilCL, n.d. [1866], VHS.

53. Marshall McDonald to Mary E. McCormick, 22 January 1866 [1867], Marshall McDonald Papers, Duke.

54. Marshall McDonald to Mary E. McCormick, 1 February 1867, Marshall McDonald Papers, Duke.

55. *Father*, 369.

56. *Father*, 320.

57. Catesby Jones to Robert D. Minor, 9 April 1867, Minor Papers, VHS.

58. Lucius Desha to Hugh Moran, 23 June 1872, W&L.

59. Lucius Desha to Hugh Moran, 16 August 1871, W&L.

60. Chester, "At College," 2.

61. Allan, *March Past*, 205–6.

62. Mrs. REL to Mrs. R. H. Chilton, 10 March 1867, The Museum of the Confederacy.

63. *Father*, 252.

64. REL to Markie, 14 April 1868, by permission of The Huntington Library, San Marino, Calif., HM 8841.

65. Mrs. REL to Cora Caroline Peters, 16 January 1867, W&L.

66. MacDonald, 258.

67. Chester, "At College," 2.

68. Mrs. Rees Turpin, quoting MilCL, to Dr. Leslie Lyle Campbell, 26 May 1941, Rockbridge Historical Society, W&L.

69. MilCL's account at end of Journal, 21 August 1888, VHS.

70. REL to Mrs. REL, 26 November 1867, VHS.

71. REL to Mrs. REL, 29 November 1867, VHS.

72. *Father*, 358.

73. *Father*, 360.

74. Elizabeth Preston Allan, *The Life and Letters of Margaret Junkin Preston* (New York: Houghton Mifflin & Co., 1903), 221.

75. REL to MilCL, 8 January 1870, VHS.

76. REL to MilCL, 27 January 1867, VHS.

77. REL to MilCL, 21 [December 1866], VHS; REL to Markie, 22 December 1866, by permission of The Huntington Library, San Marino, Calif., HM 8838; *Father*, 346.

78. *Father*, 302.

79. *Father*, 304.

80. MilCL's account at end of Journal, 21 August 1888, VHS.

81. MilCL's account of trip with REL to Peaks of Otter, summer 1869, VHS.

82. Freeman, 4:322.

83. MilCL's account of trip with REL to Peaks of Otter, summer 1869, VHS.

84. Mrs. REL to Harry Lee, n.d. [1869], W&L.

85. *Father*, 366–67.

86. Christiana Bond, *Memories of General Robert E. Lee* (Baltimore: Norman Remington Co., 1926), 33–34.

87. Riley, *General Robert E. Lee*, 130.

88. *Father*, 81.

89. REL to Mrs. REL, 2 April 1870, VHS.

90. *Father*, 391.

91. Ibid., 393, 394.

92. Ibid., 399.

93. Mrs. REL to MilCL, 9/13 May [1870], VHS.

94. MCL to Jo Lane Stern, 30 August [1870], W&L.

95. MacDonald, 278.

96. MilCL's account at end of Journal, 21 August 1888, VHS.

97. Ibid.

98. William Edmondstoune Aytoun, *Lays of the Scottish Cavaliers and Other Poems* (Edinburgh: William Blackwood & Sons, 1849), 9–10.

99. MilCL's account at end of Journal, 21 August 1888, VHS.

100. Ibid.

101. Ibid.

102. Ibid.

103. Ibid.

104. MCL to Jo Lane Stern, 8 May [1871 or 1872], W&L.

105. *Green Mount After the War: The Correspondence of Maria Louisa Wacker Fleet and Her Family, 1865–1900*, ed. Betsy Fleet (Charlottesville: University Press of Virginia, 1978), 71.

106. Ibid., 75–76.

107. MCL to Jo Lane Stern, 19 February 1872, W&L.

108. Mrs. REL to "Letty," 22 May [1872], L-J.

109. Mrs. REL to Norvell [Caskie Jones], 5 January 1873, W&L.

110. Mrs. REL, quoting MCL, to Miss Lella Pendleton, n.d. [winter 1872], W&L.

111. REL to Miss Charlotte Haxall, 12 August 1870, VHS.

112. Mrs. REL to Mrs. Richardson, 10 June [1868], The Museum of the Confederacy.

113. Mrs. REL to Mrs. Cocke, 20 June 1873, John Hartwelle Cocke Collection, #5680, University of Virginia Library, Charlottesville, Va.

114. MilCL's account at end of Journal, 5 February 1884, VHS.

115. Ibid.

116. MilCL's account at end of Journal, 22 January 1887, VHS.

117. Death record listed at Bureau of Vital Statistics, Virginia State Library, Richmond, Va.

118. MilCL's account at end of Journal, 22 January 1887, VHS.

Chapter 7. "The Pathways of Life Alone," 1873–1918

1. Annie Moore Parker, "Personal Recollections," *The St. Mary's Muse* 11, no. 4 (December 1906): 23.

2. David H. Strother, 7 April, 17 April 1885 diary, West Virginia and Regional History Collection, West Virginia University Library.

3. Allan, *March Past*, 198.

4. MilCL to Harry Lee, 28 December [1873], W&L.

5. MilCL to Mrs. Margaret Junkin Preston, 29 November [1873], Margaret Junkin Preston Papers, UNC.

6. MilCL to the Rev. Samuel H. Chester, 19 March 1884, W&L.

7. MilCL's account at end of Journal, 21 August 1888, VHS.

8. MilCL to Mrs. Emily Hay, 18th [n.d.], W&L.

9. Mrs. Cornelia Phillips Spencer, "The Young Ladies' Column," *North Carolina Presbyterian*, 18 May 1870.

10. Allan, *March Past*, 199.

11. Ollinger Crenshaw, *General Lee's College: The Rise and Growth of Washington and Lee University* (New York: Random House, 1969), 178.

12. GWCL to Mrs. Seddon Jones, 20 August 1895, W&L.

13. MilCL to Mrs. Emily Hay, 22 April [n.d.], W&L.

14. MilCL to Mrs. Emily Hay, 1 March [n.d.], W&L.

15. MilCL to Mrs. Emily Hay, 23 April [n.d.], W&L.

16. MilCL to Mrs. Emily Hay, 1 March [n.d.], W&L.

17. MilCL to [Mrs. Emily Hay], 21 April [n.d.], W&L.

18. Caroline Johnston to Mrs. William Preston Johnston, 22 July [1882], letter in possession of heirs of Mrs. Forest Fletcher, Bel Air, Md.

19. John M. Glenn to Dr. James Lewis Howe, 14 April 1939, W&L.

20. MilCL to Mrs. Margaret Junkin Preston, 28 July [1887], Margaret Junkin Preston Papers, UNC.

21. MilCL to Mrs. Emily Hay, 6/18 January [1879], W&L.

22. MilCL to Mrs. Margaret Junkin Preston, 28 July [1887], Margaret Junkin Preston Papers, UNC.

23. MilCL to Mrs. Emily Hay, 6/18 January [1879], W&L.

24. MilCL to Mrs. Margaret Junkin Preston, 14 May [1887], Margaret Junkin Preston Papers, UNC.

25. MilCL to Mrs. Margaret Junkin Preston, 2 February 1892, Margaret Junkin Preston Papers, UNC.

26. From *Virginia* copyright 1913, 1930, 1938, 1941 by Ellen Glasgow; renewed 1958, 1966 by Richmond, Virginia SPCA. Reprinted by permission of Harcourt Brace Jovanovitch, Inc., 148, 152.

27. MilCl's account at end of Journal, 20 July 1890, VHS.

28. Background on MCL's travels from Scrapbook 1732–1892, 113, 129.

29. Samuel Wickliffe Melton to his wife, 12 July 1878, Samuel Wickliffe Melton Papers, USC.

30. William B. Hesseltine and Hazel C. Wolf, *The Blue and the Gray on the Nile* (Chicago: University of Chicago Press, 1961), 232–33.

31. Fanny Stone to Charles P. Stone, 10 February [1878], letter in possession of Jane Stone Marfield, Washington, D.C.

32. Andrews, *Poor Relation*, 193–94.

33. Scrapbook 1816–1892, 29.

34. *New York Daily Tribune*, 15 June 1902.

35. Andrews, *Poor Relation*, 195.

36. Personal interviews by author with Mrs. Forest Fletcher, Miss Ellen Anderson, Earl S. Mattingly, all of Lexington, Va.

37. MilCL's account at end of Journal, 16 October 1891, VHS.

38. Ibid.

39. MilCL to the Rev. Samuel H. Chester, 20 October [1891], W&L.

40. MilCL to [Mrs. Emily Hay], 18th [n.d.], W&L.

41. Ibid.

42. Crenshaw, *General Lee's College*, 180.

43. MilCL to William A. Anderson, 7 July 1897, W&L.

44. Diary of William L. Wilson, 10 March [1897], W&L.

45. L. M. Harris, quoting GWCL, to "Captain" Greenlee Letcher, 14 April 1940, W&L.

46. GWCL to P. A. Green, 24 April 1899, W&L.

47. MilCL to Miss Mary Cocke, n.d. [1897], The Museum of the Confederacy.

48. James Lewis Howe, "George Washington Custis Lee," *Virginia Historical Magazine of History and Biography* 48 (October 1940): 315–27.

49. MilCL to Mrs. Emily Hay, 29 November [n.d.], W&L.

50. Ibid.

51. *New Orleans Picayune*, 29 March 1905.

52. *Rockbridge County News*, 6 April 1905.

53. Minutes of Faculty of Washington and Lee University, 1891–1912, 449, W&L.

54. Shepherd, *Life of Robert Edward Lee*, 150.

55. "In Memoriam of Mildred Childe Lee," published by the Mary Custis Lee Chapter, U.D.C. of Lexington, Va.

56. *Ring Tum Phi* [W&L student newspaper] 8, no. 22 (1 April 1905): 2.

57. *New York World*, 22 October 1914, reprinted in *The Lexington Gazette*, 28 October 1914.

58. MCL to Dr. Henry Louis Smith, 15 December 1917, W&L.

59. MCL to T. W. Gilliam, Secretary [of the student body], Washington and Lee University, 27 December 1917, W&L.

60. Will of MCL, Office of Register of Wills, Washington, D.C., copy on file at W&L.

61. Ibid.

Select Bibliography

This short bibliography is intended for persons wishing to learn more about the family of Robert E. Lee and to study the Lee ladies as representative of Southern women from the 1830s to World War I.

MANUSCRIPT SOURCES

The Lees wrote thousands of letters, most of which are now housed at the following libraries and historical societies:

Virginia Historical Society. The Lee Family Papers and the George Bolling Lee Collection constitute by far the largest collection of letters, journals, and other unpublished Lee material, including Agnes Lee's journal, Mildred Lee's various reminiscenses, and Mary Custis Lee's scrapbooks.

Library of Congress. Much of the material now housed in the original at the Virginia Historical Society is on microfilm in the Library of Congress' deButts-Ely Collection.

Washington and Lee University. In the Special Collections of the university's library are hundreds of letters to and from Lee family members, as well as notes, dance cards, and other samples of social life from 1865 to 1880.

University of North Carolina at Chapel Hill. The Southern Historical Collection in the university's library includes Lee family letters pertaining to lost and stolen items from Arlington, letters from Mildred Lee to Margaret Junkin Preston, and correspondence between Mrs. Lee and the wife of her nephew Louis Marshall.

Duke University. The Robert Edward Lee Papers in the manuscript department of the university library contain, among other items, letters from Custis Lee to his father and sisters. The Gertrude Jenkins Collection and the Marshall McDonald Papers are also housed here.

Huntington Library. Here are housed some of Robert E. Lee's early letters to his wife, as well as his correspondence with Martha Custis Williams.

Arlington House–The Robert E. Lee Memorial. At the mansion are family letters and memorabilia, as well as the unpublished manuscript by Murray H. Nelligan, "'Old Arlington': The Story of the Lee Mansion National Memorial."

Allan, Elizabeth Randolph Preston. *A March Past*. Richmond: Dietz Press, 1938.

Andrews, Marietta Minnigerode. *Memoirs of a Poor Relation: Being the Story of a Post-War Southern Girl and Her Battle with Destiny*. New York: E. P. Dutton, 1930.

"Arlington and Mount Vernon 1850, as Described in a Letter to Augusta Blanche Berard," with introduction and notes by Clayton Torrence. *Virginia Magazine of History and Biography* 57 (1949): 140–75.

Avary, Myrta Lockett. *Dixie After the War*. New York: Doubleday, Page & Co., 1906.

Beymer, William G. *On Hazardous Service: Scouts & Spies of the North & South*. New York: Harper & Brothers, 1912.

Bond, Christiana. *Memories of General Robert E. Lee*. Baltimore: Norman Remington Co., 1926.

Chesnut, Mary Boykin. *A Diary from Dixie*. Boston: Houghton Mifflin Co., 1949.

Chester, Samuel H. "At College Under General Lee." MS, ca. 1920, University Library, Washington and Lee University, Lexington, Va.

Craven, Avery, ed. *"To Markie": The Letters of Robert E. Lee to Martha Custis Williams*. Cambridge, Mass.: Harvard University Press, 1934.

Crenshaw, Ollinger. *General Lee's College: The Rise and Growth of Washington and Lee University*. New York: Random House, 1969.

Cuthbert, Norma B. "To Molly: Five Early Letters from Robert E. Lee to His Wife, 1832–1835," *Huntington Library Quarterly* (May 1952): 257–76.

deButts, Mary Custis Lee, ed. *Growing Up in the 1850s: The Journal of Agnes Lee*. Chapel Hill: University of North Carolina Press, 1984.

DeLeon, T. C. *Belles, Beaux, and Brains of the 60's*. New York: G. W. Dillingham Co., 1909.

———. *Four Years in Rebel Capitals*. Mobile: Gossip Printing Co., 1890.

Dowdey, Clifford. *Lee*. Boston: Little, Brown & Co., 1965.

———, and Louis H. Manarin, eds. *The Wartime Papers of R. E. Lee*. Boston: Little, Brown & Co., 1961.

Fleet, Betsy, ed. *Green Mount After the War: The Correspondence of Maria Wacker Fleet and Her Family*. Charlottesville: University Press of Virginia, 1978.

Flood, Charles Bracelon. *Lee: The Last Years*. Boston: Houghton Mifflin Co., 1981.

Freeman, Douglas Southall. *R. E. Lee: A Biography*. 4 vols. New York: Charles Scribner's Sons, 1934.

"Glimpses of the Past: Letters of Robert E. Lee to Henry Kayser, 1838–1846," *Supplement of the Missouri Historical Society* (January–February 1936): 1–43.

Grey, Nellie. *A Virginia Girl in the Civil War, 1861–1865: Being a Record of the Actual Experiences of the Wife of a Confederate Officer*. Edited by Myrta Lockett Avery. New York: D. Appleton & Co., 1903.

Harrison, Constance Cary. "A Virginia Girl in the First Year of the War," *The Century Illustrated Monthly Magazine* 30 (August 1885): 606–14.

———. *Recollections Grave and Gay*. New York: Charles Scribner's Sons, 1911.

Jones, J. William. *Life and Letters of Robert Edward Lee: Soldier and Man*. New York: Neale Publishing Co., 1906.

———. *Personal Reminiscenses, Anecdotes, and Letters of Gen. Robert E. Lee*. New York: D. Appleton & Co., 1874.

Jones, Katharine M. *Heroines of Dixie*. Indianapolis: Bobbs-Merrill Co., 1955.

———. *Ladies of Richmond*. Indianapolis: Bobbs-Merrill Co., 1962.

Langhorne, Orra. *Southern Sketches from Virginia, 1881–1901*. Edited by Charles E. Wynes. Charlottesville: University Press of Virginia, 1964.

Lee, Robert E., Jr. *My Father, General Lee*. Garden City, N.J.: Doubleday & Co., 1904, 1924, 1960.

Lee, S. L. "War Time in Alexandria," *South Atlantic Quarterly* 4, no. 3 (July 1905): 234–48.

MacDonald, Rose Mortimer Ellzey. *Mrs. Robert E. Lee*. Boston: Ginn & Co., 1939.

Mason, Emily V. *Popular Life of Gen. Robert Edward Lee*. Baltimore: John Murphy & Co., 1872.

Massey, Mary Elizabeth. *Bonnet Brigades*. New York: Alfred A. Knopf, 1966.

McDonald, Cornelia. *A Diary with Reminiscences of the War and Refugee Life in the Shenandoah Valley, 1860–1865*. Nashville: Cullom & Ghertner Co., 1935.

Montgomery, Lizzie Wilson. *The Saint Mary's of Olden Days*. Raleigh, N.C.: 1932.

Nelligan, Murray H. "'Old Arlington': The Story of the Lee Mansion National Memorial." Unpublished diss. on file at Arlington, ca. 1954.

Putnam, Sallie Ann Brock. *Richmond During the War: Four Years of Personal Observation by a Richmond Lady*. New York: G. W. Carleton & Co., 1867.

Riley, Franklin L., ed. *General Robert E. Lee After Appomattox*. New York: Macmillan Co., 1922.

Sanborn, Margaret. *Robert E. Lee*. 2 vols. Philadelphia: J. B. Lippincott Co., 1966–67.

Scott, Anne Firor. *The Southern Lady*. Chicago: University of Chicago Press, 1970.

Spencer, Cornelia Phillips. "The Young Ladies' Column," *North Carolina Presbyterian*, 1870–76.

Stiles, John C. "One of War's Mysteries," *Confederate Veteran* 29 (June 1921): 225, 238.

Stoops, Martha. *The Heritage: The Education of Women at St. Mary's College, Raleigh, North Carolina, 1842–1982*. Raleigh: Saint Mary's College, 1984.

Thomas, Emory M. *The Confederate State of Richmond*. Austin: University of Texas Press, 1971.

Webster, T. J. "Another Chapter on the Mystery," *Confederate Veteran* 29 (June 1921): 341–42.

Wickham, Henry Taylor. "Address, Delivered Before the Joint Session of the General Assembly of Virginia." Virginia State Document No. 10. Richmond: 1940.

Williams, G. A. "Light on a War Mystery," *Confederate Veteran* 29 (July 1921): 363–64.

Index